# BACK ON THE RIGHT TRACK READING LESSONS

An Effective Step-by-Step Reading Remediation Program for Older Students and Adults

*mail@righttrackreading.com*
*Right Track Reading LLC*
*Box 1952*
*Livingston, MT 59047*

Easy-to-use tools to help a struggling reader acquire skills and get back on track to proficient reading!

By Miscese R. Gagen
©2006

Copyright © 2006
Miscese R. Gagen
All Rights Reserved

All rights reserved. No part of this book may be reproduced by any means without written permission from the author with the following exceptions: A parent who has purchased this book may reproduce pages expressly and exclusively for his/her own children and a teacher who has purchased this book may reproduce pages expressly and exclusively for use within his/her own classroom.

ISBN 978-0-9763290-1-5

First Printing      February 2007

Published by Right Track Reading LLC
Livingston, Montana
www.righttrackreading.com

Proudly Printed in the U.S.A. by
Morris Publishing
3212 East Highway 30
Kearney, NE 68847
1-800-650-7888

# Acknowledgements

With grateful appreciation, I would like to thank:

- My three precious children, Mike, Jessica and Kayla: My son's request of "Mommy, show me how to read" sparked my expanding adventure and passion in teaching children how to read. My children were my first and best instructors in teaching me how children learn to read. Their ongoing enthusiasm for reading continues to inspire me to the importance of making sure children learn to read proficiently.

- The students I have worked with on reading remediation: Their reading difficulties convinced me of the critical need for effective instruction. They taught me many details on the specific types of errors students make and helped me learn how we need to instruct students to avoid problems, build necessary skills and insure reading success. Their proud smiles and newfound enthusiasm for reading showed me without a doubt how specific instruction methods have a dramatic influence on success. These individual students I had the privilege of working with and the numerous others struggling with reading, are my motivation for publishing this book. We can help students achieve success by developing necessary skills. We can improve reading proficiency one student at a time!

- The parents and teachers who believe in the potential of their children: These parents and teachers are searching for effective ways to help students succeed at reading. My objective is to empower parents and teachers with information and effective tools so they are able help their children and students succeed at reading. This easy-to-use program provides the means to directly develop skills necessary for reading success.

- And most importantly, I would like to offer a special thanks to my wonderful husband, Mike, who always supports and encourages me in everything I do. His constant love and unwavering support made this book possible. Without his support and encouragement this book would have just remained an idea. More important than this book, his hard work and commitment to his family allowed me to be at home with our children and do things like teach them to read. I am truly blessed.

# TABLE OF CONTENTS

PREFACE ............................................................................................... 6

OVERVIEW OF READING ................................................................... 7-10
    A. Introduction ............................................................................. 7
    B. Important Background About the English Language ............... 8
    C. Biologic Process of Proficient Reading
         & Difficulty Reading (Dyslexia) ............................................. 9
    D. Effective Reading Programs Can Develop Proficient Reading .... 10

SKILLS NECESSARY FOR PROFICIENT READING .............................. 11-18
    A. Fundamental Skills Necessary for Phonologic Processing ...... 11
    B. Combining Fundamental Skills and Developing Correct
         Efficient Phonologic Processing ............................................ 14
    **Figure 1** - *Overall Process Required for Proficient Reading* ......... 15
    C. Proficient Reading is More than Phonologic Processing ........... 16
    D. Summary ................................................................................ 18

ELEMENTS OF AN EFFECTIVE READING REMEDIATION PROGRAM 19-26

STEPS TO GET STUDENTS ON TRACK TO READING SUCCESS 27-29
    A. Evaluate the Student ............................................................... 27
    B. Set Remediation Plan Targeted to the Students Needs ............ 28
    C. Explain Remediation Plan to the Student ................................ 28

EXPLANATIONS & INSTRUCTIONS FOR READING LESSONS 30-44
    A. Overall Structure and Format of the Reading Lessons ............. 30
    B. Materials Needed .................................................................... 30
    C. General Instructions for All the Lessons ................................. 33
    D. Instructions for Specific Activities ........................................... 35
    E. Additional Tips ........................................................................ 43

# READING LESSONS .................................................................................. 45-236

## Outline of Reading Lesson Content ........................................................... 45
- Section 1: Basic Sounds and Critical Subskills (Lesson 1-9) ........ 48
- Section 2: Additional Sounds (Lesson 10-17) ............................... 77
- Section 3: Vowel Combinations (Lesson 18-43) ........................... 95
- Section 4: R-Controlled Vowel Combinations (Lesson 44-56) ...... 135
- Section 5: Silent Letters, Infrequent Sounds and Common Endings (Lesson 57-65) ............................ 161
- Section 6: Reading Multisyllable Words (Lesson 66-77) ............... 180
- Section 7: Instructions for Guided Reading ................................. 222
- Section 8: Building Fluency .......................................................... 226
- Section 9: Developing Reading Comprehension Skills ................. 228
- Section 10: Expanding Vocabulary Knowledge ............................. 233

# SPELLING SECTION ............................................................................... 237-256
- A. General Information ............................................................... 237
- B. Recommendations for Teaching Spelling ............................... 238
- C. Recommendations for Learning Spelling ............................... 240
- SPELLING LESSONS - Spelling Guidelines and Patterns
  Spelling Lessons 1-31 ............................................................ 241-256

# APPENDICES:
- APPENDIX A: Sound Pronunciation ............................................. 257
- APPENDIX B: Evaluation Tools .................................................... 268
- APPENDIX C: Lesson Progress Chart .......................................... 284
- APPENDIX D: Letter Formation Instructions ................................ 285
- APPENDIX E: Summary of Spelling Patterns for Sounds ............ 287

Order and Information Page ..................................................................... 290

# PREFACE

Congratulations! This easy to use, direct-systematic-phonics program gives you tools to get your child or student back on the right track to reading success.

Research clearly shows direct-systematic-phonics programs can not only improve reading skills but can actually develop proficient reader neurologic processing pathways. *Back on the Right Track Reading Lessons* is specifically designed to improve reading skills of older struggling readers in a one-on-one tutoring situation. This complete step-by-step program is easy to use for parents who have never taught reading before as well as seasoned educators. This program empowers you with tools to get a student back on track to proficient reading.

While my desire to teach my own children to read triggered the original *Right Track Reading Lessons*, my experiences successfully tutoring older students who struggled with reading inspired *Back on the Right Track* remedial reading program. More than half of all children and adults in this country do not read proficiently. This *Back on the Right Track Reading Lessons* program is an effective, affordable, and easy-to-use reading remediation program designed to quickly get these older students back on track to proficient reading.

*Back on the Right Track Reading Lessons* directly teaches specific skills necessary for proficient reading. Carefully designed multisensory activities intentionally develop phonologic processing pathways needed for proficient reading. The program directly builds skills in phonemic awareness, knowledge of the complete phonetic code, proper tracking, smooth blending, careful attention to detail and correct phonologic processing. In addition, this program teaches students how to handle multisyllable words and provides direct instruction in developing advanced skills in fluency, vocabulary and comprehension. It also includes a section on spelling. This program is based on the direct systematic phonics approach proven effective by validated research and applies neurobiologic scientific findings of exactly how individuals learn to read proficiently. In addition, the presentation of this solid direct systematic phonics program was developed working with students who struggled with reading. The activities were designed based on careful observation of the difficulties students faced and the specific techniques that helped them master essential skills and overcome their reading difficulties.

Remediation with this effective direct systematic phonics program absolutely can make a difference. I have witnessed the dramatic effectiveness of *Back on the Right Track Reading Lessons*. Time after time struggling readers have gained essential skills to help them learn to read proficiently. Students struggle with reading because they lack specific skills. By directly teaching necessary skills you can help a student advance their reading skills.

This book empowers you with information and highly effective tools to build necessary skills and help a student overcome reading difficulty. You **can** help your student advance their reading skills and get back on track to proficient reading.

Reading success can be achieved, one student at a time!

*Note: In this book sounds are indicated between slashes / /. For example, the letter m has the sound /m/.

# OVERVIEW OF READING

## A.  Introduction

We all want our children to read proficiently. They need to be able to look at black squiggly marks on a page and translate this written code into our English language. Reading is the key that unlocks the door to the vast wealth of information and literature. Reading is critical to a successful education. If a child, or adult, struggles with reading, they suffer in other areas of education because they cannot easily access information contained in our written language.

Unfortunately, difficulty reading is a significant and serious problem throughout our country. If your student struggles with reading he or she is not alone. In 2005, 69% of the 4th graders in this country were NOT at the proficient level. Even more alarming 36% of the 4th graders were below basic level.[1] The 8th grade reports show similar rates. Even the "top in the nation" states still have alarming failure rates. For example, while Montana is above the national average, 64% of Montana 4th graders do not read proficiently and an alarming 29% can not even read at a basic level.

The fact is many students in the United States never learn to read proficiently. While the accuracy of various testing measures can be debated, the undeniable proof of this prevalent reading failure is reflected in the adult literacy rates. Difficulty reading is far greater than the limited scope of a student's ability to read stories, complete classroom assignments or pass a standardized test. The end result is limited literacy skills that handicap the individual's educational potential, future employment opportunities, earning potential, and ability to function as a fully productive member of society.

Approximately, 50% of American adults have significantly limited literacy skills. Adults are no longer classified as 'literate' or 'illiterate'. Classifications are based on an individual's ability to complete different types of real-life literacy tasks. Adults within the lowest literacy levels 1 and 2 face difficulty performing day to day literacy functions. For example, they may face difficulty filling in forms such as a social security card application, finding information in text, locating an intersection on a street map, interpreting a table of employee benefits or understanding written directions. Literacy Level 3 is identified as the *minimum* standard for success in today's labor market. The National Institute for Literacy (NIFL) states "Literacy experts believe that adults with skills at Levels 1 and 2 lack a sufficient foundation of basic skills to function successfully in our society." [2]

The purpose of this book is not to debate the failure of our education system to teach many children to read or to discuss the serious consequences of poor literacy rates, but rather to provide parents and teachers effective tools to help individual students overcome their reading difficulties. The bottom line is reading *is* difficult for many students. It is critical to get these struggling students on the "right track" to reading success. When a student struggles, we need to intervene and take direct, effective action to develop the exact skills necessary for proficient reading. We can effectively help a student learn to read proficiently by intentionally teaching exact necessary skills in a direct, systematic and complete manner. This program tackles the literacy issue from the bottom up, one individual at a time.

While 'reading' obviously is more than decoding, this decoding or changing print into words of our language is a necessary foundational skill. The decoding needs to be effortless so the student has mental energy left over for the higher process of what and why they are reading. The student must master accurate and effortless decoding in order to achieve comprehension, enjoyment, content learning, critical analysis and the other higher level objectives of reading. Although proficient decoding is not the reason why we read, it is a foundational skill essential to reading success.

---

[1] The 2005 National Assessment of Educational Progress (NAEP) Reading Report Card www.nces.ed.gov/nationsreportcard/reading.
[2] National Institue for Literacy: The State of Literacy in America, 1992 National Adult Literacy Survey (NALS)  www.nifl.gov

# B. Important Background About the English Language

There are several important facts we need to understand about our wonderful English language.

**1. English is a phonetic language with a phonetic alphabet:** English is a phonetic language, meaning words are made up of sounds blended together. English words consist of various combinations of 44 sounds. The alphabetic characters, the 26 different artificial black squiggly marks, are the way we show this phonetic language on paper. The printed letters and combinations of letters represent specific sounds. The linguistic fact is written English is a phonetic alphabet, not a pictograph or other symbolic writing system. In linguistic history, written phonetic alphabets replaced pictographs precisely because there were too many words to represent by pictures. Written English is a phonemic code. When the complete code is known, the vast majority of English words are decodable. In addition, even irregular words are mostly decodable. To read, we need to translate or decode these black squiggly marks back into the sounds that blend to form specific words. Decoding the sounds is the essential foundation for proficient reading. The more advanced skills in fluency and comprehension are dependant on first mastering phonetic decoding.

**2. Written English is NOT simple. It uses a complex code:** Unfortunately, English phonetic writing is not restricted to a simple one-to-one relationship between one specific printed symbol and one unique sound. English contains numerous complexities. The 26 written symbols and combinations of these symbols represent 44 sounds. There is overlap where a sound is represented by more than one symbol (/k/ can be written 'c', 'k', 'ck' and in a few words the Greek 'ch'). Specific symbols often represent more than one sound (c=/k/ & /s/; o= /o/, /oa/ & /u/). Symbols combine to represent different sounds than the individual components (t=/t/ h=/h/ but th=/th/). Many combinations of symbols represent multiple sounds (ow=/ow/ & /oa/; ea = /ee/, /e/ & sometimes the unexpected /ay/). Some symbols influence and modify other symbols creating new sounds (w+a; a+l; the r-controlled vowel combinations). English also contains some irregular words that at least partially do not follow the phonemic code. An finally to top it off, English language has incorporated and assimilated components of Greek, Latin, German, French, Spanish, Native American and other languages. While these contributions add to the richness of English, they do complicate reading. To read proficiently the student needs to learn these complexities.

**3. Reading is a complex artificial skill:** Reading our complex artificial system of recording the English language on paper is absolutely NOT a part of natural biologic development. While speech is a natural biologic process, reading our man-made arbitrary system of artificial black squiggles is not innate. All components of writing and reading our language are contrived. For example, even the basic left-to-right directional processing of print is not natural. Think about it. In the natural world, the best way to gather information is to look all over. In contrast, to read English you must process the alphabetic symbols in an artificial, straight-line, left-to-right manner. Other languages apply up-to-down or right-to-left processing rules. While we obviously use our biologic functions of vision and hearing to read, there is nothing natural about learning to read. Because reading is not a biological developmental process, children do not necessarily acquire these skills. Like all complex learned skills, reading it is best taught step-by-step with practice and mastery of individual steps before moving on to advanced skills.

**4. Children are naïve about how reading works and can easily end up on the incorrect track:** It is important to realize not only is reading unnatural but children are naïve about written language. Much of what skilled readers take for granted is NOT evident to children. Think about it from a child's point of view. Printed letters are simply black abstract squiggles. Usually the least interesting thing on the page of a children's book is the print. Adults glance at a page and come up with a terrific story. Many are not aware of how our reading system functions with printed letters representing sounds blended into the words of our language. Therefore, children easily adopt incorrect strategies which lead to reading difficulty. Reading instructional programs that are incomplete, include incorrect reading strategies, contain potentially misleading information, fail to teach all necessary skills or teach skills using analytical, embedded, implicit and other indirect instruction methods are ineffective with many children. It is true that *some* children figure out the necessary process and become good readers under any reading program. However, *many* do *not* learn and develop serious reading difficulties. If the child gets on the "wrong track" on their approach to reading, they face serious and persistent difficulties. The reason some children fail while others succeed has nothing to do with intelligence or ability, but rather with how different children learn and process information. Many children struggle with reading simply because they miss acquiring necessary skills. It is risky to leave it to chance for students to acquire the complex skills necessary for proficient reading on their own.

## C. Biologic Process of Proficient Reading & Difficulty Reading (Dyslexia)

New scientific research on neurological processes involved in proficient reading is fascinating. Scientific advances allow neuroscientists to view images of the brain as it reads and actually map out these neural functioning pathways. Amazingly, researchers can actually see how the brain reads! We are learning much about the distinct neural processes involved with both proficient reading and difficulty reading. Sally Shaywitz describes this information in her book *Overcoming Dyslexia A New and Complete Science-Based Program for Reading Problems at Any Level*.[3] I highly recommend this informative book to anyone wanting to learn about the science of reading. I also recommend reviewing specific research summaries and articles on neural imaging/phonologic processing, dyslexia and phonologic based reading. Links to a selection of these informative research articles can be found at www.righttrackreading.com.

**1. Neuroscientists have learned proficient readers use phonologic pathways**: Scientist have mapped out neural functioning pathways involved in proficient reading. Researchers found proficient readers convert print to sound using phonologic processing pathways. In contrast, struggling readers have difficulty turning print to sound and aren't using phonologic processing pathways. We now have biologic proof the key to proficient reading is phonologic processing. Scientists learned these neural phonologic processing pathways necessary for proficient reading first form in beginning readers. Scientists are learning how 'fast' fluent reading develops word by word and is dependent on accurate phonologic processing. While actual neural processing is complex and involves multiple areas of the brain, the bottom line is proficient reading requires phonologic processing of the print. By converting print to sound the student taps into the brain's natural systems for efficiently processing spoken language. Phonologic processing is literally the pathway to proficient reading. To read proficiently, the student must use the brain's phonologic processing pathways and turn print into sound.

**2. Dyslexia/Reading Difficulties:** Dyslexia is defined as a problem learning to read despite normal abilities and intelligence. In other words, it is when someone who has no specific physical or mental limitations has difficulty reading. These reading problems have nothing to do with intelligence or ability but rather with how the person processes the print. Thanks to the scientific advances, we now have neurobiologic evidence of why individuals have difficulty reading. The researchers discovered dyslexic readers use different neural pathways than proficient readers and these improper neural pathways form because the individual does not recognize the sound structure of words and process print phonetically. *Dyslexics have problems turning print into sound* and consequently do not develop proficient phonologic processing pathways. This brain imaging shows literally struggling readers are on the "wrong track".

Research reveals neural processing pathways first form in beginning readers. Therefore, individuals who fail to develop correct phonologic 'proficient' reading pathways continue to face serious and persistent difficulties. This helps explain the evidence most students who fall behind in reading skills never catch up. We now know difficulty reading persists because they are not processing the print correctly using proficient phonologic processors. Instead they use less efficient and effective neural processing areas.

---

[3] Shaywitz, Sally. *Overcoming Dyslexia A New and Complete Science-Based Program for Reading Problems at Any Level*. New York: Alfred A Knopf, 2004.

Sometimes students 'get by' with incorrect processing in the lowest grades (K, 1st). The easy reading material, illustrations, context clues, oral directions and limited depth of content can disguise their difficulty decoding print. For example, if the child looks at the picture or memorizes repetitive text it appears he can 'read'. However, students who have not developed necessary phonologic processing rapidly run into problems as vocabulary expands. The incorrect strategies of 'whole word' visual memorization, word guessing, context clues and predictable text fail as reading level advances. This is often why 'reading problems' often become evident in 2nd or 3rd grade. In reality, the 'difficulty' processing print already existed. To read proficiently, the student must process print phonetically. Students who don't develop phonologic processing pathways face persistent difficulty reading.

If your child has been labeled 'dyslexic' or you suspect they are facing difficulties reading, read Sally Shaywitz's book *Overcoming Dyslexia*. This informative book contains the solid science of dyslexia. Many books on dyslexia only contain information on how to manage poor reading skills. In contrast, *Overcoming Dyslexia* provides specific information on the science of dyslexia and the exact skills your student needs to acquire to develop proficient reader processing and overcome their reading difficulty.

## D. Effective Reading Programs Can Develop Proficient Reading

Very importantly, research provides neurobiological proof effective instruction using direct-phonological-based reading programs can develop neural pathways for proficient reading in both children and adults. Effective programs that specifically taught letter-sound correspondence not only noticeably improved reading skills in struggling readers, but actually changed neural activity from incorrect neural pathways to the "correct" pathway that good readers use. The proven ability of direct systematic phonics based reading instruction to actually develop correct proficient reader phonologic pathways in dyslexic individuals is the most exciting element of the fascinating neurobiologic reading research.

This brain imaging research on dyslexia further validates and supports the existing results based evidence. Valid results based research shows direct systematic phonics programs are the most effective approach for teaching children to read. This brain research shows us *why* the direct systematic phonics programs work. The neurobiologic details on exactly how proficient reading neural pathways function, provide a wealth of information on how best to design effective reading programs. Remember, reading is not a natural biologic process. To effectively and efficiently perform this artificial task of turning man-made black squiggles into language, the student needs to tap into the existing brain functioning areas naturally designed to efficiently process spoken language. By directly teaching the student to convert print to sound you intentionally develop these proficient processing pathways.

The terrific news is we now know a highly effective direct systematic phonics program of reading instruction can help children and adults develop correct phonologic processing pathways and build proficient reading skills. Scientific evidence clearly shows the specific program of reading instruction has significant effect on rates of reading success. There is a "right way" to teach reading and to ensure the correct 'good reader' neural pathways are activated. The brain research reveals why many children fail to learn to read with the popular methods of reading instruction such as 'whole language', 'literature based' and 'balanced' approaches. These well intentioned methods allow and often encourage development of incorrect neural pathways or at best fail to intentionally develop correct pathways. It is like a railroad tracks leading from a beginning point, if the student accidentally gets on the 'wrong track' they most likely will never make it to the proficient reader station, unless direct appropriate intervention occurs. In contrast, an effective phonologic based program helps ensure the student is on the "right track" to reading proficiency.

Most struggling readers lack specific necessary skills. This reading program is specifically designed to help your struggling student acquire those necessary skills and develop proficient reader neural pathways and get *"Back on the Right Track"* to reading success.

# SKILLS NECESSARY FOR PROFICIENT READING

This section lists and describes individual skills and elements necessary for developing proficient reading. The student needs to master and integrate these skills in order to develop proficient reading. Remember, reading English is a complex learned skill. The most effective and efficient way to ensure a student learns all these necessary skills is to directly teach these skills to the individual.

The following list of essential skills necessary for proficient reading was compiled from the validated scientific research found in the National Reading Panel's "Teaching Children to Read" Summary Report (www.nationalreadingpanel.org/publications/summary.htm), the University of Oregon "BIG IDEAS in Beginning Reading" (http://reading.uoregon.edu/), and various research articles on the amazing neruoscientific research on how the brain functions in proficient reading. In addition, this list is supplemented by the author's observations and experiences from carefully observing students who struggle with reading, evaluating the specific errors these struggling students made and learning the specific techniques that were successful in helping students overcome their reading difficulties.

## A. Fundamental Skills Necessary for Proficient Phonologic Processing:

### 1. Phonemic Awareness

Phonemic awareness is literally 'sound' awareness. Phonemic awareness is understanding words are made up of sounds and being able to hear, recognize and manipulate the individual sounds that form the word. Phonemic awareness is primarily an auditory skill of distinguishing and recognizing the sound structure of language. For example, phonemic awareness is realizing the word 'puppy' is made up of the sounds /p/ /u/ /p/ /ee/ or the word the word 'shape' is formed by the sounds /sh/ /ay/ /p/. Phonemic awareness is developing an 'ear for sounds' and it is critically important to reading and spelling success.

Individuals vary greatly in their natural ability to hear sounds within words. Some individuals have a definite phonological weakness and do not realize the words they hear break apart into smaller hunks of sound. Hearing the individual sounds within a word **is** difficult because spoken language is so seamless. When we speak, we naturally and effortlessly blend all the sounds together to say and hear the overall word. The natural ease of seamless speech hides the phonetic nature of our spoken language. For example: The child says and hears the word "puppy" as one seamless word /puppy/ and does not recognize or distinguish the separate sounds /p/ /u/ /p/ /ee/ that make up the word.

Research shows children with poor phonemic awareness struggle with reading and spelling. Individuals who do not distinguish and manipulate the sounds within spoken words have difficulty recognizing and learning the necessary link between print and sound that is critical to proficient reading and spelling. It is important to realize phonological abilities are not related to intelligence. Highly intelligent individuals can have phonological weakness that leads to reading difficulty. In addition, tendency for natural phonologic weakness may be an inherited trait as it appears to run in families.

Although some children and adults have a definite natural phonological weakness, the good news is phonemic awareness (PA) can be taught and learned. We have validated scientific evidence that PA instruction has a significant positive effect on both reading and spelling.[4] You can directly help students develop the necessary phonemic awareness skills.

PA development /instruction should include the following specific skills:
- The ability to isolate and distinguish individual sounds (fish starts with /f/, 'cat' ends with /t/)

---

[4] National Reading Panel's "Teaching Children to Read" Summary Report
www.nationalreadingpanel.org/publications/summary.htm

- The ability to identifying phonemes (the words 'bat', 'boy', and 'Billy' all start with the /b/ sound whereas 'tall' and 'toy' start with the /t/ sound)
- The ability to categorize similar sounds and recognize phonemic patterns: this includes the ability to recognize rhyming words (cat, mat, fat, and sat rhyme) and the ability to recognize similarities and differences in a group of words (bake and bike start with the same sound but they do not rhyme) or (in the group of words 'bug', 'rug', 'run' and 'hug', the word 'run' is different)
- The ability to segment phonemes in a word (the word 'cat' is made of the sounds /k/ /a/ /t/, the word 'shake' is made up of the sounds /sh/ /ay/ /k/)
- The ability to blend sounds together (the sounds /h/ /or/ /s/ put together make the word 'horse')
- The ability to delete phonemes. (Say the word 'train' without the /t/ and the student can say 'rain' or 'mud' without the /d/ is /mu/)
- The ability to manipulate phonemes making changes/substitutions (What would the word 'milk' be if it started with the /f/ sound instead of the /m/ sound? and the student can say '/filk/')

It is important to realize oral PA instruction alone is not sufficient. Research shows PA instruction is most effective when students are taught to manipulate sounds *with letters*. In other words, the greatest effectiveness in helping children learn to read occurs when essential oral PA training (recognizing the sounds) is linked directly to the printed letters (knowing the specific black squiggles). The student need to recognize the word 'fire' starts with the /f/ sound AND know this /f/ sound is represented by the printed letter 'f'. To read, the student must link oral PA skills directly to the printed phonemic code.

## 2. Knowledge of Complete Phonetic Code

The complete phonemic code is the specific print=sound relationships written English is based on. The English phonemic code is complex. Letters and sounds do not have a one-to-one correspondence. There are 26 letters and 44 sounds. Some letters represent more than one sound. Many sounds are made from a combination of letters. There is overlap where one sound can be written several ways. Then to top it off, our language includes spellings from other languages and some irregular words. Although it *is* complex, English is not complete random chaos. English *is* mostly phonetic or follows predictable patterns. If *all* sounds are learned and patterns practiced, most words *can* be phonetically decoded.

The student needs to acquire knowledge of the *complete* phonetic code. Knowledge of the basic alphabet is not sufficient. The student needs to know the multiple vowel sounds, consonant digraphs, vowel-combinations, r-controlled vowels, and other complexities that comprise the vast majority of printed words. Phonograms are the distinct printed letters or combinations of letters that symbolize specific sounds within written English words. Depending on exactly how they are classified, there are between 70 to 80 phonograms. In addition to the 26 single letters of the alphabet, the student needs to learn consonant digraphs (th, sh, ch, wh, ck, ph, wr…), vowel combinations (ee, oa, oe, ai, ay, oi, oy, ea, ow, ou, ue, au….), r-controlled vowels (ar, or, ore, er, ur, ir, ear, eer, air...) and other combinations (a+l, w+a, c+e, igh, ough…). It is no surprise the vowel combinations and other complexities are frequently the source of reading and spelling difficulties. Many students lack necessary knowledge of the complete phonetic code. Instruction often fails to teach these complexities or teaches them in an indirect, incomplete or haphazard manner. The most effective way to ensure students acquire complete and accurate knowledge of the complex phonemic code is to directly teach all phonograms to the student.

To read proficiently, the student must process print phonetically. Phonetic processing requires automatically converting and linking printed letter(s) directly to correct sound. This correct sound pronunciation is not the same as the letter name. Many students can tell you the letter name but do not know the sound the letter represents. For example, for the letter 'h' the sound is /h/ not the letter name /aych/. Correct pronunciation is also important. For example the letter 'd' has a quick sharp /d/ sound not a long /duh/. Knowledge of the printed code also needs to be direct. The student needs to accurately convert the printed phonograms directly to sound. Indirect processing such as relating print to a known object or word and then extracting the sound from that word, is much less efficient than automatically knowing the direct print=sound. For example if you see 'oy' in 'destroy' and have to think 'oy' is in the word 'boy' and therefore the 'oy' must have the /oy/ sound. These indirect processing pathways take significantly more effort than directly and automatically processing 'oy' =/oy/.

The goal is for the student to automatically know the printed alphabetic character equals sound association (*printed letter(s)=sound*) of the complete phonemic code. The student effectively learns this '*printed letter=sound*' association through direct instruction *and* repeated practice. When the sound is automatic, the student does not have to spend any effort consciously think about what it is. He can then concentrate on higher reading skills. It is comparable to learning how to type. In keyboarding, you learn the association of finger movement for a specific letter. At first, a beginner has to look at both the keyboard and their hands. After a little drill, he can type without looking by concentrating on what finger to move where. With additional direct practice, the typist improves in proficiency to the point where the keyboarding is automatic. When you are no longer spending mental energy on figuring out where to put your fingers, all your concentration can then focus on the actual writing/typing. The same concept applies to reading. The objective is for the student to establish direct automatic print=sound code knowledge.

### 3. Directional Tracking

In English, we read and write from left-to-right. Proper directional tracking of looking at and processing all the letters *in order* from left-to-right is essential for reading success. Although this simple sub-skill may appear self evident, many students do not apply this essential element. Remember, scanning left-to-right in a straight line is *not* a natural process. Instinctively, looking all over is a superior way to gather information. Left-to-right processing is one of the arbitrary artificial components of our man made written English language that the student must learn and automatically apply. Knowing the individual sounds is not sufficient. For accurate reading, the student *must* process sounds *in order from left-to-right*. The following words demonstrate order of the letters is important: (stop-pots-tops) (thorn-north) (no-on) (miles-limes-smile) (step-pets-pest) (every-very) (felt-left). Poor readers have frequent tracking errors where they improperly process letters out of order. Poor readers often exhibit erratic eye movement as they look around for 'whole words' or jump around searching for familiar hunks or word families. These incorrect tracking strategies contribute to reading difficulty. To read proficiently the student must not only know the individual sound but must process the letters in order left-to-right. The most effective way to ensure the student acquires this essential skill is to directly teach and require proper directional tracking.

### 4. Blending

To read proficiently, the student needs to learn to blend individual sounds smoothly together into words without choppy pauses between the sounds. This essential blending skill does not come easily and automatically for some students. Some student's inability to blend smoothly creates a hurdle that blocks reading development. If the student is chopping sounds apart they are not able to put all the sounds together and 'smoothly' say the word, and build fluency. They might know the sounds in isolation but are unable to 'hook' the sounds together. They may initially get by with short words but quickly run into trouble with longer words that contain four or more sounds. To avoid potential difficulty it is important to directly teach smooth blending skills from the beginning. For example this is teaching the student to read the word 'mast' with smoothly blended sounds /mmaasst/ instead of a choppy /m/..../a/..../s/..../t/. When sounding out it is essential the teacher demonstrates the correct blending skills of not stopping between the sounds. Difficulties blending are usually evident as 'choppy sounding out' when you evaluate a student. Teach smooth blending skills from the beginning and specifically work on this skill with any student that has difficulty blending smoothly.

## 5. Attention to Detail

Attention to detail is carefully looking at all the letters/sounds in a word. The details are critical to accuracy. Skilled reading involves focus on the internal details of the word. The student must process all sounds in order, without skipping any sounds or adding sounds that are not actually there. Words are too similar (insist-insect-inspect) (stain-strain) (play-ploy) (stay-stray) (form-from) (tree-three-there) (then-than) (change-charge)(strange-strong-string). Only 26 letters make up ALL our words! Listen to a student who struggles with reading and you will quickly observe how they make numerous errors because they miss details. Many struggling readers have not developed skills in paying attention to detail. Students need to learn to look carefully at the details. Despite some claims, the fact is you can not read accurately by only looking at the first and last letter. Not only are the details critical for accurate reading but careful attention to detail is also important in forming the accurate neural model of the word that allows development of fast/fluent reading. You can help a student develop the attention to detail skill that is so critical to reading success. Paying attention to detail is closely intertwined with helping the student develop skills in proper tracking and correct phonologic processing.

## B. Combining Fundamental Skills and Developing Correct Efficient Phonologic Processing

Correct phonologic processing is a complex process and requires integration of many different fundamental subskills. Students need to convert print to sound so they can tap into the brains phonologic processors designed for effortlessly processing spoken sound. To do this efficiently the student must recognize the sound structure of language (phonemic awareness), directly and automatically know the phonemic code including the complexities (knowledge of the complete code). They must process print from left to right (tracking) and pay close attention to all the letters in the words (attention to detail). Learning the individual components in isolation is not sufficient. The student must not only master these individual skills but also integrate and automatically apply these skills when they read. In addition, as with all learned skills, practice with correct phonologic processing is essential to developing proficiency.

It is important to also keep in mind this initial step of 'sounding out', the strong phonologic processing base, is essential to develop the advanced skill of 'fast' fluent reading. Neural research shows fluent or 'fast' reading is built word by word and based on repeated correct phonologic processing. Without the essential process of correct phonologic processing (sounding out) the student will not develop 'fast' reading/ fluent reading pathways. Students who do not develop and use phonologic processing may work hard and eventually learn to read accurately but they will not achieve the quick and almost 'effortless' process of skilled reading.

In summary, to become a skilled reader the student needs to develop proficient phonologic processing pathways. To develop these proficient phonologic processing pathways the student needs to integrate and apply individual skills in phonemic awareness, knowledge of the complete phonemic code, directional tracking, blending, and attention to detail in correct print to sound processing. When remediating struggling readers, it is imperative you directly help the student develop these correct phonologic processing pathways. The most effective and efficient method of insuring your student develops proficient reading pathways is to directly teach the student necessary skills. Parents and teachers can use targeted activities to extinguish incorrect techniques, directly build necessary skills and intentionally develop correct phonologic processing pathways.

**Figure 1 on the following page visually presents the necessary skills and the integration of these skills into proficient reading.**

# Overall Processes Required for Proficient Reading (Figure 1)

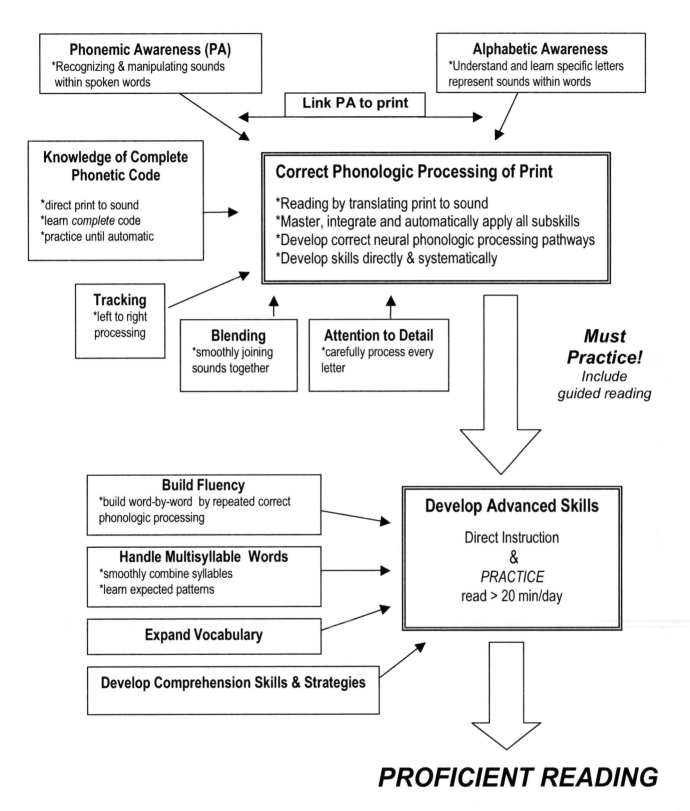

For illustration purposes, this diagram simplifies the complex process of reading. Skills are not isolated tasks. The foundational skills must be mastered, integrated, applied and PRACTICED! The correct phonologic processing of print is an essential foundation. The advanced skills in fluency, multisyllable words, vocabulary and comprehension are also critical to developing skilled proficient reading.

# C. Proficient Reading is MORE than phonologic processing.

Obviously proficient reading is more complex than knowledge of the phonemic code or even correct phonologic processing. Correct phonologic processing provides the essential foundational process of accurate and effortless decoding. Proficient reading is more complex and requires higher level skills in fluency, handling multisyllable words, comprehension, vocabulary, and skills such as the ability to extract necessary information. See *"Overall Processes Required for Proficient Reading"* on the previous page.

While a strong direct systematic phonics program will establish the foundation of correct phonologic processing, this is only the beginning. The student still needs to develop higher level advanced skills in handling multisyllable words, building fluency, expanding vocabulary and improving comprehension. These skills are all enhanced by direct instruction. The most effective way to ensure a student acquires important higher level skills is once again to directly teach those specific skills.

### 1. Skill in handling multisyllable words

The multisyllable or longer words *are* harder to read than "short" words. To read multisyllable words the student needs to apply a more advanced strategy. Some students automatically develop the proper strategies for reading multisyllable words but many do not and struggle with multisyllable words. Direct instruction and guided practice teaches the student how to handle multisyllable words. The majority of English words are multisyllable so it is critical to read them effectively.

Syllables are simply the hunks of sound within a spoken word that are said with a single puff of air. Every syllable has at least one vowel sound with or without the surrounding consonant sounds. Multisyllable words are made up of a combination of these distinct sound hunks. To read multisyllable words the student has to break the word down by distinguishing and clumping the appropriate sounds to form the correct syllables and then smoothly combining these correct sound hunks with all the adjacent syllables into one fluid word. The student needs to capture *all* the appropriate sound hunks in the word without missing one or adding one that should not be there. It is tricky and it absolutely takes practice to master this complex skill.

Many struggling readers have difficulty with multisyllable words. Also some students who have a strong reading base run into problems with higher reading levels as they begin to face many multisyllable words. These students need to learn strategies for handling multisyllable words. The general rule of thumb is $1^{st}$ graders should easily read 1 syllable words, $2^{nd}$ graders should easily handle 2 syllable words, $3^{rd}$ graders 3-syllable words and $4^{th}$ grade 4 or more syllables. It is also important to realize, this advanced skill of reading multisyllable words can not be proficiently mastered until *after* the student is able to automatically decode and blend the individual sounds.

You can help a student develop proficiency in reading multisyllable words by directly teaching strategies to handle these longer words and by providing guided practice in reading multisyllable words. Direct instruction in reading multisyllable words is particularly important when remediating struggling readers.

### 2. Fluency

Fluency is 'fast' or 'automatic' reading. Fluent readers are able to read quickly and accurately without effort. Fast oral reading with proper expression is a trademark of fluent reading. Fluency is critical to skilled reading and comprehension. By appearances, the student knows words instantly and reads the 'fast way' without slowly sounding out the word. It seems by simply 'knowing' the words the individual reads easily and quickly. However, it is important to realize appearances do **not** reveal the actual process involved in fluent reading. To help students become fluent readers, we need to learn specifically about the actual process of fluent reading and how fluent reading is developed. The necessary answers lie in the amazing field of modern neuroscience.

The remarkable advances in neural imaging research allow scientists to look closely at the process of fluent reading and how fluent reading is developed. Researchers are learning fluent or 'fast' reading utilizes a neural 'expressway' to process words. This 'fast reading area' of fluency is different from the slow phonologic processing pathways used by beginning readers. With fluent reading, a quick look at the word activates a stored neural model that allows not only 'fast' reading but also includes correct pronunciation and understanding of the word.

Importantly, the neuroscientists are learning more about how this fluency is developed. Fluent reading is established after the individual reads the word *at least* four times using accurate phonologic processing (slow accurate sounding out). Fluency is build word by word and entirely dependent on repeated, accurate, sounding out the specific word. Fluency is *not* established by 'memorizing' what words look like but rather by developing correct neural-phonologic models of the word. Repeated accurate phonologic processing is the essential precursor for developing 'fast' neural pathways. In simplified terms, the repeated accurate phonologic processing engraves a neural model of the word that then is stored in the 'fast reading area' available for rapid retrieval. We now know fluency is not the apparent visual recognition of an entire word but rather the retrieval of the exact neural model created by proper repeated phonologic processing.

Neuroscientists also discovered dyslexic readers do not develop these fluent or 'fast reading' pathways. Struggling readers do not convert print to sound using phonologic processing pathways. Consequently, they fail to develop fluent 'fast' reading pathways. Without these express reading pathways, reading remains slow and takes much effort. Because they are not utilizing phonologic processing pathways the neural 'engraving' of the word is never made and fluent reading is not developed. Even if they work hard and learn to read accurately, reading remains laborious. For reading to become 'easy' the student must first repeatedly sound out the word using phonologic processing pathways. Students who fail to use correct phonologic processing do not develop fluency. In other words reading a word over and over does not develop fluency *unless* the student is processing the print phonetically.

Effective reading instruction can directly help a student develop these fluent or 'fast' neural pathways. First, intentionally establish correct phonologic processing of print. Then provide guided practice so the student repeatedly sounds out individual words consequently expanding their storehouse of rapid retrieval neural models, allowing them to read more and more words quickly and effortlessly. Fluency is developed word-by-word and is dependent on repeated accurate print to sound (phonologic) processing.

### 3) Vocabulary

As can be expected, vocabulary knowledge is important to reading development. Vocabulary is beyond correct decoding. It is understanding the meaning of the word. Expanding the student's knowledge bank of vocabulary words is important to comprehension. The greater the student's vocabulary the easier it is to make sense of and understand text. Vocabulary is generally related to understanding individual words where 'comprehension' generally refers to understanding larger parts of the text. Vocabulary and overall comprehension are related.

Vocabulary knowledge is distinct from the skill of decoding print. A student can fully understand words that he is not able to read/decode. For example a five year old has a much larger speaking and understanding vocabulary than a printed reading vocabulary. He may not be able to decode the printed words 'gorilla', 'vacation' or 'chocolate' but has the vocabulary knowledge to understand exactly what these words mean. In contrast a student may be able to correctly decode a strange word perfectly and still now know what it means. The student may correctly decode the word 'placid', 'leviathan' or 'mizzen' but have no idea what these words mean. This would be a vocabulary knowledge issue. Of course for comprehension, the student needs to both accurately decode the word *and* know what the word means. Expanding a student's vocabulary knowledge is important to reading development.

## 4) Comprehension

Comprehension is deriving meaning from the text. Obviously, comprehension is critically important to the development of skilled reading. Comprehension is an active process that requires thoughtful interaction between the reader and the text. Vocabulary development is critical to comprehension. Comprehension, or reading for meaning, obviously is the goal of reading instruction.

Remember, to achieve comprehension, the student must *first* develop accurate phonological decoding skills and build fluency. Fluency and accuracy are critical to reading comprehension. If the student struggles with accurate fluent decoding this inability to easily convert print into language will continue to limit reading comprehension. If decoding takes significant effort, the student has little energy left to devote to thinking about what they are reading. When the student can easily, accurately and fluently decode the printed text, he then is able to focus energy on higher level comprehension skills.

Reading comprehension is a skill that needs to be developed. Comprehension is a complex higher level skill that is much greater than decoding. It is important for students to develop comprehension strategies. Comprehension strategies focus on teaching students to understand what they read not on building skills on how to read/decode. While readers acquire some comprehension strategies informally, **explicit or formal instruction in the application of comprehension strategies has been shown to be highly effective in enhancing understanding** (from the Report of the National Reading Panel). In other words you *can* take specific actions to help students develop comprehension skills.

## D. Summary

Skilled reading requires the mastery, integration and application of numerous skills and knowledge. An effective direct-systematic-phonics program explicitly teaches students to convert letters into sounds and then blend the sounds into words develops proficient phonologic processing of print. However, it does *not* constitute a complete curriculum or entire reading program. A direct-systematic-phonics program provides the essential foundation of accurate effortless decoding so the student can begin to achieve the higher goals of reading. In addition to requiring practice to build proficiency, a comprehensive reading program needs to include vocabulary, fluency and comprehension development. Other essential language curriculum areas in spelling, grammar, creative and technical writing, exposure to literature, appreciation and enjoyment of writing and ability to extract and research information from multiple sources are absolutely essential to education. The importance of these educational elements is WHY you must *first* get *all* students on the right track to reading proficiency. With the help of this program, you can get your student back on the right track to reading proficiency so the student will be able to obtain the higher skills and greater objectives.

# Elements of an Effective Reading Remediation Program
## These elements are part of *Back on the Right Track Reading Lessons* Program

**1. Teach All Skills Directly**
Always explicitly teach the student exactly what they need to know. Never leave it to chance for a student to discover essential elements on his own. Direct instruction prevents situations where the student does not learn simply because they inadvertently missed essential information or skills. While some students may be able to learn with indirect, analytic, embedded or incidental approaches, many do *not*. Statistically the majority of children fail to learn to read with indirect and embedded instructional methods. At best, these methods are inefficient. To maximize effectiveness and efficiency all skills should be directly taught to the student. Direct instruction is particularly critical in remediation as these students previously failed to acquire necessary skills. Direct instruction helps insure the student learns all necessary skills.

**2. Teach In a Systematic Manner**
Present information in a deliberate, pre-planned carefully controlled manner. This step-by-step instruction allows the student time to practice and master individual skills before additional information and complexities are taught. Start simple. Introduce new skills and knowledge a bit at a time, adding complexity as the student learns. The English language is complex. Systematic presentation helps students manage and master the complexities. A carefully designed program that directly teaches the *complete* code and progressively builds skills and knowledge in a direct systematic manner prevents the chaos and confusion that is created when you toss the entire complex English language at the student at one time. Systematic presentation helps the student make sense of our complex written language. The purpose of a carefully controlled systematic presentation is to help the student learn.

**3. Always Provide Immediate Correction**
Do not allow the student to learn or practice skills incorrectly. Immediate correction is especially critical in remediation. Correction is necessary to help the student extinguish incorrect approaches and develop necessary skills. It is a disservice to allow a student to perform a skill incorrectly. It is always easier to learn the correct way than to try and unlearn incorrect habits. If the student can not correct himself, or does not understand then you need to teach them the skill they are lacking. As the teacher, it is your job to ensure the student is learning correctly. Correction is NOT a negative action but rather a positive opportunity to help the student learn correctly.

**4. Develop Phonemic Awareness**
Directly develop phonemic awareness skills. Although some children and adults have a definite natural phonological weakness, phonemic awareness (PA) can be taught and learned. The scientific evidence proves that PA instruction has a significant positive effect on both reading and spelling. Directly teach students how to hear, recognize and manipulate sounds within words. To maximize effectiveness the program needs to directly link the phonemic awareness skills to print. When remediating older students it is particularly important not only to develop PA but to link these oral PA skills directly to the printed phonemic code.

**5. Develop and Engrain Proper Tracking**
It is essential the student develops and engrains proper directional tracking where they process letters in order from left to right. It is especially important to directly teach and emphasize proper directional tracking to remedial readers. Many struggling readers make frequent tracking errors. They try to look at all the letters at once or hop around searching for words or portions of words they recognize. Overcoming these incorrect strategies requires direct work on proper tracking skills. Physical pointing, with either the finger or other pointer, is a highly effective way to directly teach this critical skill. The multisensory benefits of having the student physically move their finger or pointer (kinetic motion) develops and engrains this essential subskill. Especially in remediation, you need to ensure the student processes *all* the letters in a word *in order from left to right*. Teach this essential skill until proper tracking is automatic.

## 6. Teach Smooth Blending

The skill of smoothly blending individual sounds together into words is critical. The student needs to learn how to say the sounds smoothly without pausing between the sounds. The instructor needs to *always demonstrate the correct blending technique* of not pausing between the sounds. Choppy/segmented sounding out makes it very difficult for some students to push the sounds back together into a word. They might know all the individual sounds but by the time they get to the end of the word with separated choppy sounding out they forget what sounds they just said or add in extra sounds when they try to put it all together. If the student keeps the sounds smoothly 'hooked' together, the word doesn't 'fall apart'. If the student has any difficulty with this essential skill, it is important to directly teach smooth blending.

## 7. Teach the Complete Phonetic Code

Directly teach the *complete* phonetic code. All necessary phonograms need to be directly and systematically taught. The phonograms are the alphabetic letters or groups of letters that symbolize the smallest speech sounds of English. The student must have knowledge of the direct print to sound relationship. Although it is best to start with the simple and most frequently encountered sounds, it is not adequate to stop there. It is essential to teach the complete code necessary to master our phonemic based written English language. This includes teaching: the sounds written with more than one letter (/th/ /sh/ /ch/ /oy/..); the multiple sounds for the vowels (o=/o/, /oa/ and /u/); the numerous vowel-combinations (ee, ea, oa, oi, ai, ou…); the multiple sounds for certain letters/combinations of letters ( s = /s/ in sit & /z/ in has); the r-controlled vowel combinations (ar, or, ir, ur, air, ear…etc) and other complexities (ph=/f/).

The student needs to look at the black printed letter(s) and immediately and directly know and process the correct sound. Teaching activities should establish this direct *accurate print = correct sound* efficient processing. The sound knowledge needs to be direct, automatic, and phonetically correct print to sound. Avoid indirect processing as it is inefficient and makes reading harder for the student. For example, activities that link the sight of printed letters to a word/object ('b' = book), or link letters or sounds to a picture 'b' or /b/ = 📖 are indirect processing.

A well designed direct systematic phonics program teaches the complete phonetic code including the multiple sounds for the vowels, the consonant digraphs, vowel combinations, r-controlled vowels and other complexities. It uses direct and accurate print to sound instruction. It includes systematic presentation and allows the student time to practice so that the sound knowledge is automatic. An effective program helps the student acquire automatic, direct knowledge of the complete phonemic code, an essential skill for proficient phonologic processing.

## 8. Use Targeted Multisensory Processes

Multisensory processes refer to utilizing the different senses to aid learning. The general concept is we learn and remember more when we involve multiple senses including visual processes (pictures, 'seeing' images), auditory/oral processes (listening and talking), and physical/kinetic processes (motion, hands on, doing). Multisensory instruction applies two or more of these senses to enhance learning. *However*, to be effective in developing reading skills these multisensory activities must be carefully targeted. Multi-sensory approaches in themselves will not help a student learn to read *unless* they directly build the exact skills necessary for proficient reading. Effective multisensory activities directly teach correct directional tracking, develop phonemic awareness, create a direct and automatic link between print and sound, teach smooth blending, and establish correct proficient phonologic processing. It is not the multisensory process itself but the application of these multi-sensory processes to the development of specific skills that is key to enhanced learning.

For instance, neural research clearly identifies the direct link between print and sound is necessary to develop proficient reading pathways. This automatic direct link between printed letter and the correct sound is the required skill activities need to target. An effective multisensory instructional activity is having the student write the printed letter while saying the sound. This simple action directly links the motion of forming the printed letter (kinetic), image of the completed letter (visual) to saying and hearing the correct sound (auditory). This targeted application and integration of the multisensory processes is highly effective in helping the student learn the necessary skill.

In contrast, multisensory activities that are not targeted to develop necessary skills (based on the science of proficient reading) have limited benefit. Activities can even be detrimental if they unintentionally create incorrect processing or utilize energy for unnecessary indirect efforts. A jumping jack, dance or hand sign are misguided application of the kinetic process because these motions are unrelated to skills necessary for reading print. These activities may actually develop indirect, inefficient processing. We know auditory and oral processes of saying and hearing sounds are critical to phonologic processing. However, saying sounds incorrectly, practicing sounds without linking them visually to the printed letters, orally chanting words or singing songs will not directly develop necessary skills of converting printed letters to their correct sound, blending these sounds into words and developing phonologic processing pathways. Similarly, looking at objects or images, color coding, and other such unrelated visual activities are misguided. Teaching a student to visual 'recognize' words by their overall appearance (sight word approach) can be detrimental because it undermines the phonologic processing essential for proficient reading. Remember to be effective, multisensory activities *must* focus on developing necessary skills.

Mixed in with the multisensory instruction, there is often a good deal of discourse about 'multiple intelligence' and 'multiple learning styles'. These terms refer to theories about how individuals have specific strengths and how some children learn better with certain styles. This theory professes views such as a student with strong 'visual intelligence' learns better with visual instructional approaches and a student with strong 'auditory intelligence' learns best with oral instructional methods. It is very important to realize while individuals absolutely do have specific strengths, this does not mean that proficient reading is achieved by many different pathways. The neural science is clear. To read proficiently the student *must* convert print to sound and develop phonologic processing pathways. An assumption such as strong visual learners would best learn to read using visual processing completely ignores the science of proficient reading. In fact, this false assumption is most detrimental to the students with the naturally strong 'visual intelligence' and weak phonemic awareness as these students are least likely to develop the necessary phonemic processing on their own. Instruction that encourages the use of visual processing actually leads these strong 'visual' students further down the incorrect processing pathways. Reading instruction needs to be designed to develop the specific skills necessary for proficient reading.

An individual's unique strengths and weaknesses make it even more important to directly develop necessary skills. It is especially important to specifically teach, emphasize and develop strong phonemic processing skills in students who are naturally weakest in these areas. Left on their own, many students with poor phonemic awareness rely on their natural strengths and fail to develop necessary phonologic processing pathways. It is also important to realize building a student's skills for proficient reading never negates or somehow minimizes their other natural strengths. For instance, if a student has strong visual skills, developing their phonemic awareness and teaching them to read with phonologic processing skills will not eliminate their strong visual skills. It will simply teach them to apply phonologic processing when reading. Effective reading instruction is not designed to match an individuals existing strengths but rather designed to intentionally develop and build skills and processes necessary for proficient reading.

In summary, multi-sensory activities are effective tools in helping students learn to read. However, these activities must be carefully designed and targeted to directly teach and reinforce the skill/knowledge necessary for proficient reading. While students may naturally have specific learning strengths and weaknesses, proficient reading requires the development of phonologic processing pathways. Effective reading programs use a variety of carefully designed and targeted multi-sensory activities to directly teach and develop the skills necessary for proficient reading.

## 9. Emphasize Attention to Detail

To read proficiently, the student needs to learn to pay attention to detail. Teach the student to carefully look at all the sounds within a word and stop him immediately if he skips details. This emphasis on attention to detail is especially important with reading remediation as you need to extinguish the old habit of not looking at all the details and replace it with the careful attention to detail. Proper tracking is also intertwined into the attention to detail skill. An effective remediation program should be designed to directly teach, develop and reinforce this critical skill that is essential for skilled reading.

## 10. Develop Phonologic Processing (Use a Direct Systematic Phonics Approach)

The student needs to learn to read by using phonologic processing. The most effective way to ensure students convert print to sound and develop the phonologic processing necessary for proficient reading is to teach them with a strong phonics-first direct systematic phonics program. Directly teach students to convert letters into sounds and blend these sounds into words. Validated research shows this type of direct-systematic-phonics instruction has significant benefits for children in K through 6th grade and in children having difficulty learning to read. [5] True phonics based programs teach students printed letters represent specific sounds and how to blend these sounds into words. To maximize effectiveness, you need to teach the student *explicitly* and *directly* in a *systematic* and *complete* manner. An important note: this absolutely is *not* a blanket endorsement for all 'phonics' programs. Many programs labeled 'phonics' use indirect, embedded methods or are in fact just sight word programs with a token addition of a few sounds. Other 'phonics' programs are incomplete or rely on indirect memorization of long complex lists of rules.

Remediation is not only teaching the correct skills but also helping the student overcome old incorrect habits. By design remediation programs need to insure the student develops and uses correct techniques. Teaching strategies must also prevent the use of incorrect strategies. Remember phonologic processing is more than knowing the sounds. Efficient phonologic processing requires integration of direct knowledge of the complete phonemic code, proper directional tracking, smooth blending, and attention to detail.

Research provides neurobiological proof effective instruction using direct-phonological-based reading programs can develop the neural pathways for proficient reading in both children and adults. Effective programs that specifically taught letter-sound correspondence not only improved reading skills in struggling readers, but actually changed brain activity form incorrect neural pathways to the "correct" pathway that good readers use.

## 11. Ensure Phonologic Processing - Avoid Sight/Whole Word Reading

It is important to avoid teaching a sight word approach where the student learns to "read" by trying to recognize what whole words "look like". Many students who struggle with reading have adopted this incorrect 'whole word' visual word recognition strategy. Remediation must focus on eliminating this detrimental habit of trying to visually recognize the entire word.

A 'whole word' approach to reading fails because there are too many words and words are too similar to learn by overall visual appearance. Initially, a simple short list can be successfully "read" by whole word strategies and guessing. For example, a short list of visually different words like …a, the, cat, ball, house, green. This whole word identification "instant reading" may be exciting at first but can encourage the child to develop incorrect reading strategies where they think "reading" equates to simply looking at what the word looks like, recognizing a few letters, and then "word guessing". Some children, especially those with strong visual memory skills, are very good at this in the beginning. However, as vocabulary expands visually similar words are encountered. The student who has adopted a whole word reading strategy is certain to fail. Not only are there absolutely too many words but words are too visually similar. A child starts school with something like a 24,000 word speaking and listening vocabulary. His vocabulary is up

---

[5] National Reading Panel's "Teaching Children to Read" Summary Report
www.nationalreadingpanel.org/publications/summary.htm

above 40,000 by 3rd grade. It is impossible to learn such an extensive vocabulary visually as whole words. Remember, only 26 letters make up all those words. To read proficiently, the student must look at each and every letter in order and process it phonologically. The neural imaging studies confirm this. The linguistic fact is our written language is NOT made up of whole word "pictures" but sounds that blend together to form spoken words. In linguistic history, written alphabets replaced pictographs precisely because there were too many words to represent by pictures.

The problem is apparent when you observe students who have been instructed in whole word methods and adopted 'whole word' visual reading strategies. Their reading errors clearly show how they mistakenly look at appearance or physical structure of the word, look only at a few letters or at part of the word, mix up the order of the letters, or simply make wild guesses. These students say "very" for the word every, "made" for dim, "doctor" for describe, "sleep" for speed, "smell" for small, "volume" for value, "have" for van, "poured" for sprout, "mile" for lime and "soft" for often. They wildly guess uncommon learned words like "chimp" for chart and "prehistoric" for plenty. Frequently, the 'wild guesses' are words they specifically have tried to visually memorize. They look at very simple phonetic words like "rod" and "fat" and say, "I don't know the word". They cannot read very simple phonetic words even when they quickly recognize a word like 'elephant'. All of these are actual examples I have observed. In closer evaluation, these students often have poor phonemic awareness, do not know many necessary sounds, do not track letters in order left to right, do not look at all the letters, and have poor segmenting and blending skills. Sadly, they never learned HOW to read and instead adopted a strategy of trying to memorize the entire look of the word - a strategy guaranteed to fail. The brain imaging research on dyslexia confirms and explains why whole word approaches fail. Proficient reading is dependant on phonological analysis. While some words are not completely phonetic and are read partly by "sight", visual recognition sight word/ whole word reading should *not* be taught as a reading strategy.

## 12. Teach Phonetically Accurate Representations of Print - Avoid teaching "word families" and "blended consonants" as unique units

Use phonetically accurate representations of print. Avoid teaching with inaccurate representations of print such as word families (at, ig, it, am & the hundreds of other possibilities) and blended consonant clusters (bl, cr, fl, sc, sl, bl & the other 60+ possible beginning and ending blended consonant sounds) *as* unique letter/sound units. There is no need to do this. All it does is *add hundreds of additional combinations* for the student to learn. Teach the necessary single sounds and blending skills and the student can then read all possible combinations. For example by knowing 6 sounds (a e m n d t) and developing blending skills the student can sound out 10 different common combinations (am, an, ad, at, and, em, en, ed, et, end). At best, the teaching of blended consonant and word family units is an inefficient and indirect way to teach the necessary blending skill. However, the serious concern is these incorrect representations actually create reading difficulties in *some* students.

Problems arise when students adopt a strategy of trying to memorize the cluster groups as a visual unit instead of processing each sound. Not only is the sheer number of combinations overwhelming but the visual similarities between the clusters make visual "what it looks like" strategies very difficult for a child to master (such as bl, pl, lb, ld). In addition, if students hop around within words looking for familiar clusters and word families, they often confuse the left to right tracking and sounding out skills that are absolutely necessary. They inappropriately pull out word family combinations from words. They pull out 'it' from wait, 'in' from coin, and 'ag' from page. These blended consonant clusters and word family units encourage some students to not look at all the letters. By overlooking the necessary attention to detail, students who learn with consonant clusters frequently insert blended sounds when they are not present. They read camp as 'clamp', tack as 'track', fake as 'flake', tide as 'tride', set as 'sent'. Because they learned the cluster as a 'hunk' they actually 'see' the cluster when it is not there. These difficulties are all actual errors made by students who were taught word family and consonant cluster techniques.

It is simpler, more effective and prevents potential reading problems to teach students the necessary sounds and develop phonemic awareness and blending skills so they are able to combine any letters. Students often do need direct practice the blended consonants sounds as individual sounds within these consonant clusters are more difficult to distinguish. For example, many children hear the first sound of 'grip' as /gr/ instead of /g/. These students need to develop phonemic awareness to distinguish the separate sounds. Always teach the blended consonants as processing and blending of the individual sounds NOT by learning cluster units. For example, teach flap as blending /f/ /l/ /a/ /p/ NOT /fl/ /a/ /p/. Same with the common "word families"; teach the blending of sounds /s/ /a/ /t/ NOT /s/ /at/.

Word families and blended consonant clusters are an inaccurate representation of our language. From the very beginning, we need to teach students to carefully process at all the letters in order by sound. Shortcuts that bypass this process can unintentionally create reading difficulties in some students. This careful attention to phonetic accuracy is particularly important in remediation situations.

## 13. Guided Oral Reading is Essential

Guided reading is reading out loud to an adult, or other proficient reader, with feedback. This is NOT independent silent reading. The key part is 'guided'. Correction and instruction helps the student learn and improve skills. The validated research shows guided out loud reading has significant beneficial impact on word recognition, fluency and comprehension across a range of grade levels.[6] Guided reading benefits both good and struggling readers. In contrast, silent independent reading may *not* actually improve reading skills for beginning readers. Numerous studies show the best readers read the most and poor readers read the least. However, these studies are all correlational. It may be the good readers simply spend more time reading. Although it sounds like a good idea to have students read more alone, there is *no* research evidence showing *independent silent reading* actually improves reading skills. If a poor reader sits flipping pages and struggling with the reading and making errors, their skills will not improve, no matter how much time they spend. In contrast, *guided* oral reading instruction helps the student improve skills. This is NOT saying students should not read to themselves, or there are no benefits for children looking at books, or students do not need to read more. Rather, it says *to improve skills*, particularly in learning stages, students need to read *out loud with feedback*. At more advanced levels, silent reading does improve the higher skills of fluency, comprehension and vocabulary.

Guided reading has a *significant* beneficial impact on developing reading skills and should be a part of reading instructional programs. Guided reading is particularly important tool in remediating struggling readers. Guided reading also is the ideal time to help students develop higher level skills in comprehension. Specific instructions for conducting guided reading are found in Section 7.

## 14. Develop Fluency

Fluency is the 'fast' or 'automatic' reading where words appear to be almost instantly recognized. Fluent readers read quickly and accurately without effort. Fluency is the objective for phonologic decoding. The critical information to keep in mind for effective reading instruction is that fluency or 'fast reading' is developed word by word based on repeated accurate phonologic processing of specific words. To build fluency, we *first* have to be sure the student is reading by correct, accurate phonologic processing (sounding out the word correctly). This foundation of correct phonologic processing is mandatory in order for the student to develop fluency. Students do not become 'fluent readers' overnight but rather build fluency word-by-word over time. With repeated practice correctly reading individual words, the student adds to their storehouse of 'fast'/fluent words. Effective tools to directly build fluency include guided oral reading and a program of spelling/writing words by sound. Specific instructions are found in Section 8.

---

[6] National Reading Panel's "Teaching Children to Read" Summary Report
www.nationalreadingpanel.org/publications/summary.htm

### 15. Teach Strategies for Handling Multisyllable Words
The majority of English words are multisyllable so it is critical to read them effectively. It is more difficult to process multisyllable words. It requires more advanced strategies and techniques than decoding simple one and two syllable words. Many struggling readers have difficulty with multisyllable words. A remediation program should include both direct instruction and guided practice in handling multisyllable words. Direct practice with common affixes is also effective in helping students learn how to handle multisyllable words. If conducted correctly, spelling can be used as an effective tool for learning how to process these longer words. Section 6 covers handling multisyllable words.

### 16. Expand Vocabulary Knowledge
Expanding a student's vocabulary knowledge is important to reading development. Vocabulary instruction leads to gains in comprehension (noted by the National Reading Panel). A comprehensive reading program needs to include vocabulary development. The student can acquire vocabulary both incidentally through exposure and through direct vocabulary instruction. It has been shown that various techniques designed to directly build vocabulary are effective in expanding vocabulary knowledge and improving reading comprehension. Optimal learning occurs when vocabulary instruction involves a combination of different techniques. Section 10 includes instructions for expanding vocabulary.

### 17. Directly Develop Reading Comprehension Skills
Comprehension is deriving meaning from text. Comprehension is a complex higher level skill. You can take direct actions to help students develop specific comprehension skills and strategies. While readers acquire some comprehension strategies informally, **explicit or formal instruction in the application of comprehension strategies has been shown to be highly effective in enhancing understanding** (from the Report of the National Reading Panel). These strategies help students think about, remember and understand what they are reading. These comprehension strategies are effective for non-impaired readers. Remember, if the student has decoding difficulties you need to *first* establish the necessary fundamental decoding skills of proficient phonologic processing. Otherwise the difficulty decoding will likely inhibit the development of the more advanced comprehension. Some students have no difficulty decoding but struggle with comprehension. These students need direct instruction in developing comprehension skills. Remediation programs should include direct instruction in developing comprehension skills. The majority of comprehension development can be accomplished as a part of guided reading. Section 9 includes specific instructions for developing reading comprehension.

### 18. Practice reading: Read! Read! Read!
Daily reading is critical. Students should read a *minimum* of 20-30 minutes every day. Of course, the more reading is better! In learning and remediation stages the majority of this reading time should be guided reading (out loud with feedback). As the student's skills develop, their reading will shift primarily to independent silent reading. Practicing correct reading skills is essential.

In general the student should read level appropriate material. Obviously, 'appropriate' is a relative term and the student's reading level will change and advance as the student gets older and as their skills advance. The appropriateness of material also varies depending if they are reading alone or reading outloud with feedback. Multiple formal methods and systems for evaluating and rating 'reading level' exist. Most are based on readability factors such as vocabulary, number of multisyllable words, sentence length and structure, grammar, and complexity of story plot. A few rating systems consider suitability of the content. Many of these systems provide numerical ratings to evaluate and compare books. These technical methods attempt to provide objective information on the actual 'reading level' of a particular book. The reading level then needs to be considered relative to the individuals' skills to determine what is 'appropriate' for the student. In addition to the formal methods, you can simply listen to your student read and then adjust material to fit.

The following simple rule of thumb can be used to help you determine if a book is the appropriate reading level for a particular student at a certain time and situation:

**Independent level:** This is material the student can read with few errors. If the student is making only a few errors on a page the material is at the independent level. This 'easy' or independent level is ideal for silent reading.

**Instructional level:** The learning level material is where the student reads with some errors and skill building. If the student is making 4 or more errors per page the material is considered instructional level and should be read to an adult as guided reading material. This instructional or learning level is ideal for guided reading so you can help the student develop skills.

**Frustration level:** This is where the material is 'too hard'. The student makes frequent errors in every paragraph. The reading level is really too advanced for the student. It is best to avoid frustration level material by finding another book. If frustration level material must be read, it is should be read as guided reading with assistance.

When a student learns to read proficiently, they should be able to read all grade level material. In other words, a 6$^{th}$ grader may have difficulty reading a college level physics textbook but should not struggle with their middle school science textbook or other classroom material. If grade level material is consistently not 'appropriate' for your student, chances are they are lacking necessary decoding skills and need direct instruction in developing the necessary phonologic processing skills.

## 19. Share the joy of reading

And as always, share the joy of reading. Reading is wonderful. Students have a natural excitement about reading that can be tapped into. Teaching students to read using a direct systematic phonics program does not preclude enjoyment and excitement with reading. In fact, it is the ability to read well that removes roadblocks and provides the route to reading enjoyment. The often quoted observation 'good readers' like to read and 'poor readers' do not enjoy reading is absolutely true. However, this is a correlational, not a cause and effect, relationship. This tendency to spend time and enjoy what we are good at is simply human nature. It is difficult to 'enjoy' an activity you don't do very well, make frequent frustrating errors and can only accomplish with difficulty and work. When students learn how to read they are able to become 'engaged' and 'excited' about reading. This is particularly evident in students who have struggled with reading. Once these students learn how to read there is often a complete 180° change in their attitude toward reading. The same 5$^{th}$ grader who in September told me she didn't like to read, literally came skipping down the hall to tell me all about the two books she voluntarily read over Christmas break. A mother of 7$^{th}$ grader I tutored told me she came home from work to find her son voluntarily reading a book, something he had previously *never* done. A year later he is an avid reader.

An effective reading remediation program intentionally develops necessary proficient reader skills. Structured reading lessons teach your student *how* to read. However, the lessons alone will not ensure your child achieves a love of reading. Parents and teachers absolutely need to encourage and promote a love of reading. Expose students to a wide variety of literature. Help them discover the amazing wealth of information contained in books. Encourage students to read. Go to the library frequently and search for books that engage the student. Check out numerous books on military aircraft. Help your daughter unpack the box of well worn favorite horse stories that her aunt sent her. Give your child a flashlight so she can re-read all the *Little House* books under the covers after lights out. Read all the *RedWall* books with him so you can discuss the details of how the brave mouse warrior and his woodland friends defeat the evil horde of vermin. Read the newspaper sports page at breakfast. Follow the latest space shuttle mission on the NASA internet site. Help her find research information. Read a nightly Bible verse. Read the same favorite book over and over. Enjoy books! However, do not skip the important step of carefully teaching students *how* to read. Help your student become a 'good reader' so they are able to enjoy reading.

Skilled reading is a key that unlocks the doors to limitless knowledge, enjoyment and adventures. Give your child or student this key by getting them on the right track to reading proficiency!

# STEPS TO GET A STUDENT BACK ON TRACK TO READING SUCCESS

## A. Evaluate the Student

An evaluation is not a 'test'. It is an informal tool to help you determine the exact skills you need help your student develop. Evaluations help you be a more effective teacher. Students who struggle with reading do so because they lack specific necessary skills. You need to know where specific deficiencies exist in order to better build the necessary skills. This is comparable to a coach watching a player perform a task so they can determine the specific weaknesses and then coaching to strengthen those areas. Evaluation results help you effectively target instruction to develop essential reading skills.

Before you evaluate your student, be sure to explain to the student that the evaluation is not a test but rather a tool to help you target your instruction. Some students, especially some who struggle with reading, are upset with anything they view as a test. Be sure you let them know that since it is not a test there are no 'wrong answers'.

An evaluation should include the following:
> **Phonemic Awareness:** Assess the student's ability to perform phonemic awareness activities. Can the student distinguish and manipulate sounds. If they have difficulty recognizing the sound structure of language, where exactly do they have difficulty? Is it with beginning, ending or middle sounds, blended consonants, blending, segmenting or sound manipulation? Results indicate what specific phonemic awareness skills you need to help the student develop. Remember phonemic awareness is essential to reading success as it allows the student to access efficient phonologic processing.
> **Knowledge of the complete phonemic code:** Evaluate the student's knowledge of the complete phonemic code. Check their direct print=sound knowledge of all basic sounds, alternate vowel sounds, vowel combinations, r-controlled vowel combinations and other complexities. Determine if they have specific gaps in their code knowledge. Also check that the code knowledge is direct and automatic. It is not a coincidence that most struggling readers have major gaps in their code knowledge especially of the vowel combinations and other complexities.
> **Spelling**: Spelling indicates how the student is transferring sound to print, the converse of reading. Give the student spelling words from an appropriate list they have NOT studied or evaluate uncorrected writing samples. Look at their exact spelling. Patterns of errors in spelling often indicate how the student is processing words. Spelling errors can also reveal phonemic weakness.
> **Reading Skills**: Have the student read some level appropriate material to you. Do not comment or make any corrections, simply record the exact errors that the student makes. Close scrutiny of the student's exact mistakes usually reveals repeated mistakes and patterns of errors. Careful evaluation of these specific errors that the student makes while reading is enlightening. Look for errors with incorrect words, skipped words, replacing one word for another, missing parts of the word and problems with multisyllable words. The particular type of reading errors can indicate deficiencies in specific skills such as tracking, blending, attention to detail, and absence of phonologic processing. The reading evaluation is particularly helpful in determining the fundamental skills that the struggling reader needs to develop.
> **Reading Comprehension**: Reading Comprehension is a higher level skill. To evaluate comprehension, the student reads some appropriate level material to you. As the student reads ask some questions about what he or she is reading. Basically, you are checking how well the student understands what they read. If they have poor comprehension skills, you then check to see if the poor comprehension skills are based on decoding/reading difficulty or on a lack of comprehension skills, or both.

**Appendix B provides evaluation tools and specific instructions for evaluating your student and interpreting the results so you can better target your instruction.**

## B. Set a Specific Remediation Plan Targeted to the Student's Needs

Use the results of the evaluation to help set a specific remediation plan. Most students who struggle with reading are missing essential fundamental skills. It is important to go back and establish the correct skills. Remember an effective remediation plan is not 'teaching down' to a lower level but rather directly teaching and developing essential skills to build up and raise the student to the proficient level. In making an effective reading remediation plan, there are several important factors to consider.

1.  **Direct intervention is essential:** In almost all cases, students do not 'outgrow' reading problems on their own. Struggling readers are lacking essential skills and need direct effective intervention. Intervene immediately to develop correct proficient reader skills. Do not wait for the student to 'pick it up' on their own. Research data reveals this rarely happens. As students get older, difficulty reading will handicap them further and further in all subject areas. The ideal situation is one-on-one direct intervention.

2.  **Effective intervention is essential:** Use an effective direct systematic phonics program to specifically develop essential proficient reading skills (direct knowledge of complete code, tracking, blending, phonologic processing). **The brain imaging research shows that effective direct systematic phonics programs not only improve reading skills but actually develop proficient reader neural pathways.** Continuing to read the 'incorrect' way, additional practice of incorrect strategies, or repeating a program that failed the student the first time around will NOT help the student overcome their difficulties. You must redirect the student and build essential skills with effective reading intervention.

3.  **An intensive remediation schedule is important:** An effective remediation program builds specific skills and brings the student up to full speed. For older students it is important to complete the remediation stage of the program as quickly as possible. Ideally 45-60 minute sessions 5 times/week. An intensive program is necessary to overcome incorrect habits and establish correct proficient reader skills. If you proceed too slowly it is difficult to help the student build necessary skills. A schedule of 1 hour 5 times a week for 4 weeks will be significantly more effective than the same 20 hour total tutoring time spread into single 1 hour sessions over a 20 week time period. An intensive schedule is not only more effective in developing skills but it allows the student to make rapid progress. This rapid progress provides additional benefits as the student sees improvement and gains confidence. It is always more effective to get a student through a reading remediation program quickly. The intensive remediation schedule allows the student to quickly get back on track with his or her classmates. The student gets past the 'learning how to read' stage and quickly moves ahead with the 'reading to learn'.

## C. Explain the Reading Remediation Plan to the Student

**Before starting be sure the student understands effective remediation directly teaches and develops essential skills to raise the student to the proficient level.** Make sure the student understands reading remediation is NOT teaching down at lower level but rather building necessary skills to help bring the student up to proficient level. The student needs to realize 1) reading problems are common 2) reading problems have nothing to do with intelligence or ability 3) difficulties reading are caused by weakness in phonologic processing and other fundamental skills 4) Effective instruction improves reading skills and 5) with some direct work you are confident they will develop proficient reader skills. Before beginning the lessons give the student a quick summary. Use your own words and include the following information:

- This reading program is designed to get you back on track to proficient reading. You have had problems reading and spelling because you are missing some essential skills. With the direct instruction in this program and work and practice on your part, you can develop the skills necessary for proficient reading.

- Reading is a complex learned skill. Think about some of the other learned skills you enjoy (Give an analogy to an activity the student enjoys: softball, soccer, basketball, piano, dance). If someone hadn't taught you the essential subskills in the beginning you would probably have difficulties performing the advanced skills. Think about trying to make a home run if you were holding the bat incorrectly, or playing a song on the piano if you never learned the basic notes, or trying to play a basketball game if you never learned how to dribble or learned the plays.

- Reading print is not a natural biologic process. Reading is complex. It requires looking at man-made, arbitrary black squiggly lines and changing that written code into our spoken language. To read proficiently you need to use the brains natural system for processing sound. These sound or phonologic processing pathways are essential to proficient reading. If you use other processes, reading will require much effort and remain difficult. Most problems with reading have nothing to do with intelligence or ability but rather by incorrect processing. Many very intelligent people face difficulty reading. You are likely having problems reading because you are not using these proficient phonologic processors. You probably were never specifically taught the necessary steps for reading proficiently or were taught in a way that accidentally allowed you to learn incorrectly.

- You are not alone in your problems reading. Approximately 69% of the students in this country can NOT read proficiently and 37% can not read at even a basic level. (If it helps show your student the actual statistics from your state located in the Reading Report Card on NAEP website. Direct links to this site can be found at the links page of www.righttrackreading.com.)

- The good news is that effective instruction improves reading. Even adults who have struggled for years can have dramatic success when they are taught with direct systematic phonics programs. Effective direct systematic phonics instruction is proven to not only improve reading skills but to actually develop the neural pathways necessary for proficient reading. This program specifically develops these phonologic 'proficient reader' processing pathways.

- Because you are older, your experience and background knowledge will help you learn quickly and progress at a much faster pace than a young child just learning to read. (Emphasize how quickly they will get back on track with an effective instruction.)

- It is my job to specifically teach you all the necessary steps to read our complex language. Before starting, I want you to know that I will stop you if you start to perform a skill incorrectly. It's my job to make sure you learn the right way and practice correctly. Remember correction is not negative. It helps you learn correctly and develop proficient reader pathways.

- Don't worry if the first lessons seem too easy. These are the 'warm up drills'. To develop proficiency it is important to learn and practice correct technique. Repeated drill in fundamental skills is necessary. The initial reading lessons make sure you master the correct techniques and basic fundamentals. Compare these initial reading lessons to the fundamental skills and drills that the student practices with their favorite sport or activity. For example, to be a skilled basketball player you must first learn to dribble and shoot free throws. Repeated drills in basic skills help you become a better player. Even the elite professional players drill fundamental skills. Like any complex skill, mastery of individual components and then repeated practice is necessary to develop proficiency. The initial lessons develop the following fundamental skills that are essential for proficient reading: phonemic awareness, direct automatic knowledge of the phonemic code, smooth blending, proper tracking, attention to detail and proper phonologic processing.

- Have patience, especially in the first few lessons. The first lesson is primarily designed to show you how the activities are structured. Lessons systematically advance. If you skip ahead you may miss something important.

- The harder you work the quicker you will develop the necessary skills and become a proficient reader. I am confident that you will excel and learn to read proficiently. Let's get started!

# EXPLANATION AND SPECIFIC INSTRUCTIONS FOR THE BACK ON TRACK READING LESSONS

## A. Overall Structure and Format of the Reading Lessons:

This program is arranged into carefully designed lessons structured for one-on-one individual instruction. The lessons use a variety of targeted multisensory activities to directly teach skills necessary for proficient reading. The activities systematically develop skills in phonemic awareness, knowledge of the complete phonetic code, directional tracking, smooth blending, attention to detail and correct phonologic processing. The advanced sections teach students how to handle multisyllable words, build fluency and develop reading comprehension. A spelling section is also included.

The lessons directly teach skills in a deliberately planned sequence. Basic sounds are presented in the first lessons, followed by multiple vowel sounds, vowel combinations, r-controlled vowel combinations and other complexities. The important tracking, blending and phonologic processing skills are developed throughout the program. The program is cumulative with word lists including newly introduced sounds as well as previous sounds. The systematic presentation allows time for the student to practice and master skills and knowledge. The first sections may seem 'easy' but are important to establishing correct phonologic processing, tracking and attention to detail. If the student has these fundamental skills he will quickly speed through these lessons. Remember fundamental drill helps improve skills.

The lessons incorporate a series of specific activities including direct instruction and practice of the sounds, sound writing, word making activities, reading word lists and writing words. Review lessons are periodically included to provide additional review and practice of sounds and skills learned to date. All these activities are carefully designed to systematically develop specific skills. Be sure and complete all activities. In addition to the structured reading lesson activities, the student should begin daily guided reading. Daily guided reading should be included a part of the reading instruction after lesson 65. Specific directions for all activities are included in subsequent sections.

When remediating older students, an intensive schedule is necessary to both establish correct skills and also overcome previous incorrect habits. The ideal remediation schedule is 45 to 60 minute sessions 4 or 5 times per week. Although there will be variation in appropriate session length for individual students, and you need to use your judgement, an intensive schedule should be used. Complete each lesson before advancing. Do NOT skip lessons. If you skip lessons the student may miss acquiring a necessary sound or sub-skill. Observe the student and adjust speed of instruction to meet the student's individual rate of learning. Repeat a lesson or portion of a lesson if the student has not yet mastered a skill or needs reinforcement. On the other hand, proceed at a faster speed, if the student fully masters the skills in the lesson. Consistency and practice is important. An intensive program allows the student to quickly see results. After years of frustration a distinctly noticeable improvement in reading skills is a great motivator for encouraging a student who was previously discouraged and frustrated with reading. The intensive schedule allows the student to rapidly establish necessary skills.

## B. MATERIALS NEEDED:

By design this reading program does NOT require purchase of expensive or complex supplemental materials. Everything you need to complete the lessons and activities is readily available and affordable. In addition to this book, you will need the following materials:

**1) Paper and Pencil**: Use regular loose-leaf paper and standard pencils.

**2) Sound Cards**: "Sound cards" are used to teach and practice the sounds. To make "sound cards" simply write the sound on an index card. For the letters and "partner letters" with multiple sounds it is helpful to note a little 2 or 3 in the bottom corner to remind the student of how many sounds that letter represents. Index cards are inexpensive, so you can make several sets for practice in alternate locations such as in the car. Keep the cards in a zip-lock bag or bound with a rubber band.

**3) Sound Tiles/ Sound Tile Kit**: The sound tiles are an integral part of the *Right Track Reading Lessons* Program. The sound tiles are an effective multisensory tool for allowing the student to 'see' and learn the correct phonetic structure of our language. Sound tiles are simply made by writing the sounds on 2" ceramic bathroom tiles with a permanent black marker. The sound tile kit includes the sound tiles and a template for word making. A plastic organizer box is also recommended.

Make either 1) the 'Complete Basic Tile Set' or 2) the 'Expanded Tile Set'. The 'Complete Basic Set' provides necessary sound tiles for conducting all word making activities in the lessons and is sufficient for most individuals tutoring one older student. The 'Expanded Set' provides double tiles for most the sounds allowing you to conduct additional activities such as matching/memory games etc. The expanded set is ideal if you tutor more than one student or plan on conducting supplemental activities.

2" square ceramic bathroom tiles – Basic white 2" ceramic bathroom tiles are available at home improvement stores for around $2.25 for a sheet of 36 tiles. You need 104 2"-tiles for a basic set (3 sheets of 36 tiles) and 131 2"-tiles (4 sheets of 36 tiles) for an expanded set. The 36 tiles are attached in a sheet with rubber tabs. I found it is easier to first break the tiles apart by bending them back and forth. After the tiles are separated, carefully cut off the excess rubber connection knobs with a pair of scissors. You can make 2" square "sound tiles" from other materials such as thick cardstock. However, I recommend 2" ceramic tiles as they are ideal for manipulation. Thin materials are difficult for students to pick up.

A permanent black marker: Use the permanent marker to write the correct letter(s) on the tiles. Always print sounds on the tiles with lower case normal/block print styles.

Make "Sound Tiles": Make either the Complete Basic Set OR the Expanded Set by printing the following sounds on the tiles with the permanent marker.
Complete Basic Tile Set:
Make 2 tiles for each of the following sounds: a e i o u y   b c d f g h j k l m n p r s t v w x th sh ch ing   or er ar
Make 1 tile for each of the following sounds: qu z wh ck tch ink   ay ai oi oy ea ee ie ei ey ou ow oa oe ue ui ew oo au aw augh igh ph wr kn ore oar oor our ur ir ear are air eer ere ire
Expanded Tile Set:
Make the basic set adding an additional ($2^{nd}$) tile for the following sounds: qu z wh ck ay ai oi oy ea ee ou ow oa ue ui ew oo au aw ore oar ur ir are air eer ear

A plastic organizer box with compartments large enough to hold the 2" tiles (Optional but highly suggested) The storage box needs a minimum of 18 compartments large enough to fit the 2"-tiles. A carrying handle is also a nice feature. I have found several affordable readily available storage box options from the $5 tackle box at the sporting goods section of a large discount store to a slightly larger and studier $10 hardware/screw organizer at a home improvement store. While this box is not mandatory it is very useful. I tried using an old shoebox and it was difficult to find the tiles needed for a specific lesson or activity. An organizer box is well worth the $10 investment.

Small labels (Optional but suggested): It is helpful to label the compartments with small round or rectangular sticky labels so you can quickly find specific tiles. This is a convenience feature to help the adult who is teaching the lessons.

**Suggested tile layout/organization for EXPANDED SET in an 18 compartment tackle box:**
(The grids on the chart represent the compartments in the tackle box. Make 2 of each sound tile unless indicated with *, then only make 1 tile for that sound)

| a e i | o u y | b c d f | g h j k | l m n p | qu r s t |
|---|---|---|---|---|---|
| v w x z | th sh wh ck | ch tch* ing ink* | ay ai oy oi | ea ee ie* ei* ey* | ou ow oa oe* |
| ue ui ew oo | au aw augh* igh* ph* wr*kn* | /or/ or ore oar oor* our* | /er/ er ur ir ear* | ar /air/ ar are air | /eer/ eer ere* ear* /ire/ ire* |

**4) Template for Word Making**: Make a template for 'word making' activities. This can be made from a piece of poster board approximately 18" long by 6" wide. When 'making words', you need to place tiles next to each other with no gaps between sound tiles. However, there needs to be a small gap on the template lines. An easy way to make the template is to place 7 tiles next to each other in a straight line and draw template lines slightly shorter than the tiles as to leave a slight gap between the template lines. Be sure and draw a large directional arrow under the tile-template to reinforce tracking.

**5) A Place to Work**: Find a quiet spot with adequate room to work. A table with 2 chairs is ideal. Sit next to the student so you can *see* and *hear* what he is doing and provide immediate feedback with both positive encouragement and corrective instruction.

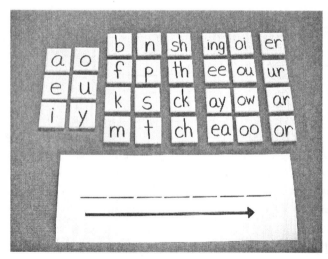

Sound Tiles and Template

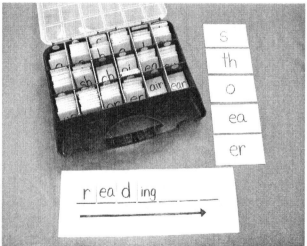

Sound Tile Kit, Sound Cards & Template

# C. GENERAL INSTRUCTIONS FOR ALL THE LESSONS

## 1. Always Make Immediate Corrections:

Immediately correct any errors. Remember corrections are a positive action and a prime learning opportunity. It is essential to make immediate corrections so the student does not learn the wrong way. Insure the student correctly performs the subskills of tracking, blending, and accurately pronouncing the sounds. All words need to be read correctly. When the student makes an error, stop them. Often all it takes is 'oops' or simply tapping the error on the page with a pencil so they look closer at the word. If they don't understand how to perform a skill or are lacking necessary sound knowledge then you must teach them how before continuing. In remediation situations, correction is essential to help the student extinguish incorrect processing and develop new efficient processing pathways.

## 2. Use Understandable Terms:

When presenting information, use understandable terms and explanations so the student will comprehend the concept. Avoid the official technical linguistic terminology such as phoneme, digraphs, diphthongs, and phonograms that are meaningless to most people. Make sure the student understands your explanations. It is always much better to say something like "this letter has the sound ___" instead of "the alphabetic characters in this phonogram symbolize the phoneme __". It is better to say "please write the partner letters 'sh' while you say the /sh/ sound" instead of saying "please encode the proper consonant digraph for the phoneme /sh/." This does not mean that you leave out all correct terminology, but rather you should explain in understandable terms and minimize unnecessary jargon.

## 3. Directly and Systematically Teach all the Sounds:

Systematically present and directly teach the direct *'printed letter(s)=sound'* relationship. By design, the lessons include a variety of highly effective multisensory activities to help the student develop the automatic direct *print=sound* relationship necessary for efficient phonologic processing. Initial lessons directly teach the basic sounds, subsequent lessons add the vowel combinations, r-controlled vowel combinations and other complexities. The sound introduction, sound card practice and writing the sound activities all provide direct print=sound practice that develops automatic knowledge. The word making and word writing activities also reinforce this direct print=sound relationship. Remember this is not 'learning the alphabet' this is the process of automatically and directly converting print to sound.

When practicing sounds make sure the student is looking at the printed letter(s), pronouncing the sound correctly and tracking under the letter with their finger or a pointer. Practice this direct *'printed letter(s)=sound'* relationship until the knowledge is automatic.

## 4. Pronounce all the Sounds Correctly:

Correct pronunciation is critical. Always make sure *you can say the sound correctly* before teaching it to the student. This needs to be the sound that letter represents in our language NOT the letter name. The sound pronunciation table is found in Appendix A.

For letter(s) with more than one sound, make sure the student properly pronounces each distinct sound separately. For example the sounds for 'o' are /o/, /oa/ & /u/ NOT /o-oa-u/ all together in one breath.

## 5. Practice the Sounds:

Practice is essential! Practice. Practice. Practice. The goal is for the student to acquire *automatic* recognition and knowledge of the sound the printed letter represents. The *'printed letter=sound'* relationship must become automatic so the student can concentrate on higher skills. To achieve this, lots of direct practice, repetition and reinforcement are necessary. Make sure all practice is direct print=sound. The multisensory activity of 'writing the sounds' is highly effective in mastering this automatic knowledge of the phonemic code.

## 6. Engrain Proper Left to Right Tracking:

Directly teach and emphasize proper directional tracking. Do not skip teaching this essential subskill. It is critical the student always looks at and process *all* the letters *in order* from left to right. To develop proper tracking, this program requires the student physically follow under the words with his finger or another pointer. This physical tracking motion is especially important in remediation, as struggling readers frequently make errors in processing order.

If older students are uncomfortable using their finger, they can use a toothpick, pencil, or another pointer of their choice. However, make sure they physically move their finger or pointer under the letters from left to right in all their reading. The multisensory benefit of kinetic motion develops and engrains this essential subskill. This finger motion is the effective tool to help a student develop proper tracking and overcome the incorrect habit of looking at all the letters at once or out of order that causes many reading errors. Only when proper tracking is automatically engrained and the student no longer makes tracking errors should the requirement of physical movement be dropped.

Directly teach, require and reinforce proper left-to-right directional tracking throughout the program. In word making activities, always have students make words in order left-to-right. Never let students make or write words out of order. In word reading, have the student physically track under the words. Have the student read word lists left-to-right across the rows. Do not let them read down the columns or skip around. During guided reading have the student physically track with their finger or a pointer.

## 7. Directly Teach Proper Blending Skills:

Smooth blending is an essential subskill to proficient reading. Many students automatically and easily learn how to blend sounds together. However, others need specific work to master this skill. If the student is separating/chopping the sounds apart instead of smoothly blending them together, *stop him immediately*. Say something like "listen to how you need to keep the sounds together without stopping". Be sure to *always demonstrate the correct blending technique* of not pausing between the sounds. Have him take a breath before starting a word. If that does not work, have him *sing* the word to you. If he is carrying a tune, it is impossible to segment the sounds. (A friend shared this simple effective technique with me.) If the student has difficulty blending sounds, immediately stop and work on this critical skill with some oral blending practice. *The student needs to master smooth blending in the initial stages.* If they can not blend smoothly it will handicap them in developing fluency.

When blending, remember sounds must always be pronounced correctly. Some of the 'fast' sounds (such as t, b c, k, d, g) can not be stretched out and said slowly, so must be quickly joined to the next sound. Learning to smoothly blend these sounds is more difficult for some students and must be practiced.

## 8. Directly Develop Phonemic Awareness Skills:

The lessons directly teach the student to recognize and distinguish the individual sounds within words and to link this phonemic awareness to print. Phonemic awareness segmenting skills are directly developed in the word making and spelling/word writing activities. The sound tiles are especially helpful in developing PA as the student is able to physically 'see' and manipulate the accurate sound structure of language.

Once again, after basic skills are established, specific attention needs to be given to the blended consonant combinations. Practice segmenting blended consonants (several lessons work specifically on blended consonants). It is often more difficult for the student to distinguish and segment blended consonant sounds, especially the blended sounds starting with "fast" sounds such as b, c, d, t (for example dr, tr, cl, br). In fact is it often harder for a student to segment or split apart these sounds than it is to read/blend them together. The student may read the word trap without hesitation but when asked to write the word he writes "tap". He needs work on hearing and segmenting the sounds out of a word. Once again make sure the consonants are taught phonetically correct as individual sounds not clusters (/f/ /l/ not /fl/).

### 9. Use Normal Print for Teaching Sounds and Writing:

Always use normal block print or similar straightforward print styles for all reading instruction activities. Do not use cursive or any of the loopy script/crossover styles. In addition, be sure to use standard block print when writing the letters on sound cards and sound tiles. The vast majority of reading material utilizes standard print styles. With regular print, letters remain fairly distinct and dissimilar from each other (except for b, d and p). However when loopy script or crossover cursive styles are used, additional letters become harder to distinguish. Loopy script and cursive-crossover print styles create letter confusion with some letters and can make reading more difficult for some students. I have observed numerous examples of letter and sound confusion I strongly believe are created directly by the loopy style of writing. For example, when k is written *k,* it looks similar to *h.* Students who learn this type of 'loopy k' routinely mix up *k* and *h,* and also *ch* and *ck.* They make frequent reading errors with the inappropriate /ch/ and /k/ sounds. Another frequent source of confusion is with the letters i, j and l. These letters are very distinct in regular block print but appear similar when loopy script is used and they become *i j l.* (The remediation for these errors is to practice printing the correct block print while saying the sound). For an adult who already reads, complicating print styles is irrelevant. For students learning the code and developing neural processing pathways, it can create unnecessary complications.

## D. INSTRUCTIONS FOR SPECIFIC ACTIVITIES:

*Back on the Right Track Reading Lessons* includes a variety of carefully designed multisensory activities that directly teach and develop skills necessary for proficient reading. The following summary gives the specific directions on how to conduct these activities. This section is organized by activity and includes instructions for conducting the activity and an explanation of the specific skills the activity targets. Most activities are directly written into the lessons. Additional activities are described so you can supplement the lessons and provide additional practice and reinforcement of skills.

Note: Although lessons include scripted wording, there is flexibility to use your own words as long as you do not alter the design of the program. For the most part this includes correct sounding out, left to right tracking, proper blending, and immediate correction of errors. Scripted instructions are provided to help start you in correct techniques not a rigid requirement that must always be followed word for word.

### 1. Teaching the Sounds

The lessons systematically introduce and directly teach the complete phonemic code. The initial lessons directly teach basic sounds, subsequent lessons add vowel combinations, r-controlled vowel combinations and other complexities. Introducing and directly teaching the sounds is a critical step. This activity directly teaches the printed letter (or partner letters)=sound relationship. Be sure the student directly links the visual image of the print to the oral and auditory process of saying and hearing the sound.

New sounds are listed at the beginning of lessons. When you first introduce a sound: Point to the print and say "This sound is __" or "this letter has the sound __". When you first introduce any multi-letter sound (such as th or ch), explain how the letters are "partners" that work together to make a sound. Use an understandable term such as "partner letters" or "buddy letters" so the student understands the concept. Once the student understands the direct relationship between print and sound you can skip the explanation and simply point at new sound and say the sound. Teach the sound to the student by saying the sound a few times as you follow under the new sound with your finger. Be sure to teach correct pronunciation. Next have the student say the sound correctly, *as* he looks at the print and follows under the sound with his finger. He must be looking at the printed letter on the page *as* he says the sound NOT just parroting the sound while looking at you or up at the ceiling. This directly links the visual image of the print to the oral & auditory process of saying and hearing the correct sound. Remember this is not 'learning the alphabet' but rather the process of automatically and directly converting print to sound.

## 2. Practice Sound Cards
The next activity in most lessons is practicing sound cards (index cards with sound written on it). The sound cards directly teach the *printed letter=sound association* and allow frequent practice so conversion from print to sound becomes automatic. Make a card for each new sound you teach. Use these sound cards as flash cards. Continue to add to the collection. The student practices newly introduced as well as previous sounds. In all practice, the student must look directly at the printed letter while saying the correct sound. To be effective make sure the student (1) looks directly at the printed letter (2) as they say the correctly pronounced sound and (3) follows under the sound with directional finger tracking. Chanting the sound while looking out the window will not build necessary skills. This simple but highly effective multisensory activity directly links the visual image of the print to the oral and auditory processes of saying and hearing the correct sound.

Repeated practice and drill with these sound cards establishes automatic knowledge of the link between print and sound. Index cards are inexpensive. Make several sets. Daily practice is important to achieve the goal of *automatic recognition and knowledge of printed letter=sound*. Older students are eager to catch up to their classmates. Emphasize the more they practice the quicker they will proceed. Help them get excited about practicing and directly learning their sounds. The older student's background knowledge enables them to rapidly advance through the sounds. Once a sound is automatic, the student no longer needs to practice it in isolation and it can be removed from the stack. Remember, automatic knowledge of the sound is a necessary sub-skill for proficient phonologic processing.

## 3. Write and Say the Sound
As discussed earlier, one of the most effective multisensory activities for directly learning the '*printed letter=sound*' relationships is to write the letter while saying the sound. In this paper and pencil activity, the student writes each sound 5 to 10 times (or more) while saying the sound. This simple act of printing the letter(s) while saying the sound effectively and efficiently establishes a direct link between print and sound. This is not a penmanship drill. To be effective the student must *say the sound* as they print the letter. The sound writing activity teaches new sounds and allows practice of previous sounds.

Sound writing/ saying is highly effective because it directly links the kinetic motion of forming the letter, visual image of seeing the completed print, oral process of saying the correct sound, and auditory processes of hearing the correct sound. These multisensory processes are all directly targeted toward developing the essential print=sound link necessary for proficient reading. Use standard block print styles and emphasize correct letter formation. Formation is especially critical with the similar appearing letters b, d and p. Explicit instruction and careful attention to how these letters are formed can prevent the common confusion that occurs in both reading and writing with these visually similar letters.

The importance of writing sounds and then later words cannot be emphasized enough. This simple yet highly effective multisensory activity forces the student to develop the necessary direct link between print and sound. It effectively and efficiently helps the student learn the phonemic code. Anytime the student does not automatically remember a sound, have him repeatedly write it while saying the sound. It works! As with sound card practice, when the student acquires automatic knowledge of the sound they no longer need to practice writing the sound in isolation.

## 4. Review Sounds
The sound review activity is periodically incorporated into the lessons. The sound review simply lists all the sounds learned to that point. This activity provides the student additional direct practice/reinforcement of the sounds. This quick review is also designed to show the instructor which sounds the student may need additional practice with. If a student does not automatically know one of the sounds on the review list, provide additional practice for that sound (practice sound card or practice writing/saying sound). Conversely, if a sound is automatic, it no longer needs to be practiced in isolation.

# 5. Making Words with the Sound Tiles

The word making activity is conducted with the 'sound tiles'. The 'sound tiles' allow the student to actually 'see' and physically manipulate the accurate phonemic structure of our language. The word making activity provides a tangible way to learn correct phonological processing. The activity forces the student to develop phonemic awareness, visualize sounds as proper printed units and physically combine these distinct printed sounds into words. By design, these activities integrate kinetic, visual and auditory processes to develop correct phonologic processing of the print. These 'sound tile' activities are especially beneficial in remedial reading situations as they directly teach and develop correct phonologic processing. As a bonus, these word making activities are fun. Even older students enjoy 'making words'.

Tell the student they are going to construct or make words by putting sounds together. The student listens to a spoken word, and then 'makes' that word with the sound tiles. This activity develops direct sound=letter knowledge, phonemic awareness of segmenting the separate sounds within a word, proper blending and tracking skills, and requires the student use correct phonologic processing.

Take out the appropriate sound tiles listed in the lesson and lay them out above the template. It is helpful to sort the sound tiles into slightly separated groups of vowels, consonants, partner letters, and r-controlled vowel combinations. The student doesn't see the listed words but rather listens carefully as you tell him the word you want him to make. For the first lesson, demonstrate how to make one of the words correctly on the template with proper sounding, blending and finger tracking.

Say "Please make the word _____". Read the first word, speaking clearly and repeating the word at least once. If necessary, speak slowly and emphasize the sounds. The student repeats the word and then starts making it. Make sure he says the individual sounds as he lays down the tiles, makes the word in order and uses proper smooth blending skills. After he completes the word, have him sound out the word to you using finger tracking and smooth blending skills. Correct any errors and give short encouraging remarks. Clear all the tiles before reading the next word on the list to the student.

In all word making activities, ensure the student:
1) Says the individual sounds out loud as he picks up/lays down the appropriate tiles.
2) Always works from left to right. Never let the student make a word out of order.
3) Blends the sounds together smoothly.
4) Accurately sounds out the word with finger tracking after completing the word with the tiles.

Immediately correct any errors. If the student picks up the wrong sound tile stop him and ask him what the sound tile says. Is he hearing the sound within the word incorrectly or does he not know the *letter=sound* relationship or did he just accidentally grab the wrong tile? With the blended sounds often the student will miss a sound such as making the word "string" as "sting". Have him read the word to you. Say, "This word says 'sting' how would you make it say 'string'?" Help him learn to hear and distinguish the sounds. Make corrections so the student learns and weak skills are strengthened.

Modify the word making activity to strengthen specific skills by selecting words from the list that contain the sounds the student needs to work on. If the student has difficulty distinguishing 'fast' blended consonant sounds then be sure and give the student words with those combinations. If the student is having difficulty with a specific sound, include words with the troublesome sound. The intent of this activity is to build specific skills. By selecting certain words you can modify the activity to best meet your individual student's needs. Likewise, if the student's skills with certain sounds are well established it is not necessary to make all the listed words.

You can make your own word building lists, just be sure you use only sounds that have been previously introduced. Take care to avoid including confusing sounds on the same list/group (such as having c, k and ck all available for selection). You never want the student to practice making a word incorrectly.

This page illustrates examples of the word making activity.

     Use Sound Tiles… u  i  ee  ay  d(2)  g  m  n  p  r  s  t  w  ch  ing

     Word List: speech  midway  greeting  indeed  stingray  praying  unseen

Lay out the template and the appropriate sound tiles listed in the lesson. Notice the separated grouping of vowels, consonants and partner letters.

Ask the student to make the first word on the list. For example, say "Please make the word 'speech'". The student does not see the printed word, he only hears it. The student 'makes' the word by translating sounds to print as he selects and places appropriate tiles on the template. The student says the sounds (not letter names) out loud as he makes the word in order from left-to-right. After completing the word, the student reads the word to you with finger tracking and smooth blending

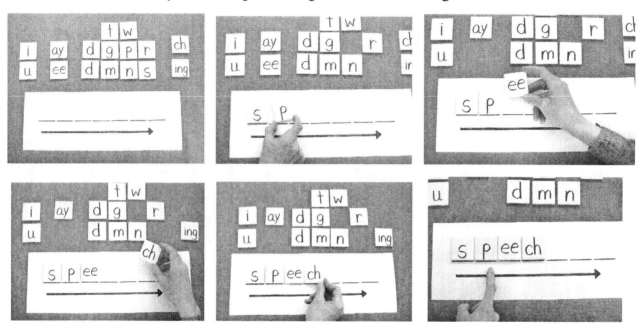

Clear the template completely and ask the student to make the next word on the list. For example, "Please make the word 'midway'". The student makes the word by translating sound to print in placing the correct tiles on the template. The advantage of the tiles is allows the student to actually 'see' and physically manipulate the accurate phonemic structure of our language. Once again when the word is completed, the student reads the word with finger tracking and smooth blending.

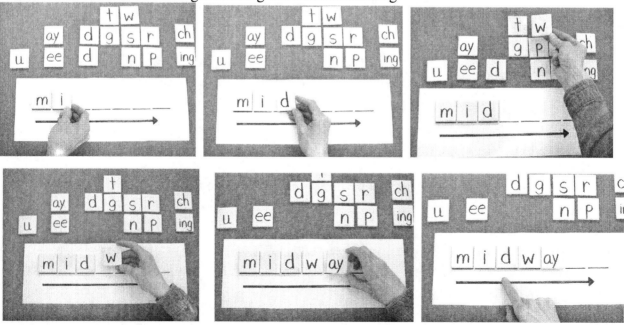

## 6. Sound Changing Activity (or other phonemic manipulation activities)

This is another word making activity with the sound tiles, except the student listens and determines how he needs to change the word one sound at a time instead of starting over. This sound changing activity gives the student direct practice in hearing and manipulating sounds, develops phonemic awareness skills, provides practice with the letter=sound relationship, and establishes correct phonologic processing. This also directly teaches the student how important each and every letter is in a word. The importance of attention to detail is demonstrated. One letter/sound changes the entire word. Once again the physical manipulation of the sound structure of language is especially beneficial in remediation.

Explain this sound tile activity is similar to the previous word making except instead of starting over each time, he *listens carefully* and only changes one sound to make the new word. Remind the student to listen carefully so he hears what sound to change. The first time you conduct this activity, demonstrate what you are asking him to do.

Say, "Please make the word _____ for me". Tell the student the first word on the list. Make sure he makes the word correctly using the techniques given in the word making activity. Then say something similar to "Great Job! You made ____." "Now please change the sound to make the word ____ ( say the next word on the list)". Be sure the student says the sounds as they pick up the tiles, makes words from left to right, and blends the sounds together correctly. Make immediate corrections if the student makes an error. When the word is completed, have the student read the word to you. With this activity, instead of clearing the tiles, leave the word in place and have the student make the necessary changes to make the next word.

For example if the sound changing activity gives the words "block > black > slack > stack": The student would make 'block' as described in the word making activity. After the student reads 'block', ask them to change it to 'black'. The student listens and makes the change removing the 'o' and replacing it with 'a'. The student points at the completed word and reads 'black' to you before you say the next word 'slack'. Once again the student listens and makes the necessary change, changing the /b/ sound to /s/ by replacing the 'b' with 's'. This word changing continues through the list of words.

You can also conduct other sound changing activities. Have the student make a word and then make specific changes to it. For example: "Please make the word 'trap'. Now what sound would you change to make the word say 'trip." "Make the word "string", now what word would it be if you took out the /r/ sound". If you made the word 'paint' and then changed the 'ai' to 'oi' sound what word would you have. If the student needs extra work in developing phonemic awareness, these types of sound manipulation activities with the tiles are a terrific method to directly develop necessary phonemic awareness skills.

## 7. Reading Word Lists

The *Right Track Reading Lessons* program makes extensive use of decodable word lists as a tool to teach student how to read correctly. These word lists are especially beneficial in remediation because they force the student to develop and use correct skills. Reading isolated words in a list effectively develops necessary phonologic processing skills as the student must look at all the sounds and use correct processing. The word cannot be guessed from pictures or context clues. Incorrect strategies will not work with random word lists. The decodable word lists in themselves may not be "exciting reading" but they are an extremely effective tool for developing correct phonologic processing. These word lists are highly effective in directly developing necessary skills.

Have the student read all the listed words in each lesson. The words are all decodable with sounds the student has systematically learned. The word lists are also cumulative, including all previously taught sounds. The student reads the listed words using correct phonologic processing, blending, tracking, and attention to detail. To develop correct skills:

- Directly teach and require proper directional tracking. The student needs to always physically track, following under the word with either his finger or a pointer as he reads each word. Once again this physical movement, directly develops correct tracking skills and is especially critical with remedial readers who previously had not acquired this essential subskill of proficient reading. In addition, to reinforce proper tracking, always have the student read the word lists from left to right across the rows, *not* down the columns.

- Directly teach and require proper smooth blending. This is where *blending skills are critical.* If the student has problems blending, have him take a breath before starting the word or have him 'sing' the word to you so that sounds do not fall apart. Do not allow choppy segmented sounding out. Be sure smooth blending is mastered from the beginning.

- Make sure each and every word is read accurately! Immediately correct any errors. It is essential to stop the student as soon as they make any error. A quick "oops" or "stop" or simply tapping the word with you pencil is often all that is needed to get the student to look closer at the word. Word reading list are designed to help the student develop and practice careful attention to detail. The student must read the word accurately. Even minor errors like saying 'run' for 'runs' must be corrected as the student needs to learn to carefully look at each and every sound. If they miss a sound or stop them and have them look again. If the word contains a newly introduced sound that the student does not yet know automatically, you many need to say something similar to 'remember this sound is __" as you point to the sound. If they say a sound that is not actually there (for example read 'sting' as 'string') stop them and have them look again. If necessary, point at the exact sound that was missed or the specific error that was made. Always have the student re-read the word correctly. In come cases, if a word is particularly troublesome for a student, you can have the student make the word with the sound tiles. This helps them 'see' the phonemic structure of the word. In the word reading, always require completely accurate decoding. This emphasis on accuracy and use of correction is critical for both extinguishing incorrect strategies and for building proficient reader skills.

**Handling Multisyllable words:** The word lists include many multisyllable words. The program systematically incorporates multisyllable words into the word lists so the student learns how to handle these longer words. Sections 1 and 2 include increasing numbers of 2-syllable words. Sections 3 through Section 5 incorporate many 2-syllable and some 3-syllable words. Section 6 is dedicated specifically to direct instruction in handling the longer multisyllable words (3+ syllables). Within each word list in Sections 1-5, the single syllable words are listed first to allow phonologic processing and practice of new sounds before requiring these sounds to be processed within the more difficult multisyllable words. The 2-syllable words are listed next and the 3-syllable words are found at the end of the list. This initial practice with 2 and 3 syllable words will help the student develop a foundation for handling the longer '3+-syllable words'. Please read the Introduction/General Information portion of **Section 6 - Reading Multisyllable Words** for a complete explanation of multisyllable words.

The technique for helping a student learn how to handle longer words is fairly simple. As the student reads the words to you, have your pencil ready. *If* the student has problems with breaking words into appropriate syllables, place a light pencil mark slashes in the appropriate syllable breaks and make a comment such as 'take another look' so he can better 'see' the syllables. For example: expensive → add the light pencil slashes to indicate → ex/pen/sive. These light pencil marks help the student begin to 'see' the appropriate breaks. Remember to make the slash marks *only* when the student needs help. While many students will easily handle the 2 and 3 syllable words without assistance, some struggle with this skill and need direct help developing this essential skill. The longer multisyllable words (3+ syllables) are addressed in Section 6.

**Building Fluency on Common Words:** The word lists incorporate frequent practice of some of the most common words. These frequently encountered words are included in the lessons after the necessary sounds are taught. Repeated and correct phonetic analysis of these common words helps the student develop accurate 'neural models' and achieve fluent 'fast reading' of these common words. Although the student needs to practice these common words, never have them shortcut the correct sounding out/phonologic processing that is essential for developing true fluency.

**Additional Practice**: Some students need additional practice to fully master reading skills. If the student has not mastered the smooth accurate decoding, provide additional practice by having the student read word lists more than once (Use a word list from any lesson you have already completed.) You can also make supplemental word lists to provide additional practice. If you make your own word lists, be sure the words are decodable, only using previously taught sounds.

## 8. Writing Words (Spelling)

The importance of writing words cannot be emphasized enough. Writing words by sound is an effective technique to intentionally help the student develop phonologic processing and improve reading skills. Reading and writing words/spelling are converse sides of the same process. If the student learns to listen to oral speech and translate those sounds into printed letters and words it greatly strengthens the reverse skill of looking at print and translating that back into the sounds of our language. Writing words is an especially appropriate and effective tool for older students as the printing process itself tends to be easy.

*Writing words or spelling by sound* effectively reinforces essential 'printed letter=sound' relationships, strengthens phonemic awareness and develops correct phonologic processing. Writing directly links and targets the processes of saying the sounds (oral), hearing the spoken sound (auditory), physically forming the letter (kinetic) and seeing printed letters (visual) to help students effectively develop phonologic processing. Word writing by sound is also an effective tool in building fluency for individual words.

For spelling to be an effective tool for reading development the student must *say the sounds as he writes the letters*. Teach the student to spell by listening to and writing the sounds of a word NOT memorization of random letters. Don't give the student words to practice. Simply select words from the lesson's word list (or other words ONLY containing sounds that have been learned). Tell the student you are starting a word writing (or spelling) activity. Give the student some paper & pencil. Say "please write the word _____". Speak clearly. Repeat the word if necessary. Speaking clearly and repeating the word are especially important if the student is still developing phonemic awareness skills to properly distinguish sounds within words. Have the student use standard print.

In the beginning, spelling should be limited to writing learned sounds. Make immediate corrections. This is not a "spelling test". It is practice turning language into print, the reverse process of reading. At first spelling needs to be simple and phonetic. As the complexity increases, minimize confusion and mistakes by telling the student what sound combination to use. If you are practicing 'ai' tell the student "we are going to write words that are written with the 'ai' partner letters. Remember you are going to write the /ay/ sound with 'ai'" and then give the words 'detain', 'train', 'explain', 'complain'." Help the student spell correctly. Don't let the student practice incorrect spelling. You can and should teach some of the common spelling patterns at this time but be sure and tell/teach it (*not* test it yet).

*Later* the student will need to practice the more complex spelling words, irregulars and learn the actual "correct" spelling option for specific words. (The /ay/ sound is spelled 'ai' in rain, 'a' in rang, 'ay' in play, and 'eigh' in eight, so which spelling do you use for a specific word?) Advanced spelling practice is necessary but don't *begin* with advanced complexities where the student *approaches* "spelling" as simply memorizing a random collection of letters. Specific spelling practice requiring memorization of correct sound combinations and irregulars is necessary at the advanced level. Additional spelling information is located in the spelling section at the end of the reading lessons.

## 9. Additional Sound Identification Activities

Additional sound identification activities can be done with word lists to provide practice and reinforcement of phonetic analysis. These activities add variety and fun to simply reading word lists.

--Identifying A Single Sound: In this activity, write a list of words that contain the different ways to represent a given sound. Then have the student underline the specific sound that you ask him to underline. For example write the list of words "boat, go, toe, show, oat, bone, hole, loan". Ask the student to underline the sound /oa/ in the words. As the student reads the words, he underlines the /oa/ sound in the word. In the example above, as he reads he would underline g<u>o</u>, t<u>oe</u>, sh<u>ow</u>, <u>oa</u>t, b<u>o</u>ne, h<u>o</u>le, l<u>oa</u>n.

--Identifying All Sounds Within a Word: Write a list of words that contain previously taught sounds (You can use words from the word read list in the lessons). Have the student underline all the sounds as they read the word. For example in the word 'chain' they would underline <u>ch</u> <u>ai</u> <u>n</u>, in 'reading' they would underline <u>r</u> <u>ea</u> <u>d</u> <u>ing</u>.

## 10. Reading Irregular Words:

Irregular words are a part of our English language. While most words are phonetic when the complete code is known, some words are not. While some words do not 'sound out' accurately and need to be learned partially by "*sight*" trying to visually memorize the whole word to 'read' should not be taught as a reading strategy. It is important to realize even irregular words are at least partially phonetic and still apply left to right tracking. For example in 'said' the 's' and 'd' are completely phonetic, /s/ is the first sound, followed by the 'irregular' /e/ and then the phonetic ending /d/. In the word 'busy' the only irregular portion is the 'u'=/i/. In 'what', only the 'a'=/u/ is irregular. The student still needs to look at and process all letters in order ('from'-'form, 'was'-'saw' are not the same). The student needs to track properly and pay careful attention to detail to develop an accurate neural model of the word. The student needs to notice and process every letter in order, even with the irregular words.

Most older students already recognize the common irregular words. If an unfamiliar irregular word is encountered, simply introduce the word as irregular. Specifically point out the irregular portion of the word to the student. Use the technique of saying "____ is an irregular word", it should sound out ____, but we say ____". Have the student read the word several times carefully noting the irregular part. Practice writing the word several times, paying attention to the sound structure and spelling that is used. Writing irregular words is an effective way to teach students irregular words without teaching the incorrect strategies of visual memorization or whole word guessing. Common irregular words are also included for frequent practice in the word list.

## 11. Guided Oral Reading:

*Guided* reading is essential to helping a student improve reading skills. This is where the student reads outloud to you with guidance and feedback. Be sure to include a *minimum* of 20 minutes of daily guided oral reading after lesson 65. At this point the student has directly learned the vast majority of the phonemic code (all but the special -tion, -cial endings.) Guided reading provides an effective learning opportunity. As the instructor, it is your job to make sure the student reads accurately and improves necessary skills. Correct any errors. In addition to strengthening phonologic processing skills, and building fluency (word by word) this guided reading provides the student an opportunity to develop reading comprehension skills and vocabulary. Guided reading is particularly important with reading remediation. Detailed instructions for conducting guided reading are located in Section 7.

# E. ADDITIONAL TIPS:

Students are all unique. I learn something every time I work with a student. The students truly have been valuable instructors for helping me learn about teaching reading. In addition, a variety of knowledgeable individuals have shared suggestions and tips with me. Thanks to my 'instructors', both big and little, I have picked up a few tips and valuable ideas for helping student develop their reading skills.

- It is helpful for the instructor to keep a pencil in hand during lessons. A pencil makes a wonderful tool not just for writing notes and making necessary breaks in the multisyllable words but to use as a pointer. I personally prefer a mechanical pencil as the lead can be retracted when using as a pointer and the fine tip allows precise pointing at specific sounds. Often when the student makes an error, I don't even need to say anything. I simply tap the pencil on the missed word. The student quickly picks on this silent 'oops-look again' signal. Somehow the pencil tap is more pleasant than a verbal correction.

- Having energetic students go outside and literally run a few laps immediately prior to sitting down for reading can be an extremely beneficial tool. In addition, if you have an especially energetic student who has difficulty sitting down, try having the student stand next to you. I have successfully used this technique with several 'lively' ones. The student MUST stand right next to me and focus and pay attention to the lesson; however they can stand and even wiggle a bit as long as it does not interfere with their reading. This standing seems to utilize some of the excess energy.

- If a student has difficulty with writing (penmanship), I recommend the *Zaner-Bloser* manuscript handwriting program. This effective handwriting program teaches the specific steps involved in correct penmanship from how to hold the pencil, to correct position, formation and spacing. I would like to thank, Mr. Clint Hackney for introducing and sharing this very effective writing program with me. The step-by-step instructions illustrating details of correct penmanship are fantastic. It sounds surprising but many students have difficulty writing because they lack basic skills. Many do not even hold the pencil correctly. Direct instruction in the exact skills of skilled writing is highly beneficial and effective in helping students improve penmanship skills. The student workbooks cost approximately $12 and are suitable and effective for individual tutoring situations. Classroom programs which include the teacher materials are also available. More information on the *Zaner-Bloser* program can be found at their website http://www.zaner-bloser.com/html/hwgen.html.

- If a student has a speech difficulty, talk with a speech pathologist for specific recommendations. Most school districts have a speech specialist or can recommend a specialist. These specialists often can provide user friendly tips and methods of helping a student make specific sounds. Additionally, a collection of some 'sound pronunciation tips' are located at the end of Appendix A. While reading instruction absolutely does *not* eliminate the need for speech assistance, the individual instruction with specific sounds as a part of the reading program provides an opportunity to help a student work on particular sounds and supplement the speech instruction.

- In addition, when correcting the reading of a student who has a speech difficulty, inability to say a sound or mispronunciation due to a speech difficulty is NOT a reading error. If the student correctly identifies and attempts to say the sound, don't correct mispronunciation as a reading error. The instructor should repeat the word pronounced correctly and help the student practice how to correctly make the sound but do not consider it 'incorrect' from a reading standpoint. For example: If the student has difficulty pronouncing /r/ and says /stwing/ for 'string' the student read the word correctly even though they did not pronounce it correctly. Do not correct these types of pronunciation errors as reading errors. In contrast, if the student misses the /r/ sound altogether and says /sting/ you would stop him and have him re-read the word picking up the 'r'.

- It is helpful to use some sort of log to keep track of the student's progress. A progress log is located in Appendix C. You can also use the lesson outline or simply record progress on a piece of paper. For the printed progress log in the appendix, note the date completed next to the lesson number. I have found the older students simply like to check the chart with handwritten date to track how rapidly they are progressing. Younger students often like to keep track of their progress with small stickers. If you are tutoring more than one student, progress logs are essential.

- In addition to a progress log, it is also helpful to keep brief notes. I record handwritten notes to myself on loose-leaf paper organized chronologically by date of the tutoring session. For each tutoring session, note information such as the exact sounds the student may need to work on, the specific errors or types of errors they are making, skills that need further development, any skill the student seems to have fully mastered, or other pertinent information. There is no required format. These 'working' notes help the instructor modify and target instruction to best meet the student's specific needs. If you are working with more than one student or have several different instructors working with an individual student these written notes are vital. The notes and progress chart can be kept in an inexpensive two pocket folder labeled with the student's name. When you go to work with a student you can simply grab their folder.

# OUTLINE OF READING LESSON CONTENT

For each lesson, this outline provides:
- The beginning page number
- The sounds that are introduced or a brief summary of the lesson
- The high frequency words that are included as the necessary sounds are introduced

*This outline lists Reading Lessons only. The separate section with Spelling Lessons starts on page 237.

| Lesson # | Page # | Sounds Introduced Summary of Lesson | High Frequency Words Practice |
|---|---|---|---|
| SECTION 1 | 48-76 | BASIC SOUNDS/SKILLS | |
| 1 | 48 | m t a s d i f | am at |
| 2 | 50 | r th l o n | that this in and on an not than |
| 3 | 52 | p e h v | him had |
| 4 | 55 | sh u b k ck | us up but |
| 5 | 58 | c g (/k/ & /g/ sounds) j w | can get got will with |
| 6 | 63 | ch tch | |
| 7 | 66 | x z qu wh | |
| 8 | 69 | Review and Practice | |
| 9 | 72 | Blended Consonants & Review | |
| SECTION 2 | 77-94 | ADDITIONAL SOUNDS | |
| 10 | 77 | s (/z/ sound) | as has his |
| 11 | 78 | e (ee sound) pronunciation /i/ - e+n e+m | me we be he she when them |
| 12 | 80 | o (/oa/ sound) o (/u/ sound) | no go old from month |
| 13 | 83 | i (ie sound) | find |
| 14 | 84 | a (/ay/ sound) pronunciation a+l a+ll pronunciation w +a | all |
| 15 | 87 | y(/y/ sound) (/ee/ sound) (/ie/ sound) | yes by my why |
| 16 | 89 | ing ink | |
| 17 | 91 | Review and Practice | |
| SECTION 3 | 95-134 | VOWEL COMBINATIONS | |
| 18 | 95 | ee | see |
| 19 | 97 | oa oe | |
| 20 | 98 | ai ay | way may |
| 21 | 100 | Review & Practice | |
| 22 | 101 | **vowel-consonant-e** | |
| 23 | 102 | a_e | make made |
| 24 | 103 | o_e i_e | |
| 25 | 105 | u_e e_e | use |
| 26 | 106 | practice all vowel-consonant-e | |

| Lesson # | Page # | Sounds Introduced Summary of Lesson | High Frequency Words Practice |
|---|---|---|---|
| 27 | 108 | **c** (/s/ sound =   c+e,i or y)<br>**g** (/j/ sound =   g+e i or y) | |
| 28 | 110 | Review and Practice | |
| 29 | 113 | **u** (oo and uu sound) | put |
| 30 | 113 | **oi  oy** | |
| 31 | 115 | **ea** | each |
| 32 | 116 | **Review & Practice** | |
| 33 | 120 | **ow** | how now |
| 34 | 121 | **ou** | out about |
| 35 | 122 | **Review & Practice** | |
| 36 | 125 | **ue ew ui** | few  new |
| 37 | 126 | **oo** | |
| 38 | 127 | **ie  ei** | |
| 39 | 128 | **ey** | they |
| 40 | 128 | **au  aw  augh** | |
| 41 | 130 | **igh** | right |
| 42 | 131 | **s** (/z/ sound) | use   these |
| 43 | 132 | Review and Practice | |
| **SECTION 4** | 135-160 | **R-CONTROLLED VOWEL COMBINATIONS** | |
| 44 | 135 | **ar** (/ar/ & /air/ sounds) | |
| 45 | 137 | **w+ar** (pronunciation) | |
| 46 | 138 | Review & Practice | |
| 47 | 139 | **or** (/or/ & /er/ sounds) | or   for |
| 48 | 142 | **5 combinations that have the /or/ sound**<br>**or  ore oar our oor** | or  for more your |
| 49 | 144 | **Review & Practice** | |
| 50 | 146 | **er** | her   other |
| 51 | 148 | **5 combinations that have the /er/ sound**<br>**er  ur  ir  ear**<br>**or** (w+or & or at end of some multi-syll.words) | her other first |
| 52 | 152 | Review & Practice | |
| 53 | 154 | **combinations that have the /air/ sound**<br>**are  ar   air  ear** (uncommon) | air |
| 54 | 156 | **3 combinations that have the /eer/ sound**<br>**ear  eer  ere** | near   here |
| 55 | 157 | **ear** | |
| 56 | 158 | **ire  & Review** | |

| Lesson # | Page # | Sounds Introduced / Summary of Lesson | High Frequency Words Practice |
|---|---|---|---|
| SECTION 5 | 161-179 | OTHER SOUNDS & PRACTICE | |
| 57 | 161 | Silent letter combos **dge mb wr kn** | write wrong know |
| 58 | 162 | Review and Practice | |
| 59 | 166 | Less frequent Sounds **ph** /f/ **ch** /k/ **y** /i/ **i** /ee/ **ai** /i/ | |
| 60 | 168 | 'Strange' & Uncommon Sounds eigh ough gn, gh, rh, pn, x | |
| 61 | 170 | Practice Common Endings -ing -er -ly | |
| 62 | 172 | Practice Plural Endings -s -es -ies | |
| 63 | 173 | Practice Past Tense Verb Ending -ed | |
| 64 | 176 | Practice -ve ending | give have |
| 65 | 177 | Review & Practice | |
| SECTION 6 | 180-221 | MULTISYLLABLE WORDS | |
| | 180 | General Information | |
| 66 | 183 | Practice Multisyllable Words | |
| 67 | 186 | Reading Compound Words | |
| 68 | 189 | Common Prefixes & Suffixes Overview | |
| 69 | 190 | Common Prefixes | |
| 70 | 200 | Common Suffixes | |
| 71 | 206 | Practice Multisyllable Words | |
| 72 | 209 | /shun/ suffixes -tion -sion -cian -sion | |
| 73 | 211 | Other Special Endings: -cial -tial; -tious -cious; -ture -sure | |
| 74 | 212 | Practice Multisyllable Words | |
| 75 | 215 | Practice Multisyllable Words | |
| 76 | 218 | Practice Multisyllable Words | |
| 77 | 221 | Continued Practice with Multisyllable Words | |
| SECTION 7 | 222-225 | GUIDED READING | |
| SECTION 8 | 226-227 | BUILDING FLUENCY | |
| SECTION 9 | 228-232 | DEVELOPING READING COMPREHENSION SKILLS | |
| SECTION 10 | 233-236 | EPANDING VOCABULARY KNOWLEDGE | |

# Section 1: Review Basic Sounds and Practice Necessary Subskills of Phonologic Processing

This section provides direct instruction and practice to develop the essential fundamental skills necessary for proficient reading: phonemic awareness, automatic knowledge and proper pronunciation of basic sounds, correct phonologic processing, proper tracking, smooth blending and careful attention to detail.

## Lesson 1:

Review Sounds:

m      This sound is /m/.

t      This sound is /t/. Always say /t/ fast.

a      This letter has two primary sounds, /a/ and /ay/. Initial practice includes the /a/ sound. Later the /ay/ and the 3$^{rd}$ /ah/ or /uh/ sound is added.

s      This letter has 2 sounds. The sounds are /s/ and sometimes /z/. Initial practice includes words with the /s/ sound. Words with the /z/ sound are added later.

d      This sound is /d/. Always say /d/ fast.

i      This letter has 2 sounds, /i/ and /ie/. Initial practice includes words with the /i/ sound. Later practice includes the /ie/ sound. (The unexpected 3$^{rd}$ /ee/ sound is not covered until lesson 59)

f      This letter has the sound /f/.

**Practice Sound Cards:** Present the sound cards (index cards w/ sound written on it) for these letters. Continue to add to this sound card collection. Practice all the sound cards until the student automatically knows the correct sound. Make sure the student looks at the print, physically tracks and pronounces the sound correctly.

**Write and Say Sounds:** Please write each sound 5-10 times. The student needs to say *the sound as he writes it*. The student needs to *print* and form the letters correctly.

**Word Making Activity:** This first lesson is primarily a practice run to demonstrate how to conduct the word making activity. See page 37-38 for complete instructions. Take out the appropriate sound tiles. Read the first word, speaking clearly and repeating the word at least once so the student is sure to hear the sounds correctly. When the student is making the word, be sure he says the individual sounds as he lays down the appropriate sound tile in order. After he completes the word, have him sound out the word to you using finger tracking and proper blending skills. Immediately correct any errors. Clear all the tiles before reading the next word on the list to the student.
**"Please make the word _____":**

Use sound tiles… a, i, dx2, f, m, s, t
    if  am  sad  sit  sat  dim  fit  sam  mad  did  fat  fast  mist  mast  fist  sift

**Reading Words:** The student reads the following words. He needs to sound out the words with physical tracking and proper blending. Correct any errors immediately.

**\*NOTE:** To reinforce tracking always read lists across the page→ not down the columns.

| at | am | it | mat | if |
|---|---|---|---|---|
| fat | did | sit | sat | add |
| mad | dad | miss | tad | its |
| sad | dim | mat | Sam | did |
| mitt | sat | mad | mat | fat |
| fit | dad | Tim | at | mist |
| fist | mast | mist | fast | staff |
| sift | mitt | stiff | mast | fist |

**Writing (Spelling) Words:** Select some words from the list above. The student writes/spells these words. The detailed directions on how to conduct this word writing activity are located on page 41 under "Instructions for Specific Activities".

# Lesson 2:

## Review Sounds:

**r** → This letter has the sound /r/.

This next sound is made up of 2 letters together. These letters are what this program calls "partner" or "buddy letters". You already know some of the common 'partner letters' such as 'th', 'sh' and 'ch'. Later you will learn many more of these 'partner' letters.

**th** → These partner letters have the sounds /th/ and /*th*/. The 'th' is pronounced slightly differently in words. When we speak we usually don't even notice the different pronunciation. Listen to the difference:
1) Usually we say /th/. This 'hard' /th/ vibrates your tongue.
(Listen to the 'hard' sound /th/ in ... the, this, that)
2) Sometimes we use a 'soft', quiet /*th*/ sound.
(Listen to the quiet sound /*th*/ in ....bath, three, thin.)

**l** → This letter has the sound /l/.

**o** → This letter has 3 sounds. The sounds are /o/, /oa/ and sometimes /u/. Initial practice includes the /o/ sound and later the /oa/ & /u/ sounds.

**n** → This letter has the sound /n/.

**Practice Sound Cards:** Add the new sound cards to your collection and practice *all* the cards. The student needs to physically track and pronounce the sound correctly.

**Write and Say Sounds:** The student writes each sound 5-10 times saying the sound as they print the letter(s).

**Word Making Activity:** Make words with the sound tiles. The student needs to say the individual sounds as he makes the words and use proper blending skills. After completing the word, he reads the word using finger tracking and proper blending skills. Correct any errors. **"Please make the word _____"**

Use sound tiles  a  i(2)  o  d  f  l  m  n  r  s(2)  t  th
   thin  moth  trim  that  than  this  fast  raft  loft  slam  lost  math  sand  flat
   slid  fist  mint  land  last  mist  slim  slot  mast  list  flint  stand  limit  solid  insist

**Reading Words:** The student reads the following words. He needs to sound out the words with physical tracking and proper blending. Correct any errors immediately.

| a | on | it | I | is |
|---|---|---|---|---|
| if | an | in | am | at |
| its | not | did | lit | tin |
| dim | and | that | ant | man |
| fit | rod | tot | tan | tom |
| ram | fat | dim | that | slim |
| ran | lot | fill | dot | fan |
| did | doll | this | than | rot |
| nod | fin | and | sod | not |
| math | slat | lost | land | than |
| slam | trim | fast | lift | fist |
| mast | mist | loft | slot | sand |
| rift | soft | raft | last | slim |
| stiff | moth | lost | staff | fond |
| smith | thin | still | fins | land |
| sift | stand | draft | dims | sniff |
| lots | strand | drift | flat | rant |
| insist | limit | solid | dismiss | landed |

**Writing (Spelling) Words:** Have the student write/spell some of these words.

# Lesson 3:

Review Sounds:

p→        This letter has the sound /p/. Always say /p/ fast.

e→        This letter has 2 sounds, /e/ and /ee/. Initial practice will be with /e/. Later words with the /ee/ sound will be added.

h→        This letter has the sound /h/. Always say /h/ fast.

v→        This letter has the sound /v/.


**Practice Sound Cards:** Add the new sound cards to your collection and practice *all* the cards. The student needs to physically track and pronounce the sound correctly.

**Write and Say Sounds:** The student writes each sound 5-10 times *saying the sound as they print the letter(s).*

**Word Making Activity:** Make words with the sound tiles. Make sure the student says the individual sounds as he makes the words and uses proper blending skills. After he completes the word, have him read the word using finger tracking and proper blending skills. Correct any errors. **"Please make the word _____"**

Use tiles...... a e i(2) o   d f h l m n p r s(2) t v
    vet spit drop spin trip prod ramp rest step vast pond melt drip pelt slap plan stamp slip stomp path help flip left nest trap pest flop spot vest strap strip hand hint strand timid invest softest solid rapid limit profit himself

**Sound Changing Activity:** In this new word making activity, the student makes a word and then listens to determine the necessary changes to make a new word. See page 39 for complete instructions. For the first time, demonstrate how you make the word and then change one sound to make the new word. Can you please make the word _____. (first word on list). When the student finishes the word do *not* clear the tiles. Instead say "good job, that word says _____, now please change the sound to make the word _____ (next word on the list). Correct any errors immediately.
Use tiles..... a i o   b f m n p s t th
    that > sat > bat > bath > math > mat > that> than > thin > fin > pin > pit > pot > pit > fit

Use tiles…..a  e  i  o    f  h  l  m  n  p    r  s  t  v

hint > lint > list > last > fast > mast > vast > vest > rest > pest > pelt > melt > felt
step > stop > slop > slip > flip > flop > flap > flat > slat > slap

**Reading Words:** The student reads the following words. He needs to sound out the words with physical tracking and proper blending. Correct any errors immediately.

| if | is | a | am | in |
| at | it | an | on | I |
| did | not | and | its | dim |
| mop | that | doll | this | lit |
| than | fed | pot | sap | pan |
| pet | pod | net | sod | map |
| and | red | dad | hit | the |
| had | hot | rod | off | its |
| thin | tap | ham | and | fan |
| let | fin | Beth | led | ant |
| off | lot | is | van | pin |
| pest | drip | fast | flip | slit |
| lost | step | test | mist | math |
| drop | slip | nest | slim | slap |
| left | melt | stop | felt | plan |
| flat | drop | land | path | list |
| snap | lint | trap | limp | vat |
| loft | sand | trim | past | pond |

| hint | stop | vest | slop | vast |
| held | last | slot | pelt | tell |
| trip | that | slam | pond | tram |
| slant | stand | stamp | plant | moth |
| strap | prod | mill | trap | frill |
| print | strip | path | limp | pelt |
| lamp | sand | stiff | self | help |
| damp | smell | ramp | hand | soft |
| drill | splint | damp | slept | still |
| depth | rinse | sprint | split | slams |

*and words* (margin note)

---

| limit | dismiss | profit | valid | lasted |
| fiddle | seven | address | rapid | riddle |
| middle | velvet | trespass | illness | laptop |
| impress | triple | simple | endless | hidden |
| restless | distress | insist | little | flatten |
| apple | landed | timid | helpless | solid |
| softest | lifted | planted | listless | invest |
| dismiss | linen | restless | misfit | handoff |
| timid | tested | himself | handed | dampest |

Writing (Spelling) Words: Have the student write/spell some of these words.

# Lesson 4:

Review Basic Sounds:

**sh** → Together these partner letters have the /sh/ sound.

**u** → This letter has 2 primary sounds, /u/ and /oo/. Initial practice will be with the /u/ sound. Later lessons will cover the /oo/ sound as well as when the 'u' sometimes has a 3$^{rd}$ sound /uu/.

**b** → This letter has the sound /b/. Always say /b/ fast.

**ck** → These partner letters have the /k/ sound. Always say /k/ fast.

**k** → This letter has the sound /k/. Always say /k/ fast.

The 'ck' and 'k' both make the same /k/ sound. This is not a problem when you read. However, it is helpful to notice the expected pattern when ck is used for spelling. You will notice the ck sound is never used at the beginning of words, but rather at the end of words or syllables that have the /a/ /i/ /o/ /u/ or /e/ (short vowel sounds) right before the /k/ sound (like sock, back, lick, deck, luck, ticket, racket, bucket). Point this pattern out as the student reads and makes words.

**Practice Sound Cards:** Add the new sound cards to your collection and practice *all* the cards. The student needs to physically track and pronounce the sound correctly.

**Write and Say Sounds:** The student writes each sound 5-10 times *saying the sound as* they print the letter(s).

**Word Making Activity:** Make words with the sound tiles. Correct any errors.
"Please make the word _____"
Use tiles.... a e i(2) o u    b d f h l m n p r s t    sh ck
   rack  rust  stub  shin  melt  stun  rash  flush  hunt  flash  shrub  lock  must  blast
   bunt  shop  runt  mash  felt  rush  punt  stack  dash  shed  truck  fleck  stick
   shock  flick  radish  unpack  finish  punish  pickup  publish  backup  habit
Use sound tiles  a  e  i(2)  o  u    b d k l m n p r s  t v  th sh
   ask  elk  desk  kept  that  task  dusk  skip  tusk  blast  silk  bust  skin  skid   this
   risk  skim  milk  dust  skit   timid  limit  rapid  invest  insult  desktop  vanish  robin

**Sound Changing Activity:** Remember with the sound changing game you will listen and make changes to the word to make a new word.

Use sound tiles... a e u b h n s t v

    vet > bet > bat > hat > hut > but > bus > bun > ban > van

Use sound tiles... a i o u b d h k l m n p r s t sh

    skid > skin > skip > slip > slop > slosh > slash > slap > slam > slum

    milk > silk > sulk > sunk > bunk > bunt > hunt > runt > rant > pant > past > mast > mask

Use sound tiles... a i o u  b l n p r s t  ck sh

    stub > stun > stan > stab > stack > stick > stock > stop

    truck > trick > track > trash > brash > brush > blush > slush > slash > slap > slack

**Reading Words:** The student reads the following words sounding out the words with physical tracking and proper blending. Correct any errors immediately.

| us | up | a | it | I |
|---|---|---|---|---|
| am | on | at | if | but |
| is | in | the | an | him |
| bit | mash | bun | fed | let |
| hut | run | hip | did | and |
| its | ash | had | bat | fun |
| that | its | lap | kit | bus |
| hill | hum | red | Kim | back |
| hid | tick | tub | mash | sick |
| not | ask | kid | ship | lock |
| this | dock | than | kiss | dish |
| elf | rust | sun | kin | sock |
| help | rut | pass | shop | elk |
| shed | lush | bash | dust | rash |

| | | | | |
|---|---|---|---|---|
| hush | bed | lash | thin | muck |
| drum | still | nest | held | slam |
| soft | trip | plum | pump | best |
| rock | kick | shut | fish | shin |
| plan | trap | hand | mist | fund |
| must | silk | bunk | kept | nick |
| milk | skin | skip | silt | sift |
| belt | fist | rush | stop | lick |
| pack | pick | bunt | hunt | kelp |
| vet | mint | band | shod | skill |
| tuck | punt | moth | trick | shush |
| kill | deck | luck | mud | trunk |
| flat | lick | past | vest | drift |
| brash | slush | plant | flash | truck |
| print | pluck | shred | thump | flint |
| stack | flick | skunk | brush | trunk |
| shrill | blunt | shell | stunt | slant |
| shift | shrub | strip | brand | stilt |
| skimp | blond | trust | stamp | shrimp |
| stump | fleck | track | split | spell |
| flunk | strap | pulse | trash | plump |

| fresh | shack | bless | helps | trust |
|-------|-------|-------|-------|-------|
| punish | vanish | laptop | finish | impress |
| insist | limit | middle | insult | robin |
| summit | ticket | publish | vanish | promise |
| until | habit | distrust | tunnel | pocket |
| finish | pickle | selfish | rapid | backup |
| problem | invest | absent | radish | triple |
| seven | hidden | restless | velvet | rocket |
| linen | habit | locket | timid | handed |
| setup | sudden | invest | product | pickup |

**Writing (Spelling) Words:** Have the student write/spell some of the listed words.

# Lesson 5:

## Review Sounds:

**c →** This letter has 2 sounds, /k/ and /s/. Always say /k/ fast. Initial practice will be with /k/ then later practice includes words where c = /s/ sound. c+e  c+i  c+y = /s/ sound. When e, i or y comes after 'c', c always has the /s/ sound. Otherwise the c has the /k/ sound.

**g →** This letter has 2 sounds, /g/ and sometimes the /j/ sound. Initial practice will be with the /g/ sound. Later practice includes words where g is followed by e, i, or y and has the /j/ sound.

**j →** This letter has the sound /j/. Always say this /j/ sound fast.

**w →** This letter has the sound /w/.

**Practice Sound Cards:** Add the new sound cards to your collection and practice *all* the cards. The student needs to physically track and pronounce the sound correctly.

**Write and Say Sounds:** The student writes each sound 5-10 times *saying the sound as* they print the letter(s).

**Word Making Activity:** Make words with the sound tiles. Immediately correct any errors. **"Please make the word _____"**
Use tiles   a i u    b c d f g  l  m n p  r s  t    sh
   cast  clump  gash  crash  shrug  glad  crush  clamp  clip  scan  clasp  gift  flag  plug
   shrimp  camps  graft  grin  flash  crust  crop  claps  grump  clash  grunt  grand  scrub
Use sound tiles…  a  e  i(2)  o  u(2)    b  c  g  j  l  m  n  p  r  s  t(2)  v  w  sh  th
   wet  jog  win  smug  wish  grub  west  twig  swim  twin  jest  gust  job  just  jump
   trust  swig  twist  panic  inject  valid  vanish  topic  rapid  subject  project  unjust
   invest  inject  within  plastic  victim  tropic

**Sound Changing Activity:** Remember with the sound changing game you listen and make changes to the word to make a new word.
Use sound tiles …… a  i    b  d  f  g  l  r    ck  sh
     fish> dish > dash > lash > bash > gash > rash > rack > shack > back
Use sound tiles….. a  e  i  u  b  c  d  g  l  m  p  r  s  t
     crisp > crimp > cramp > clamp > clump > glump > grump
     crust > crest > crept
     crab > grab > grad > glad >
     grin > grip > trip > drip > grip > slip > slim > swim > swam > swag > swig > twig > twin
Use sound tiles…… e  i  u    g  j  l  m  n  s  t  w
     just > jest > west > welt > wilt

**Reading Words:** The student reads the following list, sounding out the words with physical tracking and proper blending. Correct any errors immediately.

| it  | us   | up   | am  | if   |
| --- | ---- | ---- | --- | ---- |
| ash | in   | is   | at  | kit  |
| had | its  | that | ask | than |
| on  | cot  | him  | cut | get  |
| leg | doll | fill | tip | bag  |

| | | | | |
|---|---|---|---|---|
| wet | not | got | this | mud |
| fish | the | wag | can | wig |
| nut | pig | mug | fog | act |
| dug | cop | fed | and | hug |
| rug | back | hid | fin | well |
| Jim | jug | will | with | pup |
| jack | win | with | elk | top |
| job | web | gum | do | big |
| jig | back | jog | jet | did |
| cat | hot | met | cup | deck |
| fib | jam | tub | lash | bat |
| red | sip | fed | sick | dim |
| hit | sin | puff | lock | fell |
| dish | sun | miss | net | shut |
| gap | cash | fat | mesh | skit |
| bed | rash | band | dash | kid |
| luck | swig | just | thug | log |
| twin | wish | beg | wed | jump |
| west | swim | wilt | kin | weld |
| slum | junk | grip | flat | ship |
| bus | run | shin | led | bell |

| | | | | |
|---|---|---|---|---|
| rust | tick | sock | muck | bug |
| mash | fed | kick | fed | wish |
| neck | fish | hush | shop | milk |
| skin | skip | math | shell | clam |
| Tim | must | luck | nest | gab |
| shock | pack | dull | mash | fed |
| shut | with | clap | plan | past |
| grub | clock | gust | cast | grab |
| gimp | hunt | swish | clip | camp |
| frog | sunk | gift | grunt | slip |
| cram | pest | plum | melt | glad |
| flag | grill | truck | kept | lost |
| left | snap | cluck | glass | romp |
| skunk | swell | stub | hand | gasp |
| shred | black | stuck | shrub | fresh |
| welt | click | trick | twist | trash |
| print | grasp | flash | slept | brush |
| pluck | swung | twist | swift | track |
| splash | clamp | swept | depth | crash |
| graft | crept | grump | trust | clump |
| grand | crisp | swell | strict | sprint |

| shrimp | stump | plant | plunk | wept |
| dwell | spill | script | grant | struck |

| unjust | inject | jungle | within | credit |
| until | profit | impress | rapid | object |
| witness | clinic | distrust | insist | distract |
| himself | vanish | little | panic | valid |
| punish | inspect | magnet | select | pilgrim |
| insect | problem | address | ended | congress |
| neglect | captive | subject | insect | cattle |
| district | plastic | effect | victim | enact |
| middle | promise | public | simple | ticket |
| clinic | discuss | project | topic | pigment |
| contest | fabric | object | active | classic |
| cactus | traffic | witness | metric | nonsense |
| laptop | pickup | unpack | invest | midship |
| triple | hidden | freshen | little | progress |
| insult | handed | finish | backup | invest |
| misfit | product | desktop | solid | flatten |
| robin | publish | absent | undress | summit |
| famish | sudden | catnip | picnic | skittish |

**Writing (Spelling) Words:** Have the student write/spell some of the listed words.

# Lesson 6

Review Basic Sounds:

**ch** — These partner letters have the /ch/ sound.
(The unexpected /k/ and /sh/ sounds are not covered until Lesson 59.)

**tch** — These partner letters also have the sound /ch/. This spelling of the /ch/ sound includes the silent 't'.

The **ch** and **tch** have the same /ch/ sound. Notice the 'tch' spelling is ONLY used at the end of words or syllables that have the short vowel /a/ /e/ /i/ /o/ /u/ sounds.

**Practice Sound Cards:** Add the new sound cards to your collection and practice *all* the cards. The student needs to physically track and pronounce the sound correctly.

**Write and Say Sounds:** The student writes each sound 5-10 times *saying the sound as* they print the letter(s).

**Word Making Activity:** Make words with the sound tiles. Immediately correct any errors. **"Please make the word _____"**
Use sound tiles..... a  e  u  i    b  f  g  m  n  p  r  t  ch  sh
   inch  chat  much  punch  chug  brag  grin  finch  chin  chant  chum  ranch
   branch  brunch  pinch  chip  shrub  munch  chest  chimp
Use sound tiles    a  e  i(2)  o  u    b  c(2)  d  h  l  m  n  p  r  s  t(2)  w  tch
   latch  hitch  itch  match  pitch  notch  witch  hutch  etch  batch  ditch  patch
   stretch  plastic  until  clinic  dispatch  insect  picnic  contact  hopscotch  contract

**Sound Changing Activity:** Remember to listen and make changes to the word.
 Use sound tiles..... a  i  o(2)  u    b  c  h  m  n  p  s  t  th  ch
   chip > chap > chat > that > hat > hit > hot > cot > cat > bat > bath
   much > such > sum > chum > chub > hub > hum > bum > bun > sun

**Reading Words:** The student reads the following list, sounding out the words with physical tracking and proper blending. Correct any errors immediately.

| | | | | |
|---|---|---|---|---|
| a | I | us | up | did |
| if | am | it | get | in |
| is | this | at | an | not |

| that | and | the | chip | can |
| than | such | got | him | do |
| had | to | said | will | chin |
| on | chat | was | swim | wish |
| much | chop | inch | chap | chip |
| twin | pinch | jack | check | lunch |
| chop | such | fetch | chick | winch |
| chant | chill | chuck | chug | swig |
| grass | ranch | chum | match | well |
| much | west | chomp | chill | jump |
| with | shut | stick | thin | batch |
| crush | plug | grin | hint | stretch |
| pitch | fetch | belch | notch | chest |
| patch | bunch | latch | chess | chin |
| lunch | pitch | belch | branch | inch |
| ranch | stick | chomp | class | pinch |
| blotch | wilt | bunch | twist | clap |
| champ | chunk | snatch | black | brick |
| itch | match | switch | finch | chat |
| test | just | chest | flip | flinch |
| swift | trust | splash | crunch | stitch |

| chimp | glitch | chant | grinch | brunch |
| bunch | shelf | chump | crunch | witch |

---

| unjust | classic | contest | himself | conflict |
| insist | profit | unless | insect | gossip |
| chicken | active | ruffle | punish | channel |
| vanish | chapel | gotten | trusted | rested |
| sandwich | chapstick | himself | chipmunk | hidden |
| until | children | classic | middle | subject |
| habit | pocket | publish | shellfish | promise |
| contempt | contact | contract | select | progress |
| invest | clinic | contest | flatten | district |

**Writing (Spelling) Words:** Specifically teach the 'ch' and 'tch' spelling patterns and have the student practice writing/spelling words with these patterns.

**'ch' spelling:** The /ch/ sound is **usually** spelled with 'ch'.
- Always use 'ch' when /ch/ sound begins a word or syllable: chest, chimp, check, chum, chat, chip, chin, chess, chap, chant, chop, chick, chug, champ
- Use 'ch' when there is a consonant preceding to the /ch/ sound: lunch, pinch, ranch, branch, hunch, crunch, inch, pinch, flinch, crunch, bunch, brunch, belch, mulch
- Later you will see how the 'ch' is used after all the vowel and r-controlled vowel combinations (for example: reach, poach, pouch, march, birch, perch, porch)

**'tch' spelling:** Use the 'tch' spelling **only** when the /ch/ sound is the end of a word or syllable immediately following a single short vowel sound. Notice the 'tch' spelling where the /ch/ sound immediately follows a single short vowel sound in: batch, itch, fetch, match, notch, catch, ditch, latch, witch, patch, hutch, stitch, pitch, catching, pitching, fetching, and hatchet.

NOTE: exceptions are such, much and rich (these are spelled with the 'ch' spelling)

# Lesson 7:

Review Basic Sounds:

**qu** — These partner letters have the sound /kw/.

**x** — This letter has the sound /ks/.

**z** — This letter has the sound /z/.

**wh** — These partner letters have the sound /wh/. This is the soft whisper sound /wh/.

**Practice Sound Cards:** Add the new sound cards to your collection and practice *all* the cards. The student needs to physically track and pronounce the sound correctly.

**Write and Say Sounds:** The student writes each sound 5-10 times *saying the sound as* they print the letter(s).

**Word Making Activity:** Make words with the sound tiles. Correct any errors.
"Please make the word _____"
Use sound tiles...... a e(2) i o   c d f g l m n p  qu  s t(2) x z ck
   fox  ax  max  zip  zap  mix  zag  lamp  zest  quick  quilt  quack  tax  exit  zest  quit
   stick  fix  exit  fax  next  expand  toxin  complex  contest  expect
Use sound tiles... a  i   d l n s t v    sh ck qu
   quilt  quit  stand  quack  squid  quick  squish  squint  vanish
Use sound tiles...... a e i o u   f h k l m n p r s t    ch wh
   which  whip  chomp  ranch  whisk  print  punt  lunch  chimp  stump  itself  unrest  himself

**Sound Changing Activity:** Remember to listen and make changes to the word.
Use sound tiles..... a i o   b f qu t x ck
   quit > quick > quack > tack > tax > fax > fix > fox > box
Use sound tiles.. e i u b f k l m n s t x
   next > nest > best > belt > felt > melt > milt > milk > silk > sulk

**Reading Words:** The student reads the following list, sounding out the words with physical tracking and proper blending. Correct any errors immediately.

| | | | | |
|---|---|---|---|---|
| a | I | us | up | did |
| fix | if | am | it | ax |
| get | ox | box | in | this |
| wet | cut | this | web | zip |
| fox | tax | is | zip | buzz |
| Rex | to | not | that | pat |
| can | box | tax | chin | quest |
| than | and | with | next | such |
| zap | him | said | will | inch |
| rush | melt | plan | left | frog |
| lost | felt | pest | plum | shred |
| quit | which | math | much | whip |
| zig | quick | when | quack | six |
| whisk | squish | text | lots | best |
| track | whim | best | got | wax |
| do | lost | ask | camp | jazz |
| mix | quick | whiff | wind | fox |
| such | flex | when | luck | quit |
| bunch | quilt | Zack | inch | trash |
| branch | shrub | fresh | brick | stuck |
| squid | chip | such | shelf | trust |

| | | | | |
|---|---|---|---|---|
| with | van | max | quit | fax |
| when | zag | next | quack | mesh |
| squish | text | six | jazz | mix |
| quilt | chant | Zack | zest | quick |
| twist | ranch | wax | fuzz | milk |
| weld | zips | much | inch | next |
| ranch | chest | strip | fleck | crisp |
| punch | chap | lunch | pinch | stand |

---

| | | | | |
|---|---|---|---|---|
| vanish | extra | exact | exam | tropic |
| exit | middle | subject | ticket | longest |
| expand | valid | contact | children | express |
| finish | panic | rapid | toxin | complex |
| exact | dispatch | unless | gotten | middle |
| index | impress | clinic | witness | insist |
| object | until | unless | progress | unrest |
| profit | limit | inspect | punish | disband |
| credit | glasses | happen | fitness | lasted |
| intend | kitten | adjust | itself | within |
| uncut | problem | pocket | rested | strongest |
| contest | hopscotch | neglect | promise | kitchen |

**Writing (Spelling) Words:** Have the student write/spell some of the listed words.

# Lesson 8: Review and Practice

**Review Sounds:** The student quickly says these sounds. This provides practice plus an assessment to determine if the student needs additional practice with any sounds.

| m | t | a | s | d | i | f | r |
|---|---|---|---|---|---|---|---|
| th | l | o | n | p | e | h | v |
| sh | u | b | k | ck | c | g | j |
| w | ch | tch | x | z | qu | wh | |

**Reading/Reviewing Irregular Words:** This quickly reviews a few common irregular words you have already frequently read and spelled. Please read and then write these words noticing the specific sounds as you write.

| to | do | said | was | of |
|---|---|---|---|---|
| what | who | | | |

**Review Sound Cards:** Quickly review the stack of all sound cards. If the student automatically knows a specific sound, remove the card from the stack. If there is any hesitation (not automatic knowledge) then keep the card for further practice/repetition. At this point, many if not all of these sounds will be automatic and there is no need to continue to practice them in isolation as sound/flash cards.

**Write and Say Any Sounds that need additional practice:** Continue having the student print sounds that are not automatic 5-10 times while saying the sound.

**Reading Words:** The student reads the following list, sounding out the words with physical tracking and proper blending. Correct any errors immediately.

| a | if | am | at | I |
|---|---|---|---|---|
| us | up | it | an | is |
| on | in | get | did | can |
| and | than | to | the | not |

| | | | | |
|---|---|---|---|---|
| him | this | do | got | that |
| him | said | with | such | of |
| zap | was | pet | drip | bed |
| wag | step | jug | fox | with |
| will | elk | job | wet | doll |
| chip | such | six | quit | with |
| dim | its | ant | who | van |
| next | whip | camp | zip | just |
| chin | kick | wish | lift | bask |
| what | which | flex | much | land |
| lost | quit | when | six | path |
| fish | held | land | jump | west |
| milk | skip | clock | swig | hunt |
| clap | trip | grab | pig | snap |
| chest | math | pitch | quilt | help |
| just | slush | slept | swish | plant |
| still | dwell | fresh | clamp | flush |
| slant | swept | trust | flash | depth |
| ditch | stuck | brand | clunk | sprint |
| brisk | flesh | swell | test | finch |
| match | brush | stump | crust | shop |

| camp | swim | catch | champ | much |
| this | next | shop | inch | with |
| swift | twist | grand | squish | whisk |
| ranch | stunt | trick | shush | flash |
| brush | trunk | blond | which | drift |
| shred | clump | graft | shrimp | frost |

---

| insist | simple | profit | until | select |
| vanish | panic | within | banish | extra |
| jungle | inject | conflict | inspect | credit |
| valid | edit | insect | seven | active |
| itself | impress | hidden | velvet | children |
| pocket | clinic | livid | problem | himself |
| topic | effect | object | complex | discuss |
| happen | plastic | exit | middle | finish |
| unless | gotten | subject | lasted | disband |
| rested | trusted | himself | rapid | little |
| longest | expand | expect | promise | limit |
| catching | address | hundred | often | contest |
| sudden | limit | rested | instill | fastest |
| tropic | neglect | contest | invest | progress |

Writing (Spelling) Words: Have the student write/spell some of the listed words.

# Lesson 9:

## Practicing skills with blended consonants.

Students often need specific work on developing the phonemic awareness skills to distinguish individual sounds within blended consonant clusters (2 or 3 consonants together). The blends that include the "quick" sounds (b, d, c, g, p, t) can be particularly difficult to hear and segment. Students often have the most difficulty when these "fast" sounds lead the blended group (tr, dr, br, cr, pl... ) or where they are included in ending clusters (pt, nd, ct, mp). It IS more difficult to distinguish and recognize the individual sounds within these clusters.

Direct practice with recognizing the individual sounds within these blends helps develop phonemic awareness and improve reading and spelling skills. Although specific attention should be given to the blended consonant patters, blended consonants should always be taught as the blending of individual sounds (not as a distinct cluster of letters as a unit). This ensures the student not only develops phonemic awareness, but also adopts the attention to detail that is so important for accurate reading.

The student needs to practice both reading AND writing/spelling words that contain blended consonants. It is generally easier for students to read a word correctly (they see the letters) than it is to write/spell a word (as they may have difficulty distinguishing all the separate sounds). The word making activities with the sound tiles and writing/spelling activity help the student develop the necessary phonemic awareness skills to distinguish the individual sounds within blended consonants.

**Practice Making Words with Blended Consonants:** Have the student make the words. If the student misses a sound; have them read/sound out the word they created and then say "You made ___. You need to make ___. Can you hear what sound is missing?" (example...you give him "slick" and he makes "sick". Have him read the word making sure he is pointing at the sound tiles as he reads. "That says sick, you need to make slick." *Help the student learn to hear and distinguish the differences in the words.*

Use sound tiles.... a  i  u    c  b  d  g  l  m  n  p  r  s  t  ch
  grin  brim  clasp  damp  strap  crab  grab  grasp  scrunch  branch  scrap  cramp
  clamp  ramp  glad  drum  grump  dump  crust  brunch  stump  pinch  smug

Use sound tiles... a i o    b  d  l  m  n  p  r  s  t  w  ck
  past  stab  drop  slip  strip  trap  twin  smack  stand  strand  pond  drab  branch
  black  brick  strap  drip  slick  slack  stack  print  swim  brand

Use sound tiles... a  e i o    b  d  f  h  l  n  p  r  s  t
  land  slap  last  snap  rant  drop  lift  flap  hand  band  plant  fret  held   bland
  help  blast  flop  stand  soft  left  plan  strand  trap  felt  flip  fist  best

**Sound Changing Activity:** Remember to listen and make changes to the word.
Use sound tiles  a  i  o  u     b  c  l  m  r  s  t  ck
   block > black > slack > stack > stick > slick > click > cluck > clock >
   > clack > crack > crick > brick > brim
Use sound tiles... a  u     b  d  g  l  n  r  s  t
   gland > grand > grant > grunt > brunt > blunt > blant > slant
Use sound tiles...... a  u     c  g  l  m  p(2)  r  s  t
   stamp > stump > slump > plump > glump > grump > gramp > cramp > clamp > clump

**Reading Words With Blended Consonants:** The student reads the following list, sounding out the words with physical tracking and proper blending. Correct any errors immediately. Stop the student if they miss a sound and have them re-read the word. If necessary, point to the missing sound.

| | | | | |
|---|---|---|---|---|
| grab | frog | plant | clamp | crib |
| black | prop | snap | black | drop |
| scat | hand | clap | clod | long |
| grasp | drill | slick | frill | slit |
| brat | still | frog | trip | grill |
| crab | drip | brunch | flat | stub |
| crash | bland | smack | stand | clash |
| land | stash | trap | sand | trick |
| twin | split | twist | clasp | slash |
| best | skunk | swift | help | class |
| slant | cramp | left | raft | slap |
| felt | slack | brand | track | slick |
| ramp | truck | drum | smash | strand |
| drum | scrap | shrimp | fact | strong |

| stub | brat | brim | pact | fresh |
| crunch | strip | slant | crisp | ask |
| skunk | swept | shrill | grant | clump |
| splish | strong | split | splash | grant |
| pinch | drab | crust | branch | strand |
| clam | lunch | flesh | best | swim |
| soft | blast | stand | plump | grant |
| shred | blond | dress | graft | stunt |
| brick | drift | dump | ranch | pluck |
| print | spend | crest | strap | melt |
| black | brand | chant | stick | spin |
| slept | stomp | struck | grump | switch |
| crisp | grasp | crush | frost | stamp |
| dwell | swift | bunch | swell | smack |
| must | facts | glimpse | swung | which |
| print | grand | sprint | grip | flask |
| kept | skunk | strict | dwell | swept |
| scrap | brunch | splat | stunt | stash |
| trust | blast | flash | shelf | past |
| brick | grump | frost | clash | punch |
| brand | chest | swig | swift | slack |

| | | | | |
|---|---|---|---|---|
| shred | smell | whisk | crunch | glass |
| much | last | next | task | quilts |
| gift | shrub | grant | romp | grub |
| hand | list | black | flint | rest |
| crept | slept | glad | grand | grunt |
| clamp | flip | shrug | flask | just |
| catch | crafts | speck | swims | slick |

---

| | | | | |
|---|---|---|---|---|
| insist | impress | instill | vanish | cricket |
| picnic | unless | express | expect | clinic |
| selfish | profit | gossip | catfish | vanish |
| static | blacktop | disband | finish | inspect |
| kitten | muffin | simple | shotgun | adjust |
| fabric | bathtub | backpack | spastic | happen |
| mitten | confess | intend | index | until |
| object | splendid | itself | pistol | restless |
| credit | expect | enact | congress | promise |
| glasses | across | complex | fitness | insect |
| within | little | progress | exact | setback |
| absent | problem | ended | expand | plastic |
| dispatch | camel | solid | simple | travel |
| blacken | happen | lasted | liquid | candle |

| riddle | victim | comment | rented | relic |
| riddle | disband | gotten | subject | hopscotch |
| contest | chipmunk | neglect | promise | progress |
| kitchen | adjust | kitten | longest | laptop |
| chapel | sandwich | publish | absent | undress |
| listed | punish | picnic | product | invest |
| midship | solid | locket | handed | pickle |
| velvet | softest | flatten | lifted | hidden |
| strongest | distant | driven | insult | submit |
| madness | enact | misprint | bathtub | setup |
| catfish | blacken | catnip | travel | blacktop |
| branches | intent | stretched | himself | hundred |
| restless | pocket | classic | banish | landed |
| pickup | express | squinted | sample | unjust |
| stranded | skittish | subtext | mismatch | distract |
| desktop | sudden | blended | exit | planted |
| triple | seven | dampest | address | rapid |
| connect | inspect | inset | strictest | trusted |
| famish | scribble | sadden | absent | robin |

**Writing/Spelling Words with Blended Consonant Sounds:** Have the student write/spell some of the listed words.

# Section 2 : Additional Sounds and Further Practice with Phonologic Processing, Tracking and Blending

# Lesson 10:

**s**      The letter **s** has 2 sounds, /s/ and /z/. You have been reviewing the /s/ sound. Now you will practice the 2nd sound /z/. In fact, in English, most words with the /z/ sound are spelled with the letter s not z.

**Write and Say the Sound:** The student writes **s** 5-10 times saying the /z/ sound.

## Reading Words that have the /z/ sound for s:

Notice the /z/ sound in the following common words:

| | | | | |
|---|---|---|---|---|
| is | as | has | his | was |
| visit | resin | closet | risen | |

The /z/ sound is also found in many plural words. You usually say these without even noticing you say /z/. Please read these words noticing how the **s** has the /z/ sound.

| | | | | |
|---|---|---|---|---|
| frogs | dogs | hills | buns | pigs |
| pins | kids | jams | ribs | hums |
| bugs | tubs | digs | tags | drums |
| hugs | pills | hams | drills | hands |

The /z/ sound of s is found in many other common words. Most of the s=/z/ words contain code that has not yet been covered. These will be systematically added into the lessons as the necessary code is learned (For example use, rose, close, wise, please, choose, wisdom) If the student reads a word using the /s/ sound when it should be /z/, simply say something like, "this word uses the /z/ sound" and have the student try the word again.

**Making Words:** Make words with the sound tiles. "Please make the word _____"
Use sound tiles...... a e i(2) o u    b d f g h l n p r s t v
      is   as   hugs   has   his   bags   hands   pads   bunts   grubs   frogs   flags   visit   resin

**Reading Words:** The student reads the following list, sounding out the words with physical tracking and proper blending. Correct any errors immediately.

| | | | | |
|---|---|---|---|---|
| I | am | us | a | get |
| did | if | as | it | bags |
| was | pigs | has | than | is |
| at | an | this | not | cans |
| that | and | the | to | who |
| as | tags | hands | has | is |
| such | his | said | drums | best |
| swims | hits | sums | stiff | digs |
| drip | such | was | flip | camp |
| frogs | dogs | do | plugs | hugs |
| claps | flags | west | step | grab |
| swims | songs | visit | risen | closet |

**Writing (Spelling) Words:** Have the student write/spell some of the listed words. Focus on the 's' spelling for the /z/ sound.

# Lesson 11:

e    The letter **e** has 2 sounds, /e/ and /ee/. You have been practicing the /e/ sound. This lesson adds practice of the 2nd sound /ee/.

**Write and Say The Sound:** The student writes **e** 5 times saying the /ee/ sound.

**Reading Words that have the /ee/ sound for e:** The /ee/ sound of e is used in quite a few words. Usually when e is the only vowel it has the /e/ sound that you have already practiced. However, when **'e' is the only vowel at the end of the word or syllable** it often has the /ee/ sound. Go ahead and read these words noticing how the e has the /ee/ sound. Notice the /ee/ sound in the common **re- de-** and **pre-** prefixes.

| | | | | | |
|---|---|---|---|---|---|
| he | be | she | we | me | belong |

| | | | | | |
|---|---|---|---|---|---|
| begin | refill | rebuff | redraft | redress | refit |
| reflect | refresh | regret | rehash | reject | relapse |
| relax | remit | repress | rerun | resell | respect |
| restrict | resist | depend | demand | prefix | preset |
| prefill | predict | pretense | prevent | detest | result |
| evil | reflex | detect | secret | regress | debug |

**Pronouncing e with e+n and e+m:**

**e+ n**

**e+m** We are also going to learn something unusual about e. When the /e/ sound comes before n or m…we usually pronounce it /i/. When we say the /e/ before the n or m sound it comes out sounding like the /i/ sound. I want you to try to say the /e/ sound with /n/ and /m/. Notice how it comes out sounding like /i/. Usually in reading words we do not even notice we pronounce 'e' differently, but *it sure helps to know the short e before n or m sounds like /i/ when you try to spell the words.*

**Reading Words that have e+n and e+m :** Read a few of the words where the e comes before n or m and sounds like the /i/ sound.

| | | | | | |
|---|---|---|---|---|---|
| hem | pen | hen | end | them | send |
| went | bench | lend | vent | bend | dent |
| blend | spend | rent | trench | sent | tense |
| lent | bend | tent | stench | mend | trend |
| relent | repent | enact | extend | defend | ended |
| pretend | absent | | | | |

(+ numerous **–ment** suffixes that will be included later)

**Making Words:** Make words with the sound tiles. "Please make the word _____"
Use sound tiles…… a e(2) o   b c d(2) f g l m n p r(2) s t x ch
belong dent lend repent trench defend spend pretend trench blend relent regret relax demand reflex reflect respect preset began

**Reading Words:** The student reads the following list, sounding out the words with physical tracking and proper blending. Correct any errors immediately.

| | | | | | |
|---|---|---|---|---|---|
| am | us | did | as | it | end |
| hem | not | do | we | is | at |
| he | was | she | pigs | has | them |
| his | send | rent | sent | belt | me |
| quit | lift | shell | who | what | and |
| help | inch | went | his | bent | be |
| said | dent | to | said | lend | bent |
| bench | dogs | plugs | has | send | next |
| bend | quit | blend | sent | spend | drift |
| best | pets | elk | visit | refit | depend |
| sending | ended | refill | pretend | regret | middle |
| relish | active | relent | demand | result | prevent |
| relax | detect | secret | refresh | belong | closet |
| problem | itself | resist | trusted | rapid | simple |
| absent | reject | insult | reflect | expect | deflect |

**Writing (Spelling) Words:** Have the student write/spell some of the listed words.

# Lesson 12:

o → The letter /o/ has 3 sounds, /o/, /oa/ and sometimes /u/.
You have been practicing words with the /o/ sound.
This lesson adds practice with the 2nd /oa/ sound and 3rd /u/ sound.

**Write & Say The Sound:** The student prints **o** 10 times saying /oa/ and /u/ sounds.

**Reading Words that have the /o/ sound for o:** Most the time when an o is the only vowel it has the /o/ sound you already practiced. However, there are still quite a few words that the single o will have the /oa/ sound. You will start to notice some patterns where o has the /oa/ sound in 'old' and 'ost' words and also where **o is the only vowel at the end of the word or syllable.** Read these words noticing the /oa/ sound.

| go | no | old | most | cold | colt |
| sold | fold | post | gold | bolt | told |
| mold | host | bold | so | hold | volt |
| stroll | roll | total | folded | untold | oldest |
| golden | protect | program | protest | prolong | focus |
| coldest | retold | posted | boldest | | |

**Reading Words that have the /u/ sound for o:** Sometimes the o has the /u/ sound. In fact the second most frequent way we write or spell the /u/ sound in English is with the letter o. When we read, we often do not even notice that we modify the sound to /u/. However, it is important to remember the o often has the /u/ sound in spelling. In addition many multisyllable words where 'o' has an /u/ pronunciation are the 'schwa' or unstressed syllable in multisyllable words (See notes on the schwa in Appendix A -Sound Pronunciation). Read these words specifically noticing how the o has the /u/ sound.

| from | son | front | ton | month | from |
| won | consist | compass | random | convict | method |
| consent | common | wagon | ribbon | second | lemon |
| bishop | blossom | robot | custom | oven | lesson |
| seldom | collect | compress | construct | constrict | consult |
| contempt | contend | control | dragon | | |

We are going to review a few other common words that have the /u/ sound for o. These words are slightly **'irregular'**, not because of the /u/ sound for o, but because they have a 'no reason' e at the end of them. Read these familiar words and specifically notice how the o has the /u/ sound and the e is silent.

| some | come | done | none |

**Making Words:** Make words with /oa/ or /u/ sound for o. "Please make the word ___"
Use sound tiles...... a e o   b c d f g l m n p r(2) s t(2) th
from  most  gold  son  sold  ton  front  mold  post  fold  lemon  boldest  protect
oldest  program  coldest  consent  protest  seldom  method  second  retold  contempt

**Reading Words:** The student reads the following list, sounding out the words with physical tracking and proper blending. Correct any errors immediately.

| am | us | no | as | go | he |
| ton | not | do | son | is | was |
| most | so | them | me | old | she |
| visit | dogs | trash | done | has | send |
| his | bend | to | he | went | we |
| his | said | front | ton | mold | has |
| host | from | with | gold | kids | go |
| most | damp | fold | frogs | sent | bold |
| did | that | hold | task | post | from |
| hold | hills | from | this | gift | lost |
| glass | shop | get | left | bolt | come |
| stroll | hold | from | some | has | send |
| contest | uncut | resist | lemon | unclasp | common |
| oldest | total | demand | belong | pretend | belong |
| trusted | unless | consist | complex | hidden | depress |
| muffin | selfish | prolong | second | method | untold |
| custom | wagon | program | fondness | problem | coldest |
| protest | random | ribbon | golden | absent | protect |
| depend | folded | retold | posted | focus | extend |

**Writing (Spelling) Words:** Have the student write/spell some of the listed words.

# Lesson 13:

 The letter i has 2 sounds, /i/ and /ie/. You have been practicing the /i/ sound. This lesson includes practice with the 2nd /ie/ sound.

**Write and Say The Sound:** The student prints i 10 times saying the /ie/ sound.

**Reading Words that have the /ie/ sound for i:** Often when 'i' is the only vowel it has the /i/ sound you already practiced. But sometimes it has the /ie/ sound. You will start to recognize the common patterns of 'ild' and 'ind' where i has the /ie/ sound. Also when **'i' is the only vowel in a syllable and it comes at the end of the syllable, the 'i' usually has the long /ie/ sound**. Read these words noticing the /ie/ sound.

| wild | kind | child | bind | mild | rind |
| pint | find | grind | wild | mind | child |
| blind | bind | remind | unkind | childish | wildest |
| virus | silent | titan | Bible | behind | biped |
| bridle | hijack | migrant | micron | pilot | rifle |

**Making Words:** Make words that have the /ie/ sound for i.
Use sound tiles...... e i   b d f g h k l m n p r s t w ch
       wild  kind  child  bind   pint  find  grind  blind  wind  behind  remind  wildest

**Reading Words:** The student reads the following words, sounding out with physical tracking and proper blending. Correct any errors immediately.

| do | us | no | as | go | most |
| is | he | was | his | wild | front |
| from | find | them | we | child | she |
| old | most | then | has | ton | end |
| kind | send | pint | fist | gasp | the |
| sold | said | child | mind | its | wild |
| we | some | with | gift | come | find |

| | | | | | |
|---|---|---|---|---|---|
| will | grind | told | bind | none | bent |
| month | went | send | tense | trench | spend |
| blind | string | behind | wildest | remind | kindest |
| instill | rumble | belong | little | method | common |
| simple | finish | program | rifle | visit | demand |
| extend | depend | relapse | oldest | trusted | silent |
| reflex | pretend | regret | defend | second | method |
| defense | result | protect | common | spending | focus |
| protest | untold | prevent | debug | closet | coldest |
| absent | secret | active | sending | protect | random |
| wagon | gotten | often | unless | problem | sudden |

**Writing (Spelling) Words:** Have the student write/spell some of the listed words.

# Lesson 14:

**a →** The letter **a** has 2 primary sounds, /a/ and /ay/. You have already practiced the /a/ sound. This lesson covers practice of the 2$^{nd}$ /ay/ sound. This lesson also includes when 'a' is pronounced with the alternate /aw/ or /ah/ sounds.

**Write and Say The Sound:** The student writes **a** 5 times saying the /ay/ sound.

**Reading Words that have the /ay/ sound for a:** Most of the time when 'a' is the only vowel it has the /a/ sound you already practiced, but sometimes it has the /ay/ sound. You will start to notice the common patterns where single **a** has the /ay/ sound in 'ank', 'ang' and 'able'. Also when **'a' is the only vowel in a syllable and it comes at the end of the syllable, the 'a' usually has the long /ay/ sound.** Read these words noticing the /ay/ sound.

| | | | | | |
|---|---|---|---|---|---|
| rang | sank | bang | tank | sang | clang |

| | | | | | |
|---|---|---|---|---|---|
| bank | fang | crank | hang | blank | frank |
| thank | native | plank | basic | blanket | drank |
| able | table | stable | fable | cable | basic |

**Pronouncing a when  a + l, a + ll:** We are also going to review and practice the different way we usually pronounce 'a' when it comes immediately before l or ll.

**a + l or a + ll**   When the /a/ sound comes before l or ll we usually pronounce it /aw/ as in 'all'. Listen to a few words where the 'l' modifies the 'a' that we pronounce as /aw/: (emphasize the /all/ sound so the student hears) all  ball  call  always  almost  salt.

**Reading Words that have a+l or a + ll:** Read words where the a comes before l or ll. Notice how we pronounce the **a** with the /aw/ sound.

| | | | | | |
|---|---|---|---|---|---|
| all | tall | ball | also | call | talk |
| almost | balk | stall | calm | walk | salt |
| walk | fall | stalk | hall | mall | halt |
| malt | chalk | small | all | also | chalk |
| install | almost | called | tallest | fallen | smallest |

**Pronouncing a when it is w + a:** We are also going to review and practice the different way we pronounce a when it comes after w.

**w + a**   When the single short 'a' comes after 'w', the 'w' modifies the 'a' and we pronounce it /ah/. Listen to a few words with w + a: (Emphasize the /ah/ sound so the student hears) wasp  waffle  wand  wad  wash  watch.

**Reading Words that have w + a:** Read these words where the a comes after w and we pronounce the a with more of an /ah/ sound.

| | | | | |
|---|---|---|---|---|
| wad | wasp | wand | wash | watch |
| swap | wallet | walrus | swan | swamp |
| washing | watched | watching | waffle | |

**Other times we say /ah/ or /uh/ for a:** There are quite a few words where we pronounce 'a' with an /ah/ or /uh/ sound such as **father, about, away.** You'll read more of these words as you advance into the complexities. Many of the /ah//uh/ pronunciation of short 'a' are the 'schwa' or unstressed syllable in multisyllable words (See notes on the schwa in Appendix A -Sound Pronunciation). Most of the time, as you read the word you modify to the correct pronunciation without even noticing.

| | | | | |
|---|---|---|---|---|
| adapt | attach | extra | tundra | affect |
| postal | attend | adopt | attack | compass |
| attempt | attract | amend | affront | alas |
| across | among | ultra | atomic | pasta |

**Word Making Activity:** Make a few words that have the /ay/ and /ah/ sound for a. Use sound tiles...... a i   b c g k l m n p r s t w  sh
rang  sang  bank  sank  tank  blank  crank  balk  swan  shank  calm  salt  wash  wasp  malt  basic

**Reading Words:** The student reads the following list, sounding out the words with physical tracking and proper blending. Correct any errors immediately.

| | | | | | |
|---|---|---|---|---|---|
| rang | sank | all | tank | also | talk |
| bank | bang | tall | salt | wasp | wash |
| ball | wad | wash | call | calm | said |
| mall | hang | fall | wand | walk | this |
| crank | blank | able | plank | stall | from |
| wallet | sense | watch | sang | ball | who |
| she | end | me | hang | call | done |
| child | some | wild | old | most | all |
| salt | wasp | swamp | child | find | told |
| balk | that | cold | tank | went | hang |
| grand | branch | strong | depth | which | hands |

| | | | | | |
|---|---|---|---|---|---|
| walrus | rested | himself | object | gossip | simple |
| promise | silent | index | second | ribbon | rapid |
| prolong | extra | almost | install | unkind | oldest |
| behind | protest | prefix | remind | result | until |
| reflect | pretend | evil | belong | program | focus |
| adapt | stable | tallest | native | children | across |
| contend | total | unless | confess | hidden | pretest |
| trusted | itself | complex | active | prevent | reflex |
| defend | secret | among | control | classic | complex |
| listed | middle | respect | affect | watching | blanket |
| contempt | request | amid | random | abrupt | convict |

**Writing (Spelling) Words:** Have the student write/spell some of the listed words.

# Lesson 15:

## Sound:

**y**   Y is an unique letter. It can be a vowel or a consonant. Y has 3 sounds, /y/ /ee/ and /ie/. When y is a consonant, usually at the beginning of a word the sound is /y/. When y is a vowel, it is most frequently used as the final /ee/ sound in multi-syllable words. If y is the only vowel at the end of a 1-syllable word (or sometimes ending a syllable) the sound is /ie/.

**\*\*The letter y also has an uncommon 4th sound of /i/. Only a few words of Greek origin contain this unexpected use where y has the /i/ sound. This is discussed in Lesson 59.

**Practice Sound Cards:** Practice the sound cards for: y, vowels and any previous sounds the student needs additional practice with.

**Write and Say Sounds:** The student prints **y** 10 x saying *the sounds as they write.*

**Reading Words that have the /y/ sound for y:** If the y is at the beginning of a word (or sometimes a syllable) it is a consonant and the sound is /y/.

| yes | yell | yet | yap | yelp | yuck |
| yum | yam | yip | yo-yo | yak | yen |
| yank | yodel | beyond | yelling | yucca | |

**Reading Words that have the /ee/ sound for y:** If the y is found at the end of a multi-syllable word it usually has the final /ee/ sound. This final /ee/ sound is the most frequent use of the letter y in English.

| fifty | foggy | sixty | gravy | lucky | sadly |
| kitty | only | snappy | cozy | muddy | lady |
| puppy | hungry | very | baby | Billy | pony |
| pesky | nasty | silly | happy | daddy | navy |
| candy | nosy | Lilly | dusty | salty | rusty |
| tricky | thickly | thinly | tasty | sunny | dizzy |
| crusty | only | funny | windy | chunky | picky |
| twenty | messy | sticky | dusty | quickly | calmly |
| crafty | simply | kindly | boldly | crunchy | sloppy |
| windy | mostly | gusty | empty | entry | shaggy |
| fondly | jumpy | softly | swiftly | trusty | lumpy |
| simply | study | sixty | smelly | angry | grumpy |

**Reading Words that have the /ie/ sound for y:** If the y is the only vowel at the end of a short (1 syllable) word it usually has the /ie/ sound. Y also has the /ie/ sound if it is the only vowel ending a syllable within a few other words.

| my | by | try | why | sky | fry |
| shy | cry | fly | my | try | sly |

dry    sly    ply    by    my    python
-----------------------------------------------------------------
satisfy    justify    classify    notify

## Making Words: "Please make the word _____"
Use sound tiles… a e  o u  y   b d f  l m n p r  t ck sh wh
    yum  yet  yap  yelp  yuck  yam  beyond  my  cry  shy  try  fly  why  by

Use sound tiles ….a  i  u   y   b(2)  c d f g h  l(2) m  n  r  s  t w  z
    baby  crazy  hungry  sadly  madly  misty  nasty  gladly  nifty  dusty  crusty  swiftly

# Lesson 16:

**ing**     You are very familiar with how these partner letters work together to represent the sound /ing/. Even though the sounds in '**ing**' are actually /ee/+ /ng/, we practice '**ing**' as a unit because they work together. The 'ing' is one of the most common endings so it helps to quickly identify and process it as a unit.

**ink**     These partner letters work together to have the sound /ink/. It is actually the /ee/ + /nk/ nasal sound.

Note: The **ng** combination is technically the /ng/ nasal sound instead of separate /n/+/g/ sounds. The nasal /ng/ is found in 'ing', 'ang', 'ong' & 'ung'. Most individuals will not notice this slight pronunciation variance as blending /n/+/g/ results in the nasal /ng/.

## Practice Sound Cards: Practice the sound cards for: ing  ink  y, vowels and any previous sounds the student needs additional practice with.

## Write and Say Sounds: The student prints and says each of the sounds 5 to 10 times: ing, ink, y, (plus any other sound that the student needs to practice).

## Making Words: Make words with the sound tiles. "Please make the word _____"
Use sound tiles… a  i  o    ing  ink   b d f g k l  r s t w  sh
    sing  king  going  bring  swing  string  fling  wing  sting  sling  fishing
    wishing  lashing  sink  rink  blinking  drinking  stink  slink  brink  blasting  flashing

## Sound Changing Activity: Remember to listen and make changes to the word.
Use sound tiles….. ing  ink  b d  l r s t w
    stink > sting > swing > sling > slink > blink > brink > drink

Reading Words with ing:

| ring | sing | king | wing | fling | bring |
| ding | sting | string | sling | swing | cling |
| standing | fishing | sitting | wishing | lasting | rushing |
| clapping | rocking | going | banking | smelling | slanting |
| jumping | shifting | smashing | gusting | backing | flipping |
| sagging | asking | hugging | spinning | tapping | washing |
| finding | blasting | grinning | swinging | clapping | chanting |
| swimming | camping | shutting | slipping | stopping | crushing |
| brushing | hitting | shopping | crashing | nesting | stepping |
| blocking | bringing | hopping | pinching | dripping | dusting |
| holding | passing | spelling | tossing | tracking | blending |
| planting | tipping | singing | twisting | testing | hunting |
| yelping | dusting | bringing | winning | humming | drilling |
| telling | setting | yelling | running | rubbing | catching |

Reading Words with ink:

| rink | sink | brink | wink | blink | link |
| clink | shrink | pink | slink | stink | drink |
| drinking | trinket | blinking | sprinkle | preshrink | sinking |
| inkjet | sprinkles | uplink | twinkle | blinked | shrinking |

Writing (Spelling) Words: Have the student write/spell some of the listed words.

# Lesson 17: Review and Practice

**Review Sounds:** Use the review to check if the student needs any additional practice with a certain sound. At this point, many of these sounds will be automatic and there is no need to continue to practice them in isolation.

| m | t | a | s | d | i | f |
|---|---|---|---|---|---|---|
| r | th | l | o | n | p | e |
| h | v | sh | u | b | k | ck |
| c | g | j | w | ch | tch | x |
| z | qu | wh | y | ing | ink | |

**Reading Words:** The student reads the following list, sounding out the words with physical tracking and proper blending. Correct any errors immediately.

| I | a | we | can | am | the |
|---|---|---|---|---|---|
| at | if | did | it | and | on |
| its | that | this | is | in | not |
| had | us | up | but | to | than |
| said | do | can | get | got | him |
| will | with | was | of | which | me |
| what | shop | as | has | his | when |
| met | back | plan | left | shut | cup |
| old | from | he | son | all | she |
| post | hot | land | red | drop | no |
| shin | next | list | band | crash | with |
| nest | stop | run | shed | rash | be |
| drum | hunt | deck | lock | kiss | chin |

| skin | shop | cast | gift | camp | much |
| clap | west | jump | gust | flag | catch |
| fix | buzz | try | blast | which | lunch |
| six | quick | whip | what | chest | quit |
| inch | who | crash | send | dogs | sing |
| come | most | from | wild | mind | sink |
| some | rang | blind | crank | stall | watch |
| fly | calm | also | wasp | walk | rink |
| bring | yet | you | task | clock | sense |
| walks | kind | west | jack | frogs | crept |
| bent | front | child | king | strip | yes |
| all | from | stamp | plant | math | shrub |
| thump | stump | shrimp | trunk | track | string |
| clump | crash | skunk | bunch | find | able |
| walk | swim | chess | crunch | print | blind |
| squish | twist | trust | smell | pick | song |
| bank | flask | yuck | black | help | rock |
| chips | child | box | desk | fetch | bring |
| ball | lady | find | bunch | sand | trip |
| baby | cry | class | bell | drip | stress |
| who | silly | blank | done | rang | shed |
| fry | scratch | punt | chest | tense | lunch |
| distant | also | baby | hidden | consult | cozy |
| going | picnic | finish | almost | lemons | table |

| | | | | | |
|---|---|---|---|---|---|
| punish | children | select | stinky | little | bucket |
| running | subtract | seven | biggest | express | very |
| inches | lumpy | hungry | extra | vanish | basic |
| hunting | muffins | open | insect | pony | extra |
| messy | empty | illness | triple | study | contact |
| candy | happy | wallet | only | sitting | famish |
| apples | deflect | impress | consist | undress | rapid |
| insect | reflect | wildcat | classic | respect | unrest |
| willing | retest | reject | insist | within | problem |
| rapid | robot | crushing | vanish | closet | evil |
| credit | basic | misspell | helping | invent | sudden |
| limit | instill | intend | standing | random | trusty |
| seven | ugly | blocking | address | frequent | contrast |
| resist | defend | program | discuss | protest | nonsense |
| detect | demand | slipping | credit | spastic | almost |
| metric | protest | drafted | result | intend | puzzle |
| pilgrim | active | witness | expect | respond | secret |
| focus | attract | epics | detest | direct | adopt |
| regret | attend | thinking | funny | trusted | beyond |
| withstand | setup | lesson | desktop | bathtub | uncap |
| sandbox | submit | collect | travel | liquid | basic |
| lasted | rented | candle | adjust | squinted | hundred |
| kitchen | misprint | disrupt | wildland | subtext | softness |
| dentist | transmit | risen | sudden | begin | extend |

| insult | pocket | dispatch | select | distant | wildest |
| prolong | blanket | hopscotch | madness | trinket | collect |
| across | victim | tennis | express | flimsy | abrupt |
| signal | nasty | chicken | gossip | profit | regret |
| secret | relax | pretend | absent | trusted | program |
| demand | crashing | method | seldom | golden | remind |
| simply | coldest | migrant | thankless | almost | watching |
| attack | grumpy | backdrop | adapt | respect | kindly |
| standing | seldom | insect | plastic | hunting | reset |
| tundra | yelping | tallest | empty | beyond | unkind |
| behind | senseless | abrupt | waffle | called | wagon |
| titan | blinded | boldest | ribbon | trinket | shutting |
| promise | resist | depress | smallest | total | calmly |
| crusty | flashing | uplink | discuss | misfit | congress |
| request | bigot | cactus | blacksmith | sadden | tasty |
| becalm | dazzle | behold | bedrock | prevent | untold |
| address | topic | fastest | insist | backpack | absent |
| complex | liquid | simple | stable | fitness | fabric |

--------- 3 syllable words ---------

| domestic | aggressive | establish | difficult | unwilling | probably |
| finishing | develop | diagram | expanding | medical | prolific |
| punishment | adjustment | resident | deposit | president | visible |
| equipment | refreshment | sensitive | umbrella | reminded | critical |
| satisfy | fantastic | qualify | replica | expensive | possible |

# Section 3: Vowel Combinations

## General Information on Vowel Combinations

This section starts a new group of sounds, the vowel combinations. Lack of complete knowledge of the vowel combinations often contributes to reading difficulties. Students need to directly learn these complexities that are so prevalent in our English language.

Explain: This section covers a group of sounds called vowel combinations. These letters are 'partner' vowels that work together to make a sound. Your reading will improve greatly as you learn these vowel combinations. There are a few important points to understand:

1. As you know, the vowels are a, e, i, o, and u and sometimes y.
2. The vowels often pair up as partners and work together to make certain sounds.
3. It is very helpful to know "When 2 vowels go walking (paired together) the 1st one usually does the talking (but not always!)"
4. The vowel combinations can be complex. However, you will learn the complexities of these vowel sounds.

# Lesson 18:

ee    These partner letters have the sound /ee/.

Practice Sound Cards: Practice the sound cards for: ee, ing, ink, y and any previous sounds the student needs work on.

Write and Say Sounds: Please write and say each of the sounds 5 to 10 times: ee plus any other sound that the student needs practice with.

Making Words: Make words with the sound tiles. "Please make the word _____"
Use sound tiles.... ee o u i   d(2) g k l n p r s t(2) w sh th ch ing
   three  speed  green  sweet  sheet  speech  sleep  greed  teeth  street
   indeed  keeping  unseen  greeting  upkeep  treetop  sweeping  needing

Noticing How the 'ee' works: Read the following pairs; specifically point out and 'see' how the sound changes from /e/ to /ee/ with the 'ee' vowel combination.

ned -- need        met--meet        sped -- speed        fed--feed

ten -- teen        pep -- peep      bet -- beet          wed -- weed

## Reading 'ee' Words:

| | | | | | |
|---|---|---|---|---|---|
| see | bee | tree | need | eel | deep |
| meet | seed | beep | feed | keep | teen |
| weed | sheep | teeth | jeep | deed | greed |
| queen | speech | bees | seen | peep | feet |
| screen | beef | creep | sleep | weep | peel |
| breed | speed | sweep | week | sheet | three |
| sweet | wheel | green | creep | free | keeps |
| cheek | sleeps | peel | street | meek | seem |
| tweed | steep | freeze | seep | screech | cheese |
| bleed | sheets | deeds | tweet | greets | seems |
| green | wheel | teen | sneeze | beet | steel |
| weeds | breeze | speech | reel | street | spree |
| need | squeeze | steed | sweet | free | sleet |
| indeed | sheepish | creepy | unseen | deeply | agree |
| keeping | between | needy | sweetly | greedy | freezing |
| asleep | greeting | freedom | needing | weekly | bleeding |
| needing | upkeep | coffee | canteen | between | feeding |
| sleepless | decree | weeding | sweetest | freely | esteem |
| degree | weekend | speeding | unseen | sleepy | misdeed |
| sweeping | treetop | teething | between | sixteen | speechless |
| freely | speeches | agrees | beetle | feeling | needy |
| duckweed | breezy | reseed | deepest | fifteen | preteen |

**Writing (Spelling) Words:** Have the student write/spell some of the listed words.

# Lesson 19:

**oa**          These partner letters have the sound /oa/.

**oe**          These partner letters also have the sound /oa/.

**Practice Sound Cards:** Practice the sound cards for: oa oe ee, ing, ink, y and any previous sounds the student needs work on.

**Write and Say Sounds:** Please write and say each of the sounds 5 to 10 times: oa oe ee ing, ink, y, plus any other sound that the student needs practice with.

**Making Words:** Make words with the sound tiles. "Please make the word _____"
Use sound tiles... e u oa b c d f g l m n p r s t(2) th ch ing
     goat coat coast loaf roast goal float boast soap foal groan
     throat toasting unload foaming reload coaching encroach

## Reading Words that have the **oa** spelling:

| | | | | | |
|---|---|---|---|---|---|
| oat | loaf | coat | goal | float | foal |
| soak | coal | roam | moat | poach | foam |
| boat | boast | goat | coach | oak | groan |
| cloak | soap | croak | float | toast | goal |
| moan | throat | groan | roast | goad | roach |
| load | coast | road | loan | toad | stoat |
| goals | shoal | bloat | coats | soapy | foamy |
| toasting | reload | floating | unload | roasted | loaned |
| coaching | roaming | coastal | soaking | boasting | encroach |
| freeload | soapbox | uncloak | afloat | roadless | bloated |

## Reading Words that have the **oe** spelling: **\*\*Notice: he 'oe' partner letters are not very common.** (In the word shoe, the 'oe' has an unexpected /ew/ sound)

| | | | | | |
|---|---|---|---|---|---|
| doe | woe | toe | hoe | foe | roe |

**Writing (Spelling) Words:** Have the student write/spell some of the listed words.

# Lesson 20:

**ai**      These partner letters have the sound /ay/.

**ay**      These partner letters also have the sound /ay/.

**Practice Sound Cards:** Practice the sound cards for: ai ay oa oe ee ing ink y and any previous sounds the student needs work on.

**Write and Say Sounds:** Write each of the sounds 5 to 10 times: ai, ay, oa, oe, ee.

**Making Words:** Make words with the sound tiles. "Please make the word _____"
Use sound tiles  e o ai   b c d f g l m n p r(2) s t w x
     stain  waist  paint drain faint  strain  brain  grain saint  braid explain retain
     refrain  remain  detail  regain  reclaim  retrain  repaid  derail  complain complaint
Use sound tiles... e i ay    b c d l m  n p r s t w  ing
     bray  stray  maybe  praying  inlay  delay  saying  midway  stingray  decay
     repay  betray  replay  staying

## Reading Words that have the **ai** spelling for the /ay/ sound:

| | | | | | |
|---|---|---|---|---|---|
| aim | aid | rain | wait | rail | gain |
| bait | main | paid | jail | chain | maid |
| sail | pain | waist | faint | grain | plain |
| stain | raid | train | hail | drain | snail |
| praise | strain | slain | trait | brain | pail |
| saint | braid | quaint | mail | faint | waive |
| faith | raise | gains | Spain | claim | trail |
| vain | fail | laid | strait | aims | maize |
| frail | waits | sprain | taint | traits | daisy |
| raisin | rainy | contain | afraid | refrain | plainly |
| reclaim | explain | unchain | detail | retain | derail |
| complaint | retrain | maintain | faithful | waiting | regain |
| draining | maiden | unpaid | mainly | aiming | engrain |

| | | | | | |
|---|---|---|---|---|---|
| raining | fainted | reclaim | baiting | abstain | aided |
| gained | complain | ailment | proclaim | domain | dainty |
| detain | abstain | remain | braided | unpaid | sustain |
| mainland | daily | waitress | painful | training | rainfall |
| prepaid | mailed | detain | claimed | saintly | exclaim |
| acclaim | acquaint | constraint | sprained | faithful | |

Reading Words that have the **ay** spelling for the /ay/ sound:

| | | | | | |
|---|---|---|---|---|---|
| way | may | bray | play | ray | bay |
| clay | pay | pray | say | stay | day |
| slay | tray | stray | hay | sway | lay |
| spray | fray | jay | pays | days | always |
| today | playpen | delay | prayed | relay | display |
| maybe | replay | prepay | decay | hallway | praying |
| delay | staying | pathway | away | midway | essay |
| subway | roadway | railway | decay | mainstay | inlay |
| layoff | payment | saying | playoff | daylong | hayloft |
| halfway | swaying | always | playful | paying | stingray |
| prepay | freeway | ashtray | spillway | essay | haystack |
| weekday | mislay | repay | betray | byway | holiday |

**Writing (Spelling) Words:** Have the student write/spell some of the listed words. **\*\*Directly teach the expected spelling pattern. Both ai and ay have the /ay/ sound. The 'ai' spelling is used more frequently than the 'ay' spelling. Notice the 'ai' is found at the beginning or middle of a syllable. The ai is NEVER used at the end of a word. Remember NO English words can end in 'i', therefore the 'ay' or another spelling pattern (they, sleigh) must be used for the /ay/ sound at the end of a word. In contrast, the 'ay' spelling is found at the end of the word or syllable.

# Lesson 21: Practice

**Reading Mixed List of Words:** The student reads the following words, sounding out with physical tracking and proper blending. Correct any errors immediately.

| | | | | | |
|---|---|---|---|---|---|
| wait | sprint | three | boat | train | claim |
| play | speed | soak | three | went | green |
| gain | roast | goal | teeth | rain | seem |
| faint | tray | fleet | sleep | bring | chain |
| cheese | drain | float | way | keep | braid |
| need | brain | throat | praise | small | watch |
| loan | faith | coast | black | month | grind |
| strong | twist | quilt | swift | sleet | sway |
| faint | strain | spray | boast | sweet | shrimp |
| squish | pray | squint | loan | bunch | stalk |
| plain | when | cold | blink | wheel | wash |
| rail | deep | three | both | yells | able |
| between | inches | explain | away | finish | almost |
| hiding | shaggy | fabric | dusty | pumpkin | hungry |
| thickly | freedom | insect | begin | singing | mostly |
| blended | conflict | contain | waiting | select | sunset |
| credit | panic | within | exit | nesting | banish |
| little | aided | insult | buddy | detail | byway |
| quickly | sleepy | maybe | handbag | defrost | recall |
| problem | unseen | blocking | willing | esteem | crusty |
| demand | keeping | unload | coaching | gladly | going |

| | | | | | |
|---|---|---|---|---|---|
| beyond | seven | feeding | delay | regain | unfold |
| sudden | intend | softly | spending | common | breezy |
| respect | sitting | sixteen | inspect | blending | prefix |
| wallet | talking | inject | rapid | expect | subtract |
| invent | reflect | detect | stinky | weekend | coffee |
| neglect | expand | relax | thankful | tricky | blessed |
| abrupt | result | wisdom | hidden | publish | degree |
| distrust | direct | remain | complex | quickly | extra |
| decree | among | contest | belong | oldest | upkeep |
| engrain | decay | encroach | explain | famish | freeload |

# Lesson 22: The vowel-consonant-e combinations

The next vowel combinations are slightly different than most vowel combinations as the vowel partners are separated by a consonant. Although these vowels are NOT right next to each other these 2 vowels *are* partners. It is important to recognize that the 1st vowel and the e work together as partner letters. The e makes the first vowel "say its name" (the long sound). The e is the 'silent' partner.

Use the following examples to overview the vowel-consonant-e pattern. **Read** each word to the student pointing at the sounds as you go. *Show how the partner e changes the sound* from /a/ to /ay/, /o/ to /oa/, /i/ to /ie/, /u/ to /oo/, and /e/ to /ee/. Show the student how the partner vowels work together. (Sometimes it helps to underline the e as you read the word to emphasize how the e makes the a,i,o,u or e change its sound.)

| | | | |
|---|---|---|---|
| a_e | at---ate | tap--tape | mad---made |
| o_e | hop---hope | not---note | con---cone |
| i_e | tim---time | hid---hide | spin---spine |
| u_e | cub---cube | cut---cute | tub---tube |
| e-e | pet---pete | | |

# Lesson 23: a-consonant-e combination

**a_e**   Although they are split by a consonant the a and the e are working together. The e makes the a have the /ay/ sound.

**Making Words:** The student makes the words as pairs. Have him make the first word and read it. Then have him add the e to the end and point to the a and say the /ay/ sound. Physically seeing the addition of the e and how it causes the sound to change helps the student understand and learn the pattern of how the a and e work together.

Use sound tiles... a e c d f h l m n p r t v

| at--ate | man--mane | tap--tape | mad--made | van--vane |
|---|---|---|---|---|
| fat--fate | hat--hate | rat--rate | can--cane | plat--plate |

## Reading a_e Words:

| game | ate | lame | trade | make | shade |
|---|---|---|---|---|---|
| same | made | rate | base | cake | lane |
| brake | rake | crate | amaze | crane | cave |
| gate | shape | late | ape | grape | plate |
| safe | make | graze | made | lake | tape |
| name | slate | trade | plane | daze | fade |
| blade | spade | snake | shake | blaze | shave |
| slate | made | save | jade | scrape | grade |
| blame | vase | glaze | late | male | vane |
| chase | state | behave | rebate | safest | inflate |
| escape | vacate | locate | ashamed | mistake | rotate |
| latest | invade | enslave | donate | statement | prorate |
| retake | bravest | concave | safely | rename | debate |
| landscape | relate | gateway | unsafe | evade | reshape |

**Writing (Spelling) Words:** Have the student write/spell some of the listed words. **Focus on how the addition of the 'e' makes the 'a' have the /ay/ sound.**

# Lesson 24: o-consonant-e combination & i-consonant-e combination

**o_e**   Although they are split by a consonant the o and e work together.
        The e makes the o have the /oa/ sound.

**Making Words:** The student makes the words as pairs. Have him make the first word and read it. Then have him add the e to the end and point to the o and say the /oe/ sound. Physically seeing the addition of the e and how it causes the sound to change helps the student understand and learn the pattern of how the o and e work together.
Use sound tiles.....  o  e    b  c  d  h  l  m  n  p(2)  r  t(2)

| hop--hope | not--note | con--cone | tot--tote |
|---|---|---|---|
| cop--cope | mop--mope | pop--pope | cod--code |
| rob--robe | rod--rode | lob--lobe | |

## Reading o_e Words:

| home | joke | dome | rode | hope | note |
|---|---|---|---|---|---|
| cone | those | cope | dole | mope | code |
| vote | robe | hole | rope | hose | mole |
| choke | stone | stroke | stove | broke | prose |
| zone | rose | slope | grove | smoke | globe |
| tone | stole | spoke | dome | poke | pole |
| throne | dote | doze | strobe | choke | shone |
| froze | those | quote | tote | poles | drove |
| devote | homeless | remote | frozen | homerun | promote |
| broken | hopeful | revoke | console | hopeless | decode |
| Smokey | sloped | noted | revote | quoted | spoken |
| invoke | tadpole | arose | awoke | sunstroke | encode |

**Writing (Spelling) Words:** Have the student write/spell some of the listed words.
**Make sure to focus on how the addition of the 'e' makes the 'o' have the /oa/ sound.**

# i_e

Although they are split by a consonant the i and the e are working together. The e makes the i have the /ie/ sound.

**i_e Making Words:** Have the student make the words as pairs. Make the first word and read it. Then have him add the e to the end and point to the i and say the /ie/ sound. Physically seeing the addition of the e and how it causes the sound to change helps the student understand and learn the pattern of how the i and e work together.

Use sound tiles  i  e    b  d  f  g  h  k  m  n  p  r  s  t  w

| tim--time | hid--hide | bit--bite | rid--ride | fin--fine |
| rip--ripe | spin--spine | kit--kite | dim--dime | pin--pine |
| twin--twine | grim--grime | sit--site | strip--stripe | din--dine |

## Reading i_e Words:

| time | hide | bite | ride | dime | ripe |
|---|---|---|---|---|---|
| fine | kite | wine | mile | tide | smile |
| pine | tile | twine | grime | wide | lime |
| chime | crime | stripe | swine | spite | quite |
| hide | bride | gripe | dive | Mike | chime |
| spike | mine | like | glide | wife | hike |
| while | crime | wipe | chide | trite | slime |
| file | shine | side | slide | dine | bribe |
| spine | drive | strike | dime | stride | bike |
| white | strive | kite | swipe | line | pride |
| wise | prize | inside | unlike | bedtime | sunrise |
| inscribe | online | define | offline | divide | confide |
| beside | timely | daytime | sidewalk | lifetime | provide |
| pastime | sunshine | reptile | abide | collide | profile |

**Writing (Spelling) Words:** Have the student write/spell some of the listed words. **Make sure to focus on how the addition of the 'e' makes the 'i' have the /ie/ sound.**

# Lesson 25: u-consonant-e combination & e-consonant-e combinations

**u_e**  The u and the e are partners working together.
The e makes the u have the /oo/ sound.

**u_e Making Words:** The student makes the words as pairs. Have him make the first word and read it. Then have him add the e to the end and point to the u and say the /oo/ sound. Physically seeing the addition of the e and how it causes the sound to change helps the student understand and learn the pattern of how the u and e work together.
Use sound tiles... e u  b c d m r s t

| cub--cube | cut--cute | tub--tube | mut--mute | us--use | crud--crude |

## Reading u_e Words:

| use | cute | June | duke | rude | tube |
| rule | mule | Luke | tune | crude | lute |
| prune | flute | cube | mute | tube | dune |
| flume | fuse | plume | abuse | include | excuse |
| preclude | volume | costume | accuse | astute | amuse |
| consume | misuse | rebuke | transfuse | ruled | cutest |

**e_e**  The e and the e are working together.
The second e makes the first e have the /ee/ sound.

**Reading e_e Words:** Not many words have this e_e combination.

| these | Pete | eve | theme | complete | concrete |
| compete | even | delete | deplete | supreme | convene |
| obese | stampede | athlete | scalene | extreme | |

**Writing (Spelling) Words:** Have the student write/spell some of the listed words. **Make sure to focus on how the addition of the 'e' makes the 'u' have the /oo/ sound and how the addition of 'e' makes the 'e' have the /ee/ sound.**

# Lesson 26: Practice all vowel-consonant-e combinations

**Making Words:** Make words with the sound tiles. "Please make the word _____"
Use sound tiles... a e(2) i o u   c d(2) f g l m n(2) p r s t v sh
   plate  stone  crane  stripe  shave  spade  stove  pride  rule  glide  drape  shine  grime  spine
   costume  include  reptile  preclude  pastime  locate  unsafe  relate  invade  inflate
   grateful  devote  profile   insane  donate  decode  define  shameful  ungrateful

## Reading mixed vowel-consonant-e Words:

| | | | | |
|---|---|---|---|---|
| game | plate | poke | stone | rule |
| gave | hide | note | save | rode |
| crane | stripe | tune | use | time |
| line | spoke | nine | flute | spade |
| graze | prize | tube | stone | sale |
| dime | cope | plane | smoke | doze |
| note | cute | made | hive | shone |
| brake | choke | trade | snake | quote |
| grape | wide | use | graze | rude |
| make | same | these | close | take |
| skate | vote | blade | plate | tile |
| drove | stake | shave | slime | blame |
| stroke | pride | chime | quote | name |
| mile | dine | June | late | chase |
| white | smile | shake | brine | grate |
| strive | stroke | globe | strike | prime |
| grade | brave | scrape | twine | rose |
| drive | stride | throne | swipe | sprite |

106

| | | | | |
|---|---|---|---|---|
| inside | unlike | bases | amaze | online |
| confine | combine | complete | lifetime | invite |
| escape | inflate | enslave | finest | despite |
| nickname | relate | rebate | behave | donate |
| include | useful | decode | sloped | confide |
| propose | traded | inscribe | dispute | compete |
| remade | timely | abuse | safely | exclude |
| deflate | mundane | preside | supreme | insane |
| mistake | define | homemade | divide | equate |
| provide | sideline | debate | beside | timeless |
| promote | grateful | concrete | intake | finest |
| gateway | confide | describe | rotate | shady |
| probate | amaze | invade | spoken | inflate |
| broken | latest | deplete | spineless | include |
| prescribe | useless | statement | reptile | preclude |
| delete | landscape | evade | safest | inscribe |
| extreme | volume | baseball | pastime | excuse |
| daytime | offline | console | hopeless | revoke |
| sideways | migrate | complete | became | widest |
| parade | devote | profile | baseball | unsafe |

---------- 3 syllable words ----------

| | | | | |
|---|---|---|---|---|
| demonstrate | isolate | complicate | related | included |
| regulate | calculate | educate | absolute | speculate |
| devastate | unbroken | estimate | untimely | illustrate |

**Writing (Spelling) Words:** Have the student write/spell some of the listed words.

# Lesson 27

**c** — You already know the letter c has 2 sounds, /k/ and /s/. You have been practicing the sound /k/. Now you will practice the 2nd sound /s/.
The c <u>always</u> makes the /s/ sound whenever **e, i** or **y** comes after the c. (c <u>always</u> steals the /s/ sound when e, i or y comes after it). MUST have the e, i, or y after the c to have the /s/ sound.

### c+e   c+i   c+y = /s/ always

**g** — You already know the letter g has 2 sounds, /g/ and /j/. You have been practicing the /g/. Now you will practice the 2nd sound /j/.
The g <u>sometimes</u> makes the /j/ sound when **e, i** or **y** comes after the g. MUST have e, i or y after the g to have the /j/ sound.

### g+e   g+i   g+y = /j/ sometimes

**Write and Say the Sounds:** The student writes **c & g** 5 to 10 times saying the /s/ and /j/ sound as they write the letter. (Plus other sounds the student needs to practice)

**Reading Words that have the /s/ sound for c:** Remember the **e, i,** or **y** after the c tells us the c must have the /s/ sound. POINT THIS PATTERN OUT TO THE STUDENT (especially if they are saying the incorrect /k/ sound). Help the student 'see' and understand this pattern. Underline the c and the e, i or y if necessary.

| cent | pace | cell | chance | face | rice |
| nice | lace | race | mice | cinch | dice |
| since | space | ice | dance | grace | fleece |
| spice | prince | trace | price | glance | spruce |
| splice | brace | twice | place | trance | fence |
| lacy | city | acid | icing | Nancy | pencil |
| recent | civil | Cindy | faced | decent | balance |
| replace | placemat | fancy | nicely | central | recess |
| produce | decide | enhance | civic | silence | biceps |

| census | cement | sentence | concept | except | induce |
| entrance | reduce | practice | lettuce | notice | accent |
| convince | accept | invoice | success | device | tracing |
| placement | police | exceed | precise | process | succeed |
| freelance | citrus | distance | graceful | finance | proceed |
| notice | absence | backspace | enhance | justice | necklace |
| advance | disgrace | advice | embrace | citizen | policy |

## Reading Words that have the /j/ sound for g:

| age | gem | page | gel | sage | range |
| rage | change | cage | angel | agent | gentle |
| strange | lunge | stage | plunge | vintage | logic |
| engage | tragic | postage | agile | gently | magic |
| package | manage | village | rigid | fragile | teenage |
| luggage | gemstone | voltage | changed | upstage | giraffe |
| cottage | aged | hostage | rampage | image | savage |

**Making Words:** Please make words where 'c' has the /s/ sound and 'g' has the /j/ sound. "Please make the word _____"
Use sound tiles...... a(2) e(2) i o u y    b c(2) d f g l m n p r t ch
   trance  place  prance  price  chance  trace  dance  city  fancy  practice  reduce
   notice  nicely  replace  bicep  induce  placemat  graceful
Use sound tiles..... a e i(2) o u   c d f g l m n p r s t v ch
   strange  gel  change  page  range  angel  vintage  agent  rigid  logic  rampage  tragic
   fragile  upstage  magic

**Writing (Spelling) Words:** Have the student write/spell some of the listed words. Specifically teach the c+e c+i and c+y =/s/ and g+e = /j/ pattern. Before you start tell the student the /s/ sound is going to be spelled with 'c' or the /j/ sound will be spelled with 'g'. Help the student learn these patterns.

# Lesson 28   Review and Practice

Review Sounds:

| a | s | i | o | e | u |
|---|---|---|---|---|---|

c  (ce  ci  cy)        g  (ge  gi  gy)

| ch | y | ee | oa | oe | ai |
|---|---|---|---|---|---|
| ay | a_e | i_e | o_e | u_e | e_e |

**Making Words:** Make words with the sound tiles. "Please make the word _____"
Use sound tiles… a  e(2)  i  o  u  y   b  c(2)  d  f  g  l(2)  m  n  p  r  t  ch
   panic   crime   direct   change   notice   frolic   glance   directly   prince   candy   brace
   public   admit   profit   chance   gladly   crafty   tragic   graceful   produce   practice
   credit   beyond    retold   remind   nifty   inflate
Use sound tiles…. a  e(2)  i(2)  o  u  y   d(2)  g  k  l  m  n  p  r  s  t  v  ch
   strange   strike   chime   stove   angel    gusty   vastly   result   change   pesky   invade   kindly
   mostly   simply   rusty   invite   revoke   visit   almost   unlike   mistake   provide   divide

**Reading a Mixed Word List:** The student reads the following words, sounding out with physical tracking and proper blending. Correct any errors immediately.

| you | as | his | not | has | this |
|---|---|---|---|---|---|
| by | what | did | my | that | it |
| is | wait | in | on | which | and |
| than | the | was | him | had | of |
| with | but | us | can | why | do |
| will | to | said | who | we | from |
| she | go | come | all | make | race |
| like | both | cent | use | done | call |
| nice | some | plant | page | strange | rain |
| shut | back | catch | bring | meet | made |

| | | | | | |
|---|---|---|---|---|---|
| need | end | line | three | rolls | stripe |
| trace | speech | gift | time | twice | seem |
| note | play | white | space | coat | hoe |
| teeth | melt | dress | chain | grape | cheese |
| snake | globe | goal | clay | things | slide |
| paint | strike | small | child | speed | test |
| fence | lost | dime | spend | sweet | next |
| change | print | vase | praise | string | way |
| coast | grass | use | chance | same | grade |
| which | trade | cents | pink | coast | prance |
| strange | brace | speech | grain | stage | chalk |
| swipe | ranged | needing | glance | only | into |
| hungry | blanket | silly | city | afraid | expect |
| tricky | going | pony | running | also | today |
| almost | trying | table | adding | study | little |
| tasty | notice | relax | extra | unrest | playing |
| complete | thickly | swimming | practice | muffins | pretty |
| gentle | inside | picnic | central | nicely | spending |
| cricket | broken | sweetly | common | remind | simply |
| agree | compete | softly | insect | freedom | frolic |
| needy | decide | selfish | unlike | today | belong |
| demand | always | coaching | hidden | indeed | waiting |
| explain | direct | engage | central | bandage | profit |
| canvas | children | impress | reject | within | install |

| | | | | | |
|---|---|---|---|---|---|
| contain | hundred | vintage | unless | express | unfold |
| basement | sunset | placemat | postman | reject | inspect |
| direct | halfway | behind | prevent | recess | between |
| pencil | neglect | conflict | gossip | expense | divide |
| always | classic | delete | shifted | useless | beyond |
| needless | rebate | useful | blended | insult | detail |
| protest | unload | delay | unseen | mostly | painful |
| extra | smallest | washing | attack | unkind | complex |
| spoken | recall | payment | degree | debate | profile |
| sentence | became | playful | called | longest | promise |
| delete | subtract | windfall | expand | insist | problem |
| campsite | reduce | between | refresh | complex | remind |
| oxide | exclude | secret | volume | betray | quoted |
| sunshine | balance | refine | saying | practice | middle |
| adjust | landscape | reptile | homerun | conflict | plainly |
| sulfate | derail | maintain | essay | sixteen | justice |
| reflect | package | domain | invite | sustain | athlete |

---------- 3 syllable words ----------

| | | | | | |
|---|---|---|---|---|---|
| calculate | introduce | greedily | expansive | multiply | vitamin |
| complicate | isolate | demonstrate | related | principal | directly |
| hospital | digital | adjustment | sensitive | celebrate | cinnamon |
| Pacific | civilize | satisfy | punishment | prolific | notify |
| expanding | establish | finishing | unchanged | disagree | decimal |
| qualify | prohibit | prolific | diplomat | disconnect | citizen |

# Lesson 29:

**u**  The letter **u** has 2 primary sounds /u/ & /oo/. Additionally, in a few words the **u** has an unexpected /uu/ sound. You have been practicing the /u/ sound. This lesson adds practice with the /oo/ and the unexpected /uu/ sounds.

## Write and Say the Sound:  The student writes **u** 5-10 times saying the /oo/ and /uu/ sound as they write the letter.

## Reading Words that have the /oo/ sound for u:

Note: The long u actually has a /you/ variance in pronunciation in some words (mule, cute). You will notice the student modifying the sound as appropriate. If they do not achieve correct pronunciation on their own then you can help them with correct pronunciation.

| | | | | | |
|---|---|---|---|---|---|
| tune | cube | rude | mule | flute | tuba |
| lute | tube | mute | dude | cute | pupil |
| unit | reduce | unite | rudely | refute | music |
| volume | student | stupid | include | muted | exclude |

## Reading Words that have the /uu/ sound for u:

| | | | | | |
|---|---|---|---|---|---|
| put | pull | full | push | bull | bush |
| pudding | bullet | pulling | bushy | pushing | fullest |
| bully | | | | | |

## Writing (Spelling) Words: Have the student write/spell some of the listed words.

# Lesson 30:

**oi**     These partner letters have the sound /oy/.

**oy**     These partner letters have the sound /oy/.

## Practice Sound Cards: Practice sound cards for new sounds as well as any previous sounds that need work.

**Write and Say the Sounds:** The student writes **oy** and **oi** 5 to 10 times saying the /oy/ sound *as* they write. (Plus any other sounds that need practice)

**Making Words:** Make words with the sound tiles. "Please make the word _____"
Use sound tiles...... a e u oi   b  c  d(2)  f   h  j  l  m  n  p  r s(2) t v x
   foil  coin  moist  spoil  joint  point  broil  hoist  rejoin  uncoil  devoid  exploit
   adjust  avoid  reboil  subsoil  recoil  tabloid

Use sound tiles ..... oy   a    e    c   d   j   l(2)   m   n  p   r s  t
   joy  enjoy  employ  royal  loyal  Roy  destroy  deploy  decoy

## Reading Words that have the **oi** spelling for /oy/:

| oil | coin | noise | foil | moist | soil |
|---|---|---|---|---|---|
| boil | oink | coil | spoil | join | broil |
| point | toil | joint | hoist | void | voice |
| choice | poise | moist | joist | avoid | recoil |
| pinpoint | spoiled | boiling | hoisted | devoid | subsoil |
| toilet | tabloid | exploit | rejoin | uncoil | poison |
| topsoil | oilskin | anoint | adjoin | moisten | pointless |

## Reading Words that have the **oy** spelling for /oy/:

| boy | toy | joy | royal | enjoy | loyal |
|---|---|---|---|---|---|
| employ | coy | annoy | Roy | joyful | ploy |
| voyage | deploy | decoy | enjoy | destroy | flyboy |

**Writing (Spelling) Words:** Have the student write/spell some of the listed words.

**Directly teach the expected spelling pattern. Both **oi** and **oy** have the /oy/ sound. The 'oi' spelling is used more frequently and comes primarily at the middle of a syllable (occasionally at the beginning as in 'oil'). The 'oi' is NEVER used at the end of a word (remember no English words can end in 'i'). Therefore, the 'oy' spelling must be used for the /oy/ sound at the end of a word. The 'oy' spelling is found at either the end of the word or sometimes at the end of a syllable. Help the student learn this expected spelling pattern.

# Lesson 31:

**ea** These partner letters have 2 primary and one unexpected sound. Most of the time the 'ea' partners have the sound /ee/. Sometimes they have an /e/ sound. Additionally, in a few words 'ea' has the unexpected /ay/ sound.

**Practice Sound Cards:** Practice sound cards for new sounds as well as any previous sounds that need work.

**Write and Say the Sounds:** The student writes **ea** 5 to 10 times saying the /ee/ /e/ sound as they write. Plus write any other sound that needs practice

**Making Words:** Make words with the sound tiles. "Please make the word _____"
Use sound tiles...... ea  u   b  c  d(2) f   h  l  m  n(2)  p  r  s  t  ch  sh  ing
   each   peach   east   stream   dream   preach   breast   heating   unclean   teaching
   unleash   cheating   unseat   spreading   dreadful
Use sound tiles..... ea  o  y   b  d  g  h  k  l  n  p  r  s(2)  t  w  th
   great   break   steak   bread   yeast   head   breath   death   spread   season
   wealthy   ready   neatly   reason   easy   greatly   beastly

## Reading Words that have the /ee/ sound for ea:

| eat | each | lean | east | heat | peas |
|---|---|---|---|---|---|
| beat | leaf | treat | seat | steam | teach |
| reach | beam | least | dream | beast | heap |
| crease | bleak | ease | bean | peak | please |
| jeans | tease | stream | speak | cheat | sneak |
| cream | beach | scream | preach | team | read |
| clean | bleach | lease | grease | peach | wheat |
| leash | peace | breathe | feast | steal | please |
| beat | cease | feat | yeast | treat | measly |
| eating | season | reading | creamy | release | eagle |
| peanut | reason | peacock | easy | heating | reached |
| steamy | repeat | ideal | teaching | meanest | pleasing |

115

| | | | | | |
|---|---|---|---|---|---|
| unleash | defeat | unseat | measles | meantime | leaflet |
| increase | release | disease | speaking | peaceful | cheating |
| reaching | seamless | neatest | decrease | sleazy | steamship |
| treatment | beaten | weaved | weasel | dreamless | cheaply |
| seashell | treason | squeamish | daydream | sublease | ice cream |

Reading Words that have the /e/ sound for ea:

| | | | | | |
|---|---|---|---|---|---|
| head | dealt | bread | ready | spread | breath |
| dread | death | tread | thread | breast | wealth |
| stealth | heaven | steady | health | heavy | peasant |
| already | wealthy | deadly | spreading | headway | healthy |
| steadfast | instead | ready | headstrong | stealthy | unsteady |
| dreadful | breakfast | headstrong | breathless | heavenly | retread |

Reading Words that have the unexpected /ay/ sound for ea:

| | | | | |
|---|---|---|---|---|
| great | break | steak | daybreak | greatest |

Writing (Spelling) Words: Have the student write/spell some of the listed words.

# Lesson 32: Review and Practice

| | | | | | |
|---|---|---|---|---|---|
| head | price | life | made | facts | each |
| strong | beast | trace | slide | shake | sleek |
| treat | when | white | place | than | full |
| from | glaze | spice | trade | home | rain |
| stone | stroke | stride | these | strange | snack |

| | | | | | |
|---|---|---|---|---|---|
| shape | spade | crank | string | quest | team |
| strict | slept | swift | brain | waist | flute |
| smile | catch | crush | fleece | split | pulse |
| chalk | dwell | change | raise | claim | rinse |
| rude | point | state | tense | throat | great |
| stamp | choice | fleet | death | smoke | swamp |
| moist | squint | quick | grace | change | faith |
| until | active | finish | also | oldest | city |
| random | spliced | reject | today | simple | within |
| inside | propane | reptile | ready | contain | tasty |
| almost | instead | crusty | wishing | saying | panic |
| inject | adjust | asleep | afraid | dismiss | insist |
| infest | replay | coffee | delay | useful | mostly |
| fancy | cement | into | recall | unfit | prefix |
| unseen | reprint | quickly | unpack | repay | unless |
| sadly | ending | infect | punish | explain | always |
| behind | display | update | remake | contest | crunchy |
| neatest | mostly | pushing | increase | ugly | remind |
| rapid | sudden | selfish | enjoy | planet | easy |
| lately | tallest | himself | install | windy | nicely |
| relax | insult | delete | include | feeling | along |
| unload | resting | central | upkeep | hidden | changed |
| prevent | contrast | wishing | fifty | express | gentle |
| insect | elect | plastic | mistake | define | destroy |

| catfish | bedtime | blindness | sunshine | bulldog | mitten |
| blacktop | sentence | detest | inspect | reflect | recheck |
| disband | canteen | nasty | intense | regain | event |
| happen | backbone | midwife | freedom | blending | unbolt |
| inspect | playpen | angry | kitten | wildcat | recess |
| backpack | conflict | sentence | pumpkin | cupcake | endless |
| lifeboat | hungry | speeding | wishing | beside | refrain |
| closet | visit | refine | unjust | district | constant |
| muffin | defrost | escape | flapping | between | direct |
| dentist | prevent | deflect | shotgun | tangle | conduct |
| destruct | placement | illness | playful | tulip | inspect |
| focus | midway | decide | standoff | complain | consist |
| simply | spelling | update | weekend | replace | promptly |
| inset | began | program | simply | escape | contest |
| complex | along | problem | stable | project | exceed |
| rumble | impress | pulling | away | healthy | payment |
| speechless | robin | jungle | tragic | salad | instead |
| wagon | profit | express | tundra | piston | study |
| respond | pilgrim | empty | secret | velvet | riddle |
| promise | realize | heaven | handful | unkind | faithful |
| advance | triple | beyond | within | needless | pinching |
| heavenly | promote | instead | pointless | treatment | beaten |
| distance | bellboy | volume | profile | devoid | debate |
| insist | essay | student | enhance | easement | collide |

| | | | | | |
|---|---|---|---|---|---|
| salvage | demand | extreme | inflate | backspace | concave |
| preclude | laptop | voltage | travel | inscribe | balance |
| quickly | encroach | freeway | setback | engrain | misdeed |
| splendid | upkeep | byway | abstain | coastal | betray |
| exclaim | afloat | gossip | flimsy | expect | sixteen |
| freeload | promise | backup | discuss | uplink | shifted |
| seldom | convex | healthy | spoiled | exclude | topsoil |
| pushing | decent | beyond | image | complete | justice |
| absence | gateway | timely | delete | pastime | prefix |
| weekday | ailment | safest | always | nineteen | random |
| saintly | thankful | soapbox | decay | freezing | congress |
| stable | bleeding | rainfall | migrant | watching | anoint |
| pathway | screaming | catching | headstrong | smallest | practice |
| joyful | needing | seashell | peaceful | teenage | trusty |
| mistake | parade | sidewalk | global | ashamed | meantime |
| leaflet | sleeping | hostage | rudest | extreme | twenty |

---------- 3 syllable words ----------

| | | | | | |
|---|---|---|---|---|---|
| positive | speculate | establish | holiday | tabulate | expansive |
| habitat | possible | develop | electric | Pacific | satisfy |
| expanding | equipment | example | abandon | admitted | proclaimed |
| family | attempting | medical | rejected | company | consistent |
| related | united | latitude | utensil | attitude | excluded |
| expensive | notify | absolute | unbroken | prohibit | isolate |
| multiply | atomic | celebrate | relaxing | citizen | finishing |
| impressive | unloading | elected | remaining | mistaken | completed |

# Lesson 33:

**ow**    These partner letters have 2 sounds; /ow/ and /oa/.

**Practice Sound Cards:** Practice sound card for this new sound and previous sounds.

**Write and Say the Sound:** The student writes **ow** 5 to 10 times saying the /ow/ and /oa/ sounds as they write the letters. Plus write any other sound that needs practice.

**Making Words:** Make words with the sound tiles. "Please make the word _____"
Use sound tiles... ow    a e i    b c d g h l n p r s t w    sh th    ing
   howl  growl  clown  scowl  brown  township  drowning  plowing
   blown  shown  snowing  showing  growth  blowing  throwing  window  shadow
   slideshow  elbow  lowest  widow  sideshow  growing  below

## Reading Words that have the /ow/ sound for ow:

| now | cow | how | owl | plow | clown |
| town | down | drown | brown | growl | crown |
| gown | howl | chow | frown | browse | scowl |
| drown | downtown | plowing | township | growling | avow |

## Reading Words that have the /oa/ sound for ow:

| snow | slow | grow | low | mow | flow |
| own | show | shown | blow | blown | glow |
| bowl | row | crow | throw | growth | tow |
| shallow | window | pillow | rainbow | mellow | yellow |
| showing | bowling | lowest | snowy | slowly | growing |
| follow | meadow | shadow | billow | below | sideshow |
| backflow | borrow | follow | slideshow | swallow | widow |

**Writing (Spelling) Words:** Have the student write/spell some of the listed words.

# Lesson 34:

**ou** These partner letters have 3 sounds; Most of the time 'ou' has the /ow/ sound. Sometimes 'ou' has the /u/ sound and in a few words the 'ou' has the /oo/ sound.

**Practice Sound Cards:** Practice sound card for this new sound as well as previous sounds that need work.

**Write and Say the Sound:** The student writes **ou** 5 to 10 times saying the /ow/ /oo/ and /u/ sounds *as* they write. Plus write any other sound that needs practice.

**Making Words:** Make words with the sound tiles. "Please make the word _____"
Use sound tiles... ou  e(2)  o  y    c  d  f  g  l(2)  m  n(2)  p  r  t  ch
 loud  pout  noun  couch  clout  ounce  found  count  ground  pound  pouch  flounce
 proudly  grouchy  cloudy  compound  loudly  renounce  pronounce  denounce
Use sound tiles... ou  a  e  i  y    b  c  d  f  g  m  n  p  r  s  t(2)  th  ch
 you  soup  group  youth   sound  stout  trout  sprout  south  crouch  county
 cousin  young  touch  famous  country  outside  rebound

## Reading Words that have the /ow/ sound for ou:

| out | loud | pout | oust | round | ouch |
| pound | cloud | mound | proud | stout | found |
| shout | house | clout | mouse | count | south |
| couch | sound | ground | hound | vouch | snout |
| trout | pouch | noun | grouch | spout | bounce |
| ounce | grouse | mount | south | scout | flounce |
| pounce | county | about | grounded | proudly | countless |
| renounce | sounded | compound | rebound | loudest | southeast |
| outloud | thousand | around | account | pronounce | playground |
| outside | loudly | without | counted | sprouted | cloudy |
| scoundrel | proudest | groundless | houseboat | rounded | recount |

## Reading Words that have the /u/ sound for ou:

touch　　　young　　　country　　　cousin　　　couple　　　double

trouble　　　country　　　joyous　　　famous　(*and other "ous" endings)

## Reading Words that have the /oo/ sound for ou:

you　　　soup　　　group　　　youth　　　croup

**Writing (Spelling) Words:** Have the student write/spell some of the listed words.

**Reading Irregular Words:** There are a few irregular words where the 'ou' has an unexpected 'uu' sound. The words would, could and should are the most common of these.

　　would　　　　could　　　should

# Lesson 35   Review and Practice

## Review Vowels and Vowel Combinations:

a　　　e　　　i　　　o　　　u　　　y　　　ee

c   (ce  ci  cy)　　g  (ge  gi  gy)

oa　　oe　　ai　　ay　　a_e　　i_e　　o_e

u_e　　e_e　　oi　　oy　　ea　　ow　　ou

## Word Making Activity:

Use sound tiles… oi a e i(2) o u y   c(2) d(2) l(2) m  n p t v x sh
　　explicit  divide  shade  volume  implicit  notice  clash  invite  exploit
　　complex  expand  voice  exactly  excite  multiply  vanish  uncoil  devoid

Use sound tiles… ai  ou  e(2)  i  o    c  d(2) f  l  m  n(2)  p  r(2)  s  t  w  x  ch
　　refrain  contain  found  complete  decode  proud  faint  nose  chain  prime  told
　　conflict  wisdom  paint  twine  saint  sprout  mound  stripe  explain  retain  strain  chime

Use sound tiles… ow  ee  i  u   b  d  g  k  l  p  n  r  s  w  x   th  sh  ing
　　window  blowing  grown  throw  brown  green  growling  growth  upkeep  shown
　　three  sweeping  keeping  rowing  sixteen

Use sound tiles….ea  oi   i  u  y   b  c  d  h  l  M  n  p  r  s  t  v  ch  ing
　　simply  teaching  toil  heavy  bread  heating  breast  cleaning  soil
　　spreading  ready  preaching  point  steady  moist  pride  richly  dusty  unclean

**Reading Words:** The student reads the following words, sounding out with physical tracking and proper blending. Correct any errors immediately.

| you | coin | how | find | put | count |
|---|---|---|---|---|---|
| life | will | all | that | while | these |
| sleds | race | think | small | math | loud |
| snack | eat | group | out | has | from |
| found | could | please | box | toys | need |
| trade | each | great | now | brink | point |
| which | said | down | came | push | preach |
| east | smile | about | found | growl | would |
| strange | stream | screech | spread | teach | flow |
| praise | voice | growth | cheese | fresh | snow |
| head | drink | proud | talk | rain | make |
| home | watch | film | strong | wind | blow |
| town | snow | now | why | these | brown |
| branch | grows | sold | glance | wait | desk |
| chance | coast | prance | squint | south | globe |
| scribe | catch | white | price | place | grace |
| cousin | amaze | annoy | pushing | gentle | became |
| justice | contain | wisdom | maybe | pillow | afraid |
| simply | punish | infect | away | peanut | reading |
| heavy | even | divide | enjoy | going | helpful |
| coffee | boiling | little | hungry | fuzzy | notice |
| runny | easy | today | study | subtract | between |

| | | | | | |
|---|---|---|---|---|---|
| practice | problem | about | ladybugs | divide | coaching |
| teaching | weekend | funny | played | unlike | about |
| baseball | softly | spending | complete | relax | unfold |
| thickly | picnic | central | nicely | cricket | ready |
| expect | common | almost | compete | canvas | pencil |
| children | impress | reject | within | install | neglect |
| hundred | vintage | unless | express | conflict | delete |
| bandage | inspect | gossip | prevent | expect | insect |
| basement | sunset | placemat | postman | reject | direct |
| selfish | profit | expense | insist | windfall | expand |
| campsite | catfish | bedtime | intense | detest | reflect |
| recheck | disband | until | prefix | contain | define |
| canteen | ending | nasty | contrast | regain | inside |
| event | oldest | defrost | wishing | explain | healthy |
| contest | prevent | active | escape | mostly | playpen |
| crunchy | conflict | sentence | famous | refrain | tangle |
| conduct | illness | endless | elect | congress | deflect |
| endless | fancy | cement | sunshine | into | bulldog |
| recall | unfit | remind | unseen | reprint | quickly |
| unpack | repay | dismiss | insist | resting | replay |
| soapbox | betray | enhance | voltage | devoid | encroach |

---------- 3 syllable words ----------

| | | | | | |
|---|---|---|---|---|---|
| multiply | expansive | expensive | introduce | example | habitat |
| recopy | unhappy | tabulate | celebrate | develop | capital |
| relaxing | latitude | positive | uncommon | expecting | united |

# Lesson 36:

**ew**          These partner letters have the sound /oo/.

**ue**          These partner letters have the sound /oo/.

**ui**          These partner letters also have the sound /oo/.

**Practice Sound Cards:** Practice sound cards for these new sounds.

**Write and Say The Sounds:** The student writes **ue, ew,** and **ui** 5 to 10 times saying /oo/ <u>as</u> they write. Plus write any other sound that needs practice.

**Making Words:** Make words with the sound tiles. "Please make the word _____"
Use sound tiles... ue a e    b c d f g h l r s t v
       blue   hue   fuel   true   clue   glue   due   value   rescue
Use sound tiles... ew a   b   c   d   f   l   n   p   r   s   t   ch   sh
       news   flew   stew   chew   dew   drew   slew   blew   crew   screw   pew   cashew
Use sound tiles.... ui   e   c   f   n   r(2)   s   t   :   suit   fruit   ruin   recruit

## Reading Words with the 'ew' spelling pattern:

| new | flew | stew | dew | drew | slew |
| news | blew | crew | newt | stew | grew |
| few | threw | screw | pew | yew | shrew |
| chewing | cashew | unscrew | withdrew | outgrew | renew |

## Reading Words with the 'ue' spelling pattern:

| blue | clue | value | hue | fuel | Sue |
| true | glue | due | flue | untrue | rescue |
| venue | fescue | residue | avenue | continue | revenue |

## Reading Words with the 'ui' spelling pattern:

| suit | fruit | cruise | juice | bruise | recruit |

**Writing (Spelling) Words:** Have the student write/spell some of the listed words.
***The **ue, ew** and **ui** all have the same /oo/ sound. The **ui** is only used in a few words and is NEVER used at the end of a word.

# Lesson 37:

**oo** These partner letters have 2 sounds, /oo/ & /uu/. The /oo/ sound is used more frequently than the /uu/ sound.

**Practice Sound Cards:** Practice the new sounds and any others needing review.

**Write and Say the Sound:** The student prints **oo** 3 to 5 times saying the /oo/ & /uu/ sound *as* they write.

**Making Words:** Make words with the sound tiles. "Please make the word _____"
Use sound tiles... oo(2)  e u  b  d f g k l m n p r s t(2) th
  boot  pool  food spoon  loon broom stoop  proof spool  troop  soonest  smoothest  uproot
  moonset  sunroom  sunroof  foolproof look took good  stood  cookbook footrest  bookend

## Reading Words that have the /oo/ sound for oo:

| soon | boot | pool | moon | food | too |
| coon | loon | broom | boom | hoop | room |
| noon | roof | mood | spool | choose | drool |
| troop | boost | zoo | bloom | spoon | stoop |
| smooth | root | cool | tooth | moose | loop |
| proof | scoop | coolest | roomful | raccoon | uproot |
| moody | baboon | mushroom | soundproof | reboot | moonrise |
| balloon | smoothly | soonest | teaspoon | washroom | sunroof |

## Reading Words that have the /uu/ sound for oo:

| book | hook | nook | cook | foot | look |
| stood | took | hoof | good | shook | wool |
| wood | brook | hood | cooking | textbook | looking |
| football | hooking | bookend | wooly | bookstand | sainthood |

**Writing (Spelling) Words:** Have the student write/spell some of the listed words.

# Lesson 38:

**ie**     These partner letters have 3 sounds /ie/ /ee/ and occasionally /i/.

**ei**     These partner letters have 2 sounds /ee/ and occasionally /ay/.

**ie and ei are relatively uncommon.

**Practice Sound Cards:** Practice these new sounds and any others needing practice.

**Write and Say the Sound:** The student writes **ie**, **ei** 5 times.

**Making Words:** Make words with the sound tiles. "Please make the word _____"
Use sound tiles... ie a y   b c d f g k l m n p r s t   ow th ch sh
     pie die lie tie thief chief brownie shriek yield priest brief friend field shield
Use sound tiles... ei e(2) o   c(2) l n p r t v   ing th
     conceit receive ceiling protein veil rein vein

## Reading Words that have the /ie/ sound for ie:

| pie | lie | die | tie | magpie |

## Reading Words that have the /ee/ sound for ie:

| thief | belief | chief | siege | priest | niece |
| shriek | relieve | relief | brief | grief | Maggie |
| brownie | achieve | retrieve | cookie | collie | rookie |

## Reading Words that have the /i/ sound for ie:

| friend | field | shield | yield | mischief | wield |

## Reading Words that have the /ee/ sound for ei:

| neither | conceit | receive | protein | ceiling | either |

## Reading Words that have the /ay/ sound for ei:

| veil | rein | vein | beige |

**Writing (Spelling) Words:** Have the student write/spell some of the listed words. The spelling guideline " i before e except after c or sounding as /ay/ in neighbor and sleigh and a few exceptions" helps us spell these words.

# Lesson 39:

**ey** These partner letters have 2 sounds /ee/ & /ay/. Usually the **ey** follows follows the guideline "when two vowels go walking the first does the talking" and has the /ee/ sound. In a few words it unexpectedly has an /ay/ sound.

**The ey combination does not occur in many words. The most commonly encountered **ey** word is **they**.

**Practice Sound Cards:** Practice this new sound any any other needing practice.

**Write and Say the Sound:** The student writes **ey** 3 to 5 times saying the sound.

**Making Words:** Make words with the sound tiles. "Please make the word _____"
Use sound tiles... ey  o  b  h  k  m  n  p  r  th
    key  monkey  money  they  prey  honey  obey

## Reading Words that have the /ee/ sound for ey:

| key | monkey | money | honey | pulley | valley |
| alley | abbey | hockey | kidney | volley | trolley |
| donkey | chimney | jockey | keynote | | |

## Reading Words that have the /ay/ sound for ey: (**although the /ay/ sound for ey is only found in a few words you see it often in the very common word 'they')

they     obey     prey     hey

# Lesson 40:

**aw** These partner letters have the sound /aw/.

**au** These partner letters also have the sound /aw/.

**augh** These partner letters also have the sound /aw/.
The "gh" in these partner letters are "silent"

***The **aw**, **au** and **augh** all have the same /aw/ sound.

**Practice Sound Cards:** Practice these new sounds any others needing practice.

**Write and Say The Sounds:** The student writes **aw, au & augh** 5 to 10 times saying the /aw/ sound <u>as</u> they write.

**Making Words:** Make words with the sound tiles. "Please make the word _____"
Use sound tiles... aw ou i u   c d f   h j k l n p r s(2)  t w  th
     law  jaw  hawk  dawn  claw  lawn  flaw  awful  sawdust  withdraw  outlaw  southpaw
Use sound tiles... au e i o u   d(2)  f g h l n p s t(2) v  ing
     haul  fault  flaunt  vault  auto  audit  August  hauling  defraud  default  taunting
Use sound tiles... i e  augh   c  d  r  s  tx2
     taught  caught  distraught  retaught

## Reading Words that have the **au** spelling for /aw/:

| haul | fault | auto | maul | clause | sauce |
|---|---|---|---|---|---|
| pause | Paul | cause | haunt | vault | fraud |
| launch | gaunt | caulk | taunt | flaunt | paunch |
| August | laundry | faucet | audit | hauling | defraud |
| caused | default | augment | audible | causeway | jaundice |
| saucepan | vaulted | taunting | faultless | hauled | flaunted |

## Reading Words that have the **aw** spelling for /aw/:

| saw | law | jaw | paw | hawk | lawn |
|---|---|---|---|---|---|
| pawn | claw | fawn | paws | dawn | awe |
| draw | crawl | slaw | shawl | laws | drawn |
| yawn | awful | drawing | sawdust | awesome | awning |
| declaw | chainsaw | outlaw | southpaw | whipsaw | withdraw |

## Reading Words that have the **augh** spelling for /aw/:

| caught | taught | aught | onslaught | distraught | retaught |
|---|---|---|---|---|---|

Note: In the commonly encountered irregular word 'laugh' the 'augh' has an unexpected /aff/ sound.

**Writing (Spelling) Words:** Have the student write/spell some of the listed words.

# Lesson 41:

**igh**   These partner letters have the sound /ie/. (The "gh" is "silent").

**Practice Sound Cards:** Practice this new sound any others needing practice.

**Write and Say The Sound:** Write **igh** 5 to 10 times saying the /ie/ sound.

**Making Words:** Make words with the sound tiles. "Please make the word _____"
Use sound tiles... igh  e  u   b  d  f(2)  h  l  m  n  p  r  s  t(2)
   high  sigh  light  sight  right  might  fight  flight  night  bright  delight  upright
   penlight  uptight  brightest  frightful

## Reading Words:

| high | right | light | might | sigh | fight |
| bright | thigh | tight | slight | night | fright |
| plight | sight | blight | highest | lightning | lighten |
| tighten | brightest | frighten | resign | highway | tightest |
| delight | highlight | brighten | hightail | penlight | insight |
| brighten | flashlight | frightful | highjack | outright | nightgown |
| twilight | midnight | upright | mighty | thighbone | highness |
| nightlight | uptight | daylight | backlight | sighted | moonlight |

----------- 3 syllable words ----------------------------------------------------------

| delightful | tightening | insightful | enlighten | frightfully | highlighted |

**Writing (Spelling) Words:** Have the student write/spell some of the listed words.

# Lesson 42: Additional Practice with /z/ sound of s

Reading Words That have the /z/ sound for s:

| | | | | | |
|---|---|---|---|---|---|
| is | as | use | his | has | wise |
| please | rise | choose | pause | these | noise |
| those | praise | raise | was | jobs | grabs |
| swings | peas | nose | hose | browse | stays |
| news | lays | grows | keys | laws | friends |
| hands | wins | clams | holds | pose | glows |
| saves | fuse | rose | cools | noise | cheese |
| tease | spoils | ease | plans | whose | prays |
| rains | boys | ribs | does | bruise | rides |
| dreams | glides | grows | boils | plows | dogs |
| cause | close | games | planes | clause | cruise |
| tease | plays | used | cause | easy | pansy |
| husband | resent | cruise | obeys | result | daisy |
| visit | resist | music | visible | raisin | fused |
| risen | poison | disease | reason | transit | programs |
| season | begins | excuse | because | chosen | pleasing |
| revise | noisy | caused | praising | disobeys | cousin |
| music | excuse | wisdom | poison | includes | rebounds |
| result | treason | pleasing | reuse | thousand | transfix |
| flimsy | risen | transgress | wisdom | appraise | closeout |
| compose | disclose | translate | amuse | easement | expose |
| displease | abuse | appease | measles | rosebush | oppose |
| praising | enclose | weasel | misuse | resist | compose |
| measles | transverse | defuse | disclose | pleasant | caused |

# Lesson 43: Review and Practice

Review Vowels & Vowel Combinations:

| a | o | i | e | u | y |
|---|---|---|---|---|---|

c  (ce  ci  cy)    g  (ge  gi  gy)

| ee | oa | ai | ay | a_e | i_e |
|---|---|---|---|---|---|
| o_e | u_e | e_e | oi | oy | ea |
| ow | ou | ue | ew | ui | oo |
| ie | ei | ey | au | aw | igh |

**Making Words:** Make words with the sound tiles. "Please make the word _____"
Use sound tiles… a e i o u y  oi  c(2) d f g n p r t v ch
    notice  prance  reduce  practice  fancy  price  voice  grace
    point  candy  choice  trade  pride  drove  change
Use sound tiles…. oa ou  a e y   c d g l   n r s t   sh th
    cloudy  roast  toad  ground  strange  angel  count  age  shout  throat  youth
Use sound tiles…. aw ew igh   c d f h l   n r s t   th   ing
    screw  saw  news  threw  high  thawing  drew  crawling  night
    stew  lightning  lawn  right  straw  fighting

**Reading Words:** The student reads the following words, sounding out with physical tracking and proper blending. Correct any errors immediately.

Please note the unexpected sounds/spellings as you read these irregular words.

| was | to | said | you | do | who |
|---|---|---|---|---|---|
| what | some | of | would | come | done |
| should | was | could | | | |

Please read these words to practice the sounds that you have already learned.

| light | strike | game | feed | twist | call |
|---|---|---|---|---|---|
| street | now | stream | throw | great | book |

| | | | | | |
|---|---|---|---|---|---|
| found | while | right | pie | few | friend |
| wood | fault | thief | fright | toast | fight |
| cause | soup | growth | tease | breath | fringe |
| chalk | shrimp | high | down | young | noise |
| growl | broom | praise | strange | champ | wheel |
| speech | print | leave | coast | push | caught |
| stalk | squint | oust | place | yield | group |
| season | admit | easy | today | escape | money |
| profit | maybe | simply | quickly | wisdom | deeply |
| explain | softly | expect | unfold | subtract | oxide |
| relax | convex | recall | provide | prefix | today |
| tangle | annoy | amaze | justice | crusty | hungry |
| cloudy | value | fifty | combine | exist | dizzy |
| yucky | going | ready | pillow | little | almost |
| obey | awful | cousin | trouble | famous | pointed |
| lately | contain | beagle | peanut | gently | became |
| relate | afraid | confess | slipping | dentist | middle |
| growing | royal | painting | heavy | method | expand |
| control | agree | needy | changed | unlike | freedom |
| demand | waiting | detail | avoid | active | unite |
| roomful | playground | silence | promise | between | remain |
| student | replied | message | given | infest | commands |
| settle | looked | safety | nothing | couple | reflect |
| attempt | proceed | reflex | reason | sentence | below |

| subject | pleasing | outlook | handful | despite | weakness |
| recall | paycheck | money | respond | called | talking |
| approach | follow | around | beside | accept | touching |
| falsehood | treated | writing | justice | anyway | regain |
| mighty | pronounce | broken | humble | moment | betray |
| profess | follow | respect | instead | without | risen |
| window | healing | holy | healthy | priceless | lifetime |
| success | vanish | highway | twisting | practice | steady |
| allow | unload | result | reduce | invite | behind |
| thankful | defrost | update | promptly | replace | loudest |
| central | endless | neither | valley | default | joyous |
| famous | drawing | begins | prayed | quickly | combine |
| legend | product | contest | counted | packet | classic |
| indeed | weekend | traced | device | engage | display |
| rotate | speechless | remind | postage | safety | feeling |
| frozen | tundra | increase | manage | really | afloat |
| setup | adjust | program | attack | highly | away |
| amaze | using | often | training | practice | relate |

----------- 3 syllable words -----------------------------------------------------------------

| expanding | disobey | continue | company | astonish | confident |
| difficult | mistaken | notify | satisfy | agreement | recopy |
| relaxing | explained | president | enjoyed | titanic | described |
| disappoint | speculate | reminded | completely | positive | excluded |
| united | example | related | adjustment | audible | celebrate |
| establish | citizen | isolate | finishing | consistent | habitat |

# Section 4: R-controlled vowel combinations

## General Information on "r-controlled Vowel Combinations

Explain to the Student: You are going to start some new sounds called **r-controlled vowel combinations**. You don't need to remember the term. You just need to understand often vowels work together with "r" as "partner letters" to make certain sounds. You will learn a few important points about the **r-controlled vowel combinations**:

1. The **(vowel + r)** or **(vowels + r)** work together as partners. The 'r' is "bossy" and controls the sounds of vowels. You are going to directly learn the sounds these 'vowel(s) + r partners' represent.

2. Just like the vowel combinations, these "vowel(s) + r combinations" can be complex. You will learn these complexities so you can proficiently process these common phonograms.

3. A specific "vowel(s) +r combination" can represent more than one sound (For example the printed 'ar' can represent either the /ar/ or the /air/ sound.)

4. Frequently, a particular sound can be spelled by different "vowel-r letter partners". (For example, the /er/ sound can be spelled 'er', 'ur', 'ir', 'ear' and sometimes 'or'. )

# Lesson 44:

ar      These vowel+r partner letters have 2 sounds.
   1) Most of the time the **ar** has the /ar/ sound.
   2) Sometimes the **ar** has the /air/ sound.

Practice Sound Cards: Practice this new sound and any others needing practice.

Write and Say the Sound: The student writes **ar** 5 to 10 times saying the /ar/ & /air/ sound *as* they write.

Making Words: Make words with the sound tiles. "Please make the word _____"
Use sound tiles... ar   e  y      d  g  k  l  m  n  p  s  t   ch
      march   smart   market   army   chart   garden   charge   spark   large   tardy   partly
Use sound tiles... ar   i  o  y      c  d  g  l  m  n  p  r  t  sh
      carry   carrot   party   clarity   marigold   marry   tardy   sharply   parish   tarnish

Most of the time the ar makes the /ar/ sound:
Reading Words that have the /ar/ sound for ar:

| car | jar | bar | arm | tar |
| art | arch | part | far | mart |
| barn | cart | farm | mark | star |
| park | march | card | smart | large |
| mars | dart | army | dark | bark |
| chart | tart | hard | harp | lard |
| scar | harsh | charge | yard | spark |
| tarp | ark | sharp | start | shark |
| yarn | chart | harm | stark | scarf |
| Clark | cards | marsh | parch | large |
| snarl | carve | sparks | charm | marsh |
| yards | starve | barge | sharp | starch |
| garlic | hardy | cargo | carwash | parcel |
| market | alarm | carpet | target | artist |
| tardy | margin | scarlet | marble | sparkle |
| farmyard | parched | arcade | bargain | arson |
| darkroom | barked | parking | farmhouse | partly |
| yardage | cartwheel | cartoon | cartload | snarling |
| hardship | archway | charming | startle | armpit |
| enlarge | markup | apart | sparkplug | varnish |
| harvest | harshly | parking | sharpest | starving |
| harmful | hardest | startup | garnish | discard |

| | | | | |
|---|---|---|---|---|
| largest | remark | starting | armful | embark |
| hardly | marshy | garden | harshest | farthest |
| depart | particle | argument | article | artifact |
| farsighted | carnival | farfetched | enlargement | arsonist |

**Sometimes the ar makes the /air/ sound:**
**Reading Words that have the /air/ sound for ar:**

| | | | | |
|---|---|---|---|---|
| carry | carrot | Mary | carol | barren |
| scarce | marry | barrel | parish | parent |
| parrot | marrow | barracks | sparrow | caribou |
| caravan | paranoid | marathon | garrison | marigold |
| marinate | parity | clarity | parenting | paragraph |
| parakeet | parasite | paradise | paramount | parable |
| charity | barracuda | necessary | charitable | |

**Writing (Spelling) Words:** Have the student write/spell some of the listed words.

**A closer look at the word 'are':** You are already very familiar with the common word 'are'. Take a close look at the word and specifically notice the 'ar' has the /ar/ sound. The 'e' at the end of this word is the unexpected portion of the word. This 'e' is there for no reason making the word 'are' slightly irregular.

# Lesson 45:

**w+ar**      When the ar comes after w (w+ar) the ar is pronounced differently with almost the /or/ sound. Speech formation of the /w/ modifies the /ar/ sound. The pronunciation of /w/+/a/ comes out as /wor/.

**Making Words:** "Please make the word _____"
Use sound tiles... ar  e  d  m  n  p  s  t  w  th  ing
   warm   war   ward   warp   swarm   warden   warning   warmth   warmest

**Reading Words w + ar words:** Notice how you pronounce /w/+/ar/ as /wor/. While we tend to unconsciously make this sound modification when saying or reading the word it is helpful to intentionally notice the pronunciation variance for spelling.

| war | warm | wart | ward | warp |
| wars | warn | swarm | warmth | wartime |
| warden | warmest | warning | warhead | warthog |

**Writing (Spelling) Words:** Have the student write/spell some of the listed words.


# Lesson 46: Review and Practice

**Reading a Mixed Word List:** The student reads the following words, sounding out with physical tracking and proper blending. Correct any errors immediately.

| when | came | far | out | warm |
| take | off | coat | wasps | milk |
| swarm | them | tree | stripe | all |
| nest | must | high | hope | sting |
| peace | fight | mind | pray | need |
| ground | spread | east | want | howl |
| back | make | ward | tall | reach |
| large | wart | room | face | both |
| jaws | speech | are | smart | walk |
| warmth | leave | chart | grind | warn |
| yards | read | sharks | plant | some |

| | | | | |
|---|---|---|---|---|
| find | coin | hard | small | carve |
| large | would | that | spoil | warn |
| draw | teach | paint | shelf | start |
| reach | stool | carp | count | army |
| discard | remark | about | target | broken |
| ugly | carry | parent | partly | largest |
| tulips | garden | bushes | sopping | unlike |
| afraid | bargain | protect | warning | apart |
| tardy | carrots | even | drawing | growing |
| parish | artist | also | hardly | behind |
| unless | rebate | hardship | sharpen | hardest |
| sparrow | yardage | away | barren | parcel |
| warmest | depart | enhance | devoid | distance |
| delete | sixteen | byway | arson | essay |
| contest | harshly | display | healthy | respond |

# Lesson 47:

**or** — These vowel-r partner letters have 2 sounds.
1) Most of the time the **or** has the /or/ sound.
2) Sometimes the **or** has the /er/ sound. The '**or**' has the /er/ sound when the '**or**' comes after w and at the end of some multisyllable words.

**Practice Sound Cards:** Practice sound card for this new sound as well as previous sounds that need work.

**Write and Say the Sound:** The student writes **or** 5 to 10 times saying the /or/ & /er/ sound *as* they write.

**Making Words:** Make words with the sound tiles. "Please make the word _____"
Use sound tiles... or a i o y  b c d f l m n r s t(2) v th
  north  acorn  inform  stormy  comfort  thorny  flavor  format  normal  formal  fortify
  orbit  actor  favor  tractor  doctor  tornado  forbid  mortify

## Most of the time **or** makes the /or/ sound:
## Reading Words that have the /or/ sound for or:

| or | for | torn | fort | horn |
| form | lord | born | cord | torch |
| nor | port | fork | corn | dorm |
| stork | thorn | ford | north | cork |
| force | short | horse | porch | sport |
| sort | pork | snort | forge | fort |
| torch | storm | horde | orca | forgo |
| forum | torches | torso | endorse | acorn |
| passport | portray | freeform | shortfall | organ |
| format | forty | glory | forward | mortal |
| corny | forbid | forest | forget | orbit |
| stormy | inform | normal | hornet | morning |
| portal | forsake | afford | corkscrew | dormant |
| correct | worship | enforce | comfort | report |
| newborn | portray | forward | forming | Nordic |
| acorn | shortest | Morgan | forgive | formal |
| corrupt | corset | dormant | forceful | forlorn |
| torment | vortex | torrent | dorsal | northeast |
| import | cornrow | carport | moral | fortress |

| | | | | |
|---|---|---|---|---|
| history | fortify | Florida | favorite | ordeal |
| northwest | reform | cornmeal | storage | ordain |
| florist | resort | ripcord | porkchop | forgets |
| ordinary | tornado | notify | historic | mortify |
| horrible | glorify | torpedo | forgetful | ornament |
| portable | important | organic | horrify | storybook |
| memory | horizon | calorie | immortal | assorted |

When **or** comes after w (w + or) we pronounce it with the /er/ sound: (Once again it is how you SAY these sounds together) Reading Words that have w + or that we pronounce with the /er/ sound:

| | | | | |
|---|---|---|---|---|
| work | worm | word | world | worth |
| worse | worship | worthy | worst | worry |
| workhorse | network | workshop | worsen | worksheet |

Sometimes **or** at the end of multisyllable words is said with the /er/ sound. Reading Words that have the /er/ sound for or:

| | | | | |
|---|---|---|---|---|
| odor | error | mirror | doctor | favor |
| motor | labor | terror | flavor | actor |
| tractor | sailor | traitor | tailor | razor |
| color | tenor | donor | rumor | vapor |
| tumor | mayor | minor | author | factor |
| vendor | censor | insulator | conductor | instructor |
| professor | navigator | alligator | contractor | operator |

**Writing (Spelling) Words:** Have the student write/spell some of the listed words.

# Lesson 48: Vowel-r combinations with the /or/ sound

There are five ways we write the /or/ sound. Of these 5 r-controlled vowel combinations that represent the /or/ sound the **or** is the most common followed by **ore**.

**or**      You just learned how these vowel-r partner letters represent /or/.

**ore**      These vowel-r partner letters also have the /or/ sound

**oar**      These vowel-r partner letters also have the /or/ sound

**our**      These vowel-r partner letters also have the /or/ sound

**oor**      These vowel-r partner letters also have the /or/ sound

**Practice Sound Cards:** Practice sound cards for these new and previous sounds.

**Write and Say the Sound:** The student writes **or, ore, oar, oor & our** 5 to 10 times saying the /or/ sound <u>as</u> they write.

**Making Words:** Make words that have the /or/ sound. "Please make the word ____"
Use sound tiles... ore   a e i   c d f g l m n p r s t x
     store   score   more   snore   forecast   ignore   foreman   explore   implore   restore   deplore
Use sound tiles... oar   a i u   b c d l p r s
     board   aboard   boar   oar   roar   clipboard   uproar
Use sound tiles.... our   e y   c f l p s t th
     pour   four   tour   court   your   fourth   courtesy   yourself
Use sound tiles.... oor   i y   d f l n p
     poor   door   floor   indoor   poorly

## Reading Words with <u>or</u> for the /or/ sound:

| | | | | |
|---|---|---|---|---|
| cork | or | for | torn | fort |
| horn | north | sport | short | force |
| form | lord | born | cord | storm |
| nor | port | fork | corn | horse |
| porch | stork | thorn | ford | torch |
| story | orbit | forget | ordain | endorse |
| format | glory | forty | report | inform |

| normal | forbid | forest | morning | forceful |
| forgive | history | reform | retort | shortest |
| organ | torment | import | forsake | correct |

## Reading Words with **ore** for the /or/ sound:

| sore | more | core | tore | chore |
| snore | store | more | bore | shore |
| gore | score | lore | spore | swore |
| deplore | restore | ignore | implore | before |
| adore | forefront | storehouse | forehand | forepaw |
| explore | forewarn | folklore | forego | foreclose |
| foremost | foresight | foreman | forecast | explored |
| foredoom | forearm | shoreline | foretell | adored |
| foreshadow | omnivore | saddle-sore | carnivore | beforehand |

## Reading Words with **oar** for the /or/ sound:

| oar | roar | boar | board | coarse |
| soar | hoard | roaring | aboard | uproar |
| backboard | keyboard | soaring | clipboard | billboard |
| scoreboard | snowboard | blackboard | | |

## Reading Words with **our** for the /or/ sound:

| pour | four | tour | court | your |
| fourth | course | source | yourself | courtyard |
| concourse | contour | downpour | fourteen | courtesy |

Reading Words with **oor** for the /or/ sound:

| | | | | |
|---|---|---|---|---|
| door | poor | floor | moor | indoor |
| backdoor | boorish | outdoor | poorest | seafloor |
| poorly | doormat | coordinate | | |

Writing (Spelling) Words: Have the student write/spell some of the listed words.

# Lesson 49: Review and Practice

Reading a Mixed Word List: The student reads the following words, sounding out with physical tracking and proper blending. Correct any errors immediately.

| | | | | |
|---|---|---|---|---|
| read | story | horse | good | court |
| corn | book | just | short | may |
| when | came | mine | more | coast |
| course | you | far | out | grape |
| warm | chore | drink | word | floor |
| fourth | would | fresh | north | take |
| hoops | juice | point | next | growth |
| should | like | world | four | game |
| wasps | score | charge | space | worse |
| story | about | named | hungry | nicely |
| quickly | forget | practice | afraid | indoor |
| aboard | foresight | apart | forest | corrupt |
| remark | hardly | forward | enforce | restore |

| | | | | |
|---|---|---|---|---|
| newborn | printing | contain | foremost | morning |
| parent | carpet | forgive | ignore | forty |
| expand | normal | pleased | empty | mostly |
| today | forego | garden | carry | shortest |
| flavor | offshore | worship | labor | forecast |
| orbit | implore | charged | inform | highest |
| before | network | mayor | fourteen | warning |
| restore | warmest | hardship | always | cartoon |
| coastal | engrain | reptile | cartwheel | market |
| propane | destroy | sideshow | simply | value |
| downpour | shortfall | forceful | worksheet | author |
| disease | depart | misuse | closeout | translate |
| harvest | healthy | indeed | archway | parish |
| afford | mirror | format | window | volume |
| enlist | enjoy | pesky | speechless | unite |
| faithful | adore | seldom | explore | legend |
| famous | report | central | barnyard | without |
| enlarge | foremost | hardship | keyboard | ordeal |
| beyond | slightly | domain | yourself | sustain |
| package | extreme | rigid | confine | gauntlet |
| amuse | vowel | silence | fullest | headway |
| forgetful | charity | particle | farsighted | organic |
| argument | paradise | historic | instructor | courtesy |
| necessary | forgetful | notify | favorite | ordinary |

# Lesson 50:

er     These vowel-r partner letters have the sound /er/.

**Practice Sound Cards:** Practice sound card for this new sounds as well as previous sounds that need work.

**Write and Say the Sound:** Write **er** 5 to 10 times saying /er/ sound *as* you write.

**Making Words:** Use sound tiles... er   a i u   d f g h m n(2) p s(2) t w th sh
    fern   term   stern   under   miner   thunder   father   sister   faster   usher   hermit
    gather   mister   perhaps   master   inert   winter   permit   intern   hunter   wander

# Reading Words that have the er /er/ sound:

| | | | | |
|---|---|---|---|---|
| her | verb | herd | berg | fern |
| term | Bert | herb | perm | perch |
| germ | serve | terse | term | jerk |
| berm | clerk | berth | tern | verse |
| germ | stern | over | after | alter |
| pepper | wander | summer | perky | darker |
| hermit | paper | mister | order | under |
| winter | miner | butter | better | center |
| ever | corner | thunder | harder | perhaps |
| letter | marker | cracker | former | rubber |
| boxer | permit | derby | baker | diner |
| other | elder | water | person | ladder |
| intern | helper | ginger | rather | binder |
| vertex | barter | fever | sliver | fender |
| newer | clever | inert | loner | nervous |

| | | | | |
|---|---|---|---|---|
| banner | power | alert | herder | jumper |
| monster | partner | perplex | nicer | sister |
| persist | shelter | perfect | printer | plaster |
| expert | prosper | gather | corner | poster |
| usher | thermal | twister | tower | slender |
| master | teacher | beater | hunter | shorter |
| river | cider | temper | taller | tender |
| cinder | merchant | shorter | mother | zipper |
| father | border | Gerber | brother | northern |
| persist | blunder | transfer | merger | cleaner |
| derby | prayer | younger | number | reverse |
| mercy | faster | jerky | perched | percent |
| person | border | another | singer | stranger |
| permit | sticker | quicker | proper | smoker |
| center | steamer | rather | chapter | pointer |
| tender | charter | chopper | toaster | prouder |
| owner | slumber | greater | bumper | luster |
| shooter | players | winner | differ | pattern |
| member | later | anger | expert | perfect |
| offer | fighter | eastern | wonder | thicker |
| cooler | members | modern | antler | hunger |
| ranger | heater | western | farmer | chapter |
| farther | layers | softer | slower | hiker |
| dancer | driver | silver | hanger | diver |

| | | | | |
|---|---|---|---|---|
| danger | supporter | server | blinkers | southern |
| terminate | terminal | determine | energy | persistent |
| another | remember | however | different | computer |
| internet | forever | general | encounter | consider |
| together | discover | explorer | attacker | officer |
| vertical | property | overhead | recover | overtime |

**Writing (Spelling) Words:** Have the student write/spell some of the listed words.

# Lesson 51: Vowel-r combinations with the /er/ sound

There are 5 vowel+r combinations that usually represent the /er/ sound. Of the 5 ways to write the /er/ sound, the **er** is the most common followed by **ur**.

- **er** — You learned how these vowel-r partner letters have the sound /er/.
- **ur** — These vowel-r partner letters also have the /er/ sound
- **ir** — These vowel-r partner letters also have the /er/ sound
- **ear** — These vowel-r partner letters sometimes have the /er/ sound
- **or** — You already learned how these vowel-r partner letters have the /er/ sound when they come after a w and at the end of multisyllable words.

**Practice Sound Cards:** Practice sound cards for these new sounds as well as previous sounds that need work.

**Write and Say the Sound:** Write **er, ur, ir, ear & or** 5 to 10 times while saying the /er/ sound.

**Making Words:** Make words with the sound tiles. "Please make the word _____"
Use sound tiles..... er  a  i  o  ea  b  c  d  f  l  m  n  r  s(2)  t  v  w   th
   master   weather   river   faster   sister   cleaner   feather   other
   brother   mother   reader   bother   winter   streamer   silver   sliver   blinder
Use sound tiles... ur  e  i  y   b   h   n  p  r  s   t  ch(2)  ing
   hurt   burn   church   turnip   turn   return   burst   hurry   burping   urgent
Use sound tiles... ir  i  y   b  d  f  g  l  m  n  s  t   th
   bird   girl   flirt   third   stir   thirty   dirty   thirsty   firmly   infirm   dirty
Use sound tiles ..... ear   y   d  h  l  n  p  s   th   ch  ing
   learn   earth   search   pearl   earl   heard   early   learning   earning

# Reading Words with **er** for the /er/ sound:

| | | | | |
|---|---|---|---|---|
| her | verb | herd | verse | fern |
| term | perm | perch | germ | serve |
| under | terse | over | stern | pepper |
| wander | summer | butter | letter | marker |
| hermit | paper | mister | order | rubber |
| winter | miner | better | center | cracker |
| under | ever | corner | thunder | hermit |
| after | person | number | perfect | pattern |
| toaster | thermal | twister | faster | former |
| clever | inert | binder | boxer | derby |
| alter | person | newer | printer | loner |
| danger | perky | expert | elder | nervous |
| sister | master | teacher | beater | hunter |
| river | cider | temper | taller | tender |
| cinder | merchant | shorter | mother | zipper |
| father | border | brother | cleaner | hanger |
| slender | shorter | blunder | transfer | mercy |

| | | | | |
|---|---|---|---|---|
| border | persist | singer | corner | pointer |
| southern | perfect | property | consider | internet |
| remember | together | encounter | energy | computer |

# Reading Words with **ur** for the /er/ sound:

| | | | | |
|---|---|---|---|---|
| fur | cur | blur | urge | burr |
| nurse | turn | hurt | burn | furl |
| hurl | curb | curl | burp | surf |
| lurch | murk | churn | lurk | purge |
| yurt | curve | turf | surge | purse |
| spurt | burnt | slurp | lurch | burst |
| church | curve | curse | blurb | purple |
| splurge | curly | burned | concur | unhurt |
| urban | burden | furnish | murder | purpose |
| hurry | purchase | murky | turmoil | burping |
| surface | recur | turtle | furry | turnip |
| curfew | curved | gurgle | sulfur | turkey |
| uncurl | cursive | burner | survey | urgent |
| yogurt | survive | curtail | disturb | surfing |
| current | surpass | curling | turning | return |
| hurtful | burnable | furnace | bursting | murky |
| turnpike | surname | purchase | turbine | turbid |
| surreal | currency | surgery | surgical | turbulent |
| resurface | surrender | turtleneck | survival | hurricane |

## Reading Words with **ir** for the /er/ sound:

| | | | | |
|---|---|---|---|---|
| fir | bird | firm | girl | stir |
| sir | dirt | chirp | girth | thirst |
| first | shirt | skirt | third | birch |
| birth | flirt | smirk | squirm | mirth |
| squirt | swirl | circle | thirty | dirty |
| birthday | affirm | firmly | infirm | confirm |
| circus | thirsty | birthright | birdbath | birthmark |

## Reading Words with **ear** for the /er/ sound:

| | | | | |
|---|---|---|---|---|
| earl | earth | search | pearl | earn |
| learn | heard | early | research | learning |
| earthquake | earning | searchable | earthworm | |

## Reading Words with **or** for the /er/ sound: w+or and or at the end of some multisyllable words.

| | | | | |
|---|---|---|---|---|
| work | worm | word | world | worth |
| worse | worship | worst | worry | tractor |
| odor | error | mirror | doctor | favor |
| color | visitor | actor | tailor | worker |
| contractor | operator | terror | conductor | flavor |
| insulator | sailor | traitor | alligator | instructor |
| professor | navigator | workable | worldly | working |

## Writing (Spelling) Words: Have the student write/spell some of the listed words.

# Lesson 52: Review and Practice

## Review Sounds:

| oa | ai | ay | a_e | i_e | o_e | u_e |
| e_e | oi | oy | ea | ow | ou | ue |
| ew | ui | oo | ie | ei | ey | au |
| aw | igh | ar | w+ar | or | ore | oar |
| our | oor | er | ur | ir | ear | w+or |

## Reading Words: 
The student reads the following words, sounding out with physical tracking and proper blending. Correct any errors immediately.

| come | would | what | toast | they |
| right | these | from | too | turn |
| truth | first | wise | raise | force |
| are | her | easy | key | warm |
| part | done | calls | more | storm |
| door | smart | serve | score | shore |
| easy | obey | form | mark | charge |
| your | chore | sport | hard | hurt |
| door | shirt | four | board | world |
| earth | spoil | heard | which | speak |
| group | girl | said | claim | blue |
| learn | course | curve | large | lives |
| coast | fourth | drive | purse | catch |
| some | show | beach | point | heard |
| water | market | orbit | forget | forty |

| | | | | |
|---|---|---|---|---|
| winter | carry | garden | paper | favor |
| twister | purchase | border | purple | other |
| better | thirty | furnish | along | going |
| shorter | under | cleaner | doctor | worldly |
| favor | going | after | inform | because |
| partner | gather | metric | expert | never |
| eastern | already | practice | around | learning |
| persist | away | flavor | project | puzzle |
| excite | visit | explore | worship | early |
| watched | midnight | flashing | turning | tender |
| summit | pigment | plastic | exact | tundra |
| clouds | meter | rumble | thunder | distance |
| victim | radish | safety | research | surface |
| increase | crashed | ever | current | corner |
| sister | powder | account | respond | prevent |
| common | normal | involve | turning | chapter |
| pointer | northern | searching | worldly | intern |
| global | before | furnish | circle | marker |
| affirm | remark | inform | shortest | person |
| result | forward | basic | request | learned |
| nervous | scoreboard | pencil | operate | discover |
| important | exploring | distracting | together | consider |
| different | energy | instructor | encounter | forever |
| argument | expanded | president | Pacific | introduce |

# Lesson 53: Vowel-r combinations with the /air/ sound

**/air/ sound:** There are 3 vowel+r combinations that usually represent the /air/ sound.

**are** — These vowel-r partner letters have the /air/ sound (*note.. this is NOT the word "are" but the "partner letters '*are*' that make the sound /air/)

**ar** — As presented earlier, these vowel-r partners can have the /air/ sound.

**air** — These vowel-r partner letters also have the /air/ sound

There are 3 ways we usually write or spell the /air/ sound. Of the three ways to spell the /air/ sound, **are** and **ar** are the most frequent. The spelling pattern **air** is not used in many words. A few words are spelled with the unexpected 4$^{th}$ spelling pattern of 'ear'. In addition, the irregular words 'their' and 'there' contain unexpected /air/ spellings.

**Practice Sound Cards:** Practice sound card for these new sounds as well as previous sounds that need work.

**Write and Say the Sound:** Write **are, ar, & air** 5 to 10 times saying the /air/ sound as you write.

**Making Words:** "Please make the word _____"
Use sound tiles...  are   a  e  o    b  c  f  g  l  m  p  s  t  w
   glare   stare   scare   spare   flare   blare   beware   aware   software   compare
Use sound tiles...  ar   i  o  y    c  d  g  l  m   p  r  t
   carry   carrot   clarity   marigold   marry   parrot

# Reading Words with <u>are</u> for the /air/ sound:

| | | | | |
|---|---|---|---|---|
| mare | bare | dare | hare | stare |
| care | spare | share | flare | snare |
| square | pare | glare | scare | fare |
| blare | rare | aware | stared | shared |
| careless | beware | compare | careful | squarely |
| farewell | scarecrow | bareback | dared | prepare |
| software | barefoot | warfare | threadbare | careless |

Reading Words with **ar** for the /air/ sound: (Remember how the ar sometimes makes the /air/ sound -Lesson 44)

| | | | | |
|---|---|---|---|---|
| carry | carrot | carol | Mary | marry |
| carries | parrot | parent | barrel | parish |
| barren | barracks | sparrow | caravan | caribou |
| clarity | marathon | marigold | marinate | marriage |
| paradise | parakeet | parasite | barracuda | necessary |

Reading Words with **air** for the /air/ sound:

| | | | | |
|---|---|---|---|---|
| air | hair | stair | fair | pair |
| chair | fair | flair | lair | affair |
| dairy | airplane | despair | unfair | airbag |
| repair | stairway | aircraft | wheelchair | airflow |
| highchair | haircut | crosshair | airline | chairlift |
| hairband | chairman | fairground | repairing | |

Reading Words with the unexpected **ear** spelling for the /air/ sound: (this 'ear' spelling for /air/ sound is only used in a few words)

| | | | |
|---|---|---|---|
| bear | tear (rip) | pear | wear |

Writing (Spelling) Words: Have the student write/spell some of the listed words.

Other irregular words with the /air/ sound:

You already know the common words **there** and **their**. These frequently encountered words contain unexpected spellings for the /air/ sound. **There** and **their**, sound the same but have different meanings. (Words that sound the same but have different meanings are called homophones for "same sounds".) **There** means in, at or to a place. **Their** is a pronoun meaning done by or belonging to them. (Put *their* favorite book over *there* on the table.)

# Lesson 54: Vowel-r combinations with the /eer/ sound

**/eer/ Sound:** There are three vowel-r combinations/partner letter combinations that usually represent the /eer/ sound. The three ways to write the /eer/ sound are:

- **ear** — These vowel-r partner letters usually have the /ear/ sound. This is just like the 'ear' that you hear with.
- **eer** — These vowel-r partner letters also have the /ear/ sound
- **ere** — These vowel-r partner letters also have the /ear/ sound

Of the 3 ways to write the /ear/ sound. The **ear** is by far the most common. Although the **ere** is only used in a few words, you see it often in the common word **here**.

Also if you notice, the vowel combinations ea, ee and e-consonant-e that you already learned help you learn these sounds as the /eer/ sound is almost exactly the same as blending the /ee/ sound with an /r/(/ee/+/r/= /eer/)

**Practice Sound Cards:** Practice sound card for these new sounds as well as previous sounds that need work.

**Write and Say the Sound:** Write **ear, eer & ere** 5 to 10 times saying the /ear/ sound as you write.

**Making Words:** Make words with the sound tiles. "Please make the word _____"
Use sound tiles... ear  u  y   b  c  d  f(2)  l(2)  n  p  s
   nearly  year  clearly  spear  beard  fearful  bleary  unclear  nearby  dearly
Use sound tiles... eer  o  u   d  l  n  p  s  t  v  ch
   deer  cheer  leer  peer  steer  volunteer

## Reading Words with <u>ear</u> for the /eer/ sound:

| ear | dear | near | clear | tear (drop) |
| hear | year | gear | beard | spear |
| fear | sear | shear | rear | smear |
| bleary | appear | dearly | hearing | weary |
| yearly | nearby | clearly | fearful | nearly |
| clearance | nearsighted | unclear | yearbook | |

**Reading Words with <u>eer</u> for the /eer/ sound:**

| | | | | |
|---|---|---|---|---|
| deer | cheer | leer | steer | peer |
| career | sheer | engineer | volunteer | |

**Reading Words with <u>ere</u> for the /ear/ sound:** (The **ere** spelling is only found in a few words. However, you frequently see it in the common word 'here'.)

| | | | |
|---|---|---|---|
| here | mere | sincere | severe |

**Writing (Spelling) Words:** Have the student write/spell some of the listed words. Notice that of the 3 ways to write the /ear/ sound. The **ear** is by far the most common.

# Lesson 55: Review Vowel-r combination ear

**ear**     The vowel-r combination **ear** has 2 primary and 1 unexpected sound.
1) The 'ear' combination usually has the /ear/ sound.
2) Sometimes 'ear' has the /er/ sound.
3) Occasionally 'ear' has the unexpected /air/ sound.

**Practice Sound Cards:** Practice sound cards for previous sounds that need work.

**Write and Say the Sound:** Write **ear** 5 to 10 times saying the /ear/ & /er/ sounds.

**Reading Words where ear has the /eer/ sound:**

| | | | | |
|---|---|---|---|---|
| ear | dear | near | clear | tear(drop) |
| hear | year | gear | spear | beard |
| fear | bleary | appear | sear | dearly |
| shear | rear | weary | nearly | yearly |
| smear | nearby | clearly | hearing | fearful |
| hearing | clearance | nearsighted | unclear | yearbook |

Reading Words where **ear** has the /er/ sound:

| | | | | |
|---|---|---|---|---|
| earth | learn | early | search | earl |
| earn | pearl | heard | learning | unearth |

Reading Words where ear has the unexpected /air/ sound:

| | | | |
|---|---|---|---|
| bear | pear | tear (rip) | wear |

Writing (Spelling) Words: Have the student write/spell some of the listed words.

# Lesson 56: Vowel-r combination ire & Review

**ire**   These vowel-r partner letters have the sound /ire/.

Note: The vowel combination i-consonant-e that you already learned helps you process 'ire' as the /ire/ sound is similar to blending the /ie/ sound with the /r/ (/ie/+/r/= /ire/).

Practice Sound Cards: Practice sound card for this new and previous sounds.

Write and Say the Sound: Write **ire** 5-10 times saying /ire/ sound as you write.

Reading Words with the 'ire' /ire/ sound:

| | | | | |
|---|---|---|---|---|
| fire | tire | mire | hire | spire |
| tired | dire | wire | inspire | tired |
| perspire | hired | umpire | retire | rehire |
| entire | desire | empire | backfire | barbwire |
| acquire | conspire | transpire | require | wildfire |
| admire | crossfire | inquire | misfire | tightwire |

Writing Words: Have the student write/spell some of the listed words.

**Reading a Mixed Word List:** The student reads the following words, sounding out with physical tracking and proper blending. Correct any errors immediately.

| | | | | |
|---|---|---|---|---|
| work | just | need | these | term |
| smart | good | spare | warm | court |
| here | yard | large | thorn | stair |
| near | earth | range | chore | fence |
| ground | spire | scowl | spread | serve |
| youth | carve | pair | voice | board |
| world | groups | earn | north | year |
| church | please | force | drown | short |
| heard | fire | source | fault | grew |
| speak | scare | pounce | true | charge |
| tardy | employ | empty | handful | exclude |
| affront | armful | delete | return | translate |
| behind | prevent | obey | value | freedom |
| escape | exceed | better | target | loudest |
| clearance | afford | device | market | compass |
| urgent | early | crushing | sudden | elbow |
| squarely | payment | calmly | hungry | center |
| result | labor | account | detail | forward |
| parent | gentle | compare | defraud | turkey |
| complete | cursive | renew | slowly | curfew |
| newer | entire | without | indoor | today |
| enlarge | include | portray | explain | farthest |

| washroom | survey | replace | fairground | danger |
| repair | courtyard | manage | vertex | normal |
| hopeless | flavor | volume | nicer | student |
| alter | retain | acquire | expert | county |
| permit | problem | desire | warning | hairband |
| coastal | endorse | easement | career | upkeep |
| carry | healthy | transfer | divide | perfect |
| ignore | pushing | midnight | furnish | confide |
| nearly | remark | promote | disturb | corner |
| alley | beware | apart | belief | relate |
| restore | wildfire | return | textbook | ordeal |
| unclear | report | outlaw | afloat | network |
| highlight | surface | downpour | stairway | greatest |
| careless | curtail | statement | parcel | profile |
| poorest | concave | margin | faithful | warmest |
| farewell | distraught | forecast | upright | concourse |
| savage | snowboard | admire | retail | earthquake |
| barefoot | survive | improve | walking | practice |
| refrain | windfall | afraid | travel | research |
| disagree | volunteer | paradise | continue | history |
| already | however | forgetful | carnivore | property |
| workable | engineer | president | important | argument |
| consider | professor | discover | persistent | forever |
| notify | foreshadow | necessary | tornado | artifact |

# Section 5: Silent Letters, Less Frequent Sounds & Practice with Common Endings

## Lesson 57: Silent Letter Combinations

**dge** — These partner letters have the sound /j/. The 'd' is silent and the 'e' makes the 'g' have the /j/ sound.

**mb** — These partner letters have the sound /m/. The 'b' is silent and the 'm' has the expected /m/ sound.

**wr** — These partner letters have the sound /r/. The 'w' is silent and the 'r' has the expected /r/ sound.

**kn** — These partner letters have the sound /n/. The 'k' is silent and the 'n' has the expected /n/ sound.

**Practice Sound Cards:** Practice sound cards for these new sounds as well as previous sounds that need work.

**Write and Say the Sound:** Write **dge**, **mb**, **wr** and **kn** 5 to 10 times saying the sounds as you write.

**Reading Words that have the dge /j/ sound:**

| | | | | |
|---|---|---|---|---|
| bridge | edge | wedge | ledge | badge |
| dodge | fudge | lodge | fridge | grudge |
| smudge | hedge | judge | budge | abridge |
| dislodge | footbridge | porridge | dodgeball | lodgepole |

Teach the pattern & EXPLAIN WHY. Notice how the dge ending is found at end of words with the single short vowel sounds /a/, /e/ /i/ /o/ and /u/. The 'e' is needed after the 'g' to form the /j/ sound. The 'd' is added so there is a double consonant to prevent the 'e' from changing the short vowel sound to a long vowel sound. For example in page the 'e' makes the 'a' have the /ay/ long sound (vowel-consonant-e combination). But in badge the 'd' prevents or blocks the 'e' from changing the /a/ sound to the /ay/ sound.

## Reading Words that have the mb /m/ sound:

| | | | | |
|---|---|---|---|---|
| climb | dumb | crumb | limb | comb |
| thumb | plumber | numb | lamb | bomb |

## Reading Words that have the wr /r/ sound: (*write, wrong and wrote are the most commonly encountered wr words)

| | | | | |
|---|---|---|---|---|
| write | wrong | wrote | wren | wrap |
| wrath | wreck | wrench | wring | wrist |
| wreath | wrong | wrinkle | writer | wrongly |
| unknown | wrestle | wrangle | wrapper | wristwatch |
| writeup | wreckage | | | |

## Reading Words that have the kn /n/ sound: (*know and knew are the most commonly encountered kn words)

| | | | | |
|---|---|---|---|---|
| know | knew | knee | kneel | knead |
| knife | knight | knock | knuckle | knot |
| knit | knob | knack | kneecap | knockout |
| unknown | knowledge | jackknife | knucklehead | acknowledge |

**Writing (Spelling) Words:** Have the student write/spell some of the listed words.

# Lesson 58: Review and Practice

## Review Sounds:

| | | | | | | |
|---|---|---|---|---|---|---|
| m | t | a | s | d | i | f |
| r | th | l | o | n | p | e |
| h | v | sh | u | b | k | ck |

| | | | | | | |
|---|---|---|---|---|---|---|
| c | g | j | w | ch | tch | x |
| z | qu | wh | y | ing | ink | ee |
| oa | oe | ai | ay | a_e | i_e | o_e |
| u_e | e_e | oi | oy | ea | ow | ou |
| ue | ew | ui | oo | ie | ei | ey |
| au | aw | igh | ar | w+ar | or | ore |
| oar | our | oor | er | ur | ir | ear |
| w+or | are | ar | air | ear | eer | ere |
| ire | dge | mb | wr | kn | | |

## Making Words: "Please make the word _____"

Use sound tiles… ir ore ar  i e y  c d f g l m n p r  s t(2) x  th
  thirty  restore  explore  partly  implore  artist  thirsty  ignore  largely
  garlic  forearm  army  deplore  infirm  target  firmly  carpet  margin

Use sound tiles… ou igh dge  a e y  b c d f l g m n p r s t  sh ch th
  ledge  shout  badge  right  flight  sound  touch  proudly  edge  youth  group  delight
  youngest  outright  country  rebound  loudest  famous  brightest  flashlight

Use sound tiles… ow ai  i e  b d g l  m n p r(2) s  t w x  sh ing
  plowing  saint  glide  shown  strain  rainbow  window  elbow  remain  growing  raining
  below  township  retrain  slideshow  explain  detain  waiting  remaining

Use sound tiles… oo ear  a e i y  b c l n s t  ch th  wr
  earth  booth  learn  search  wrath  nearly  early  write  wrist  thinly  clearly
  soonest  smoothly

Use sound tiles…. er or oi  e i u y  c d f l  m n p r t v x  ch sh
  choice  coin  force  point  shine  shorter  price  voice  torch  corner  under  crunchy
  order  exploit  exit  shortly  former  devoid  report  inform  perform  reorder  record

Use sound tiles…. ea er  a i o y  b c d f l m n p r s(2) t v w  th
  master  weather  river  faster  sister  cleaner  feather  other  wealthy
  bother  mother  reader  brotherly  steamer  printer  ready  stealthy  transfer

**Reading a Mixed Word List:** The student reads the following words, sounding out with physical tracking and proper blending. Correct any errors immediately.

| | | | | |
|---|---|---|---|---|
| read | start | horse | good | corn |
| peace | book | just | please | group |
| youth | know | place | right | free |
| stone | make | grace | pray | twice |
| change | write | chance | roast | which |
| string | date | tool | years | world |
| come | wrong | know | edge | climb |
| perch | force | spread | fright | reach |
| ground | carve | warm | sound | raise |
| page | race | cheese | watch | search |
| slink | four | chair | your | serve |
| squirt | worse | square | near | earth |
| glory | inform | layer | turmoil | worthy |
| early | garden | warmest | forward | favor |
| carry | story | reveal | surface | record |
| ignore | active | unearth | inspire | hornet |
| talking | follow | become | after | sticker |
| perfect | remain | given | silence | looked |
| nothing | pointer | never | normal | thirsty |
| spirit | hunting | harmful | upkeep | reason |
| falsehood | about | named | hungry | until |
| itself | longest | little | problem | selfish |
| compare | almost | before | longer | active |
| pencil | relent | unleash | install | across |
| power | vowel | hidden | contest | instead |
| limit | promise | middle | simple | within |

| | | | | |
|---|---|---|---|---|
| rapid | punish | complex | without | follow |
| today | expand | never | learning | always |
| respond | prevent | results | involve | eastern |
| learning | chapter | basic | receive | instruct |
| proper | expose | improve | engage | describe |
| possible | inspect | working | credit | income |
| report | total | other | request | amount |
| climate | color | current | degree | trying |
| order | express | program | master | complete |
| gather | intense | freedom | service | highest |
| fewer | protect | shared | locate | percent |
| include | destroy | frequent | decline | traffic |
| modern | western | center | founded | trading |
| single | network | another | native | appoint |
| wealthy | created | fortress | avoid | suggest |
| agreed | control | turmoil | allow | exchange |
| reject | humid | illness | printed | enter |
| major | speaking | mainstream | himself | younger |
| aware | perhaps | rehire | parent | normal |
| ever | famous | looking | urban | growing |
| forget | expand | blasted | around | open |
| shoreline | weather | purchase | thirsty | worship |
| collapse | risen | bounced | fallen | striking |
| climate | central | sprawling | surround | civil |
| fragile | control | angle | research | trigger |
| biggest | manage | rainy | season | market |
| order | steady | charted | harmful | gather |
| dislodge | knowledge | mayor | storage | before |

# Lesson 59: Less Frequent Sounds

**ph** — These partner letters have the sound /f/.

**ch** — In the vast majority of words, the **ch** has the expected /ch/ sound. However, in some words the **ch** has the /k/ sound (The 'h' is silent and the 'c' has the /k/ sound). Occasionally **ch** has the /sh/ sound.

**y** — The letter y has 3 primary sounds, /y/, /ee/, and /ie/. In a few words, the y has a 4th sound of /i/.

**i** — The letter **i** has an unexpected 3rd /ee/ sound in some words.

**ai** — These partners primarily have the sound /ay/. Occasionally 'ai' has the /i/ sound within some multisyllable words ending in 'ain'.

*note the ph=/f/, ch= /k/, & y= /i/ sounds are all found in words of Greek origin.

## Reading Words with the ph /f/ sound:

| | | | | |
|---|---|---|---|---|
| phone | phrase | graph | phony | phase |
| sphere | nephew | prophet | phonics | pamphlet |
| orphan | trophy | gopher | graphic | photo |
| physics | phantom | pheasant | pharmacy | elephant |
| alphabet | photograph | physical | telephone | photocopy |
| phonetic | autograph | telegraph | | |

## Reading Words with the /k/ sound for ch:

The /k/ sound for ch is found in relatively few words. It is essential to learn because it occurs in some important words.

| | | | | |
|---|---|---|---|---|
| Christ | school | schedule | ache | chronic |
| chrome | scheme | scholar | Christmas | chord |
| chemist | anchor | schooner | cholesterol | chemistry |
| chlorine | chromosome | chronicle | | |

*Occasionally 'ch' represents the /sh/ sound as in: chef, chateau, chivalry, chagrin, chalet, chevron, Chicago and Cheyenne. Most of these words have French origins. Despite these inconsistencies related to the unique aspects of our diverse English language, the fact remains, 'ch' has the expected /ch/ sound in the overwhelming majority of words.

# Reading Words that have the /i/ sound for y

| | | | | |
|---|---|---|---|---|
| gym | mystery | physics | typical | myth |
| cylinder | system | pyramid | syllable | symbol |

# Reading Words that have the /ee/ sound for i:
The single 'i' has /i/ or /ie/ sound in most words. However 'i' has the /ee/ sound in some words. Note the use of 'i' for the /ee/ sound in the following words. Once again this unexpected spelling of the /ee/ sound presents more of a spelling problem than a reading problem as we often read without even noticing the i=/ee/.

Many occurrences of 'i'=/ee/ are found in words ending in consonant-y. The 'i' spelling results from changing 'y' to 'i' before adding the suffix. In these words the 'i' maintains the original /ee/ sound from the initial 'y' in the base word:

| | | | | |
|---|---|---|---|---|
| worry - worrier | city-cities | carry-carrier | dry- driest | friendly-friendliest |
| sorry-sorriest | try-tries | happy-happier | sturdy-sturdier | pretty-prettiest |
| duty-duties | shy-shiest | funny-funniest | angry-angrier | multiply-multiplier |

The -ian suffix is another pattern where the i = /ee/

| | | | | |
|---|---|---|---|---|
| guardian | barbarian | custodian | veterinarian | amphibian |
| librarian | comedian | civilian | Indian | Floridian |
| riparian | vegetarian | | | |

The -ial ending is another pattern where 'i'=/ee/

| | | | | |
|---|---|---|---|---|
| territorial | trivial | material | bacterial | imperial |
| serial | editorial | controversial | terrestrial | congenial |

The -iate ending is another pattern where 'i'=/ee/

| | | | | |
|---|---|---|---|---|
| defoliate | affiliate | intermediate | radiate | appropriate |
| abbreviate | immediate | humiliate | alleviate | |

Other words with the 'i' = /ee/

| | | | | |
|---|---|---|---|---|
| machine | trampoline | nicotine | magazine | ambiance |
| barrier | brilliant | brilliance | | |

The /ee/ in the 'ing' & 'ink' combinations was covered in Lesson 16.

# Reading Words that have the /i/ sound for ai:
In a few words, the 'ai' has the /i/ sound instead of the expected /ay/ sound. This /i/ sound is found primarily with the 'ain' ending of some multisyllable words.

| | | | | |
|---|---|---|---|---|
| captain | certain | again | mountain | curtain | fountain |
| bargain | chaplain | villain | co-captain | | |

# Lesson 60:
# Overview "Strange" combinations: eigh, ough and A Few Other Uncommon Sounds

The "strange" 'eigh' and 'ough' vowel combinations are not used in many words. While it is helpful to review these sounds, it is almost necessary to simply learn the common irregular words that contain these confusing sounds.

**eigh** These partner letters usually have the sound /ay/. This combination is NOT found in many words. The gh is silent & the ei has the /ay/ sound.

/ay/ e**igh**t e**igh**ty fr**eigh**t w**eigh**t w**eigh** sl**eigh** n**eigh**bor
(unexpected sound of /ie/ in height)

**ough** These partner letters are truly confusing. They represent 6 different sounds depending on the word. This is one of the "strange" combinations where you just have to learn the words. Luckily, not many words have this confusing 'ough' combination!

1. /aw/ **ough**t b**ough**t th**ough**t f**ough**t s**ough**t
2. /ow/ b**ough** dr**ough**t
3. /oa/ th**ough** alth**ough** d**ough** d**ough**nut
4. /oo/ thr**ough** sl**ough**(swamp;bog)
5. /off/ c**ough**
6. /uff/ t**ough** en**ough** r**ough** sl**ough** (shed;cast off)

The following sound combinations are uncommon. This brief review is provided for awareness. The majority of the words that contain these sounds are found in technical medical and scientific fields. The few more commonly encountered words that contain these uncommon sounds can be learned as 'irregular' or 'unexpected' spellings. These unusual spellings are primarily Greek origin.

**gn**  These have the sound /n/. The g is silent.
   gnat   gnaw   gnarled   gnome

**gh**  These have the sound /g/. The h is silent.
   ghost   ghetto

**rh**  These have the sound /r/. The h is silent.
   rhyme   rhythm   rhizome   rhinoceros   rhombus

**pn**  These have the sound /n/. The p is silent.
   pneumonia  pneumatic (derived from pneuma, the Greek word for air)

**x**  The /ks/ is the most frequent sound for x. However, in a few words that **begin** with the letter x, the sound is /z/.

Words that *begin with x* have the sound /z/.
   xylophone   xeric   xylem

With the exception of xylophone and xeric (dry/arid conditions), most words beginning in 'x' are technical scientific words. Look in the dictionary for examples.

NOTE: In the word X-ray, the 'X' does not represent a sound but rather is the letter name 'X'. In science and math the letter 'X' is often used to represent the unknown. The scientist who discovered this new 'unknown-ray' therefore called it the "x-ray". The name 'x-ray' stuck.

# Lesson 61: Practice Reading Common Endings

**-ing**    These partner letters have the sound /eeng/. You already learned these and know how the /ing/ sound usually comes at the end of words.

**-er**    You already learned how these partner letters have the sound /er/. The /er/ sound is a very common ending for words.

**-ly**    You can easily sound out this common ending. It says /lee/. The -/y ending is a common ending on many words. Even though you can sound it out, it helps to practice reading it quickly because it is so common.

## Practice the Common -ing ending

| | | | | | |
|---|---|---|---|---|---|
| running | meeting | going | writing | picking | yelling |
| drawing | petting | walking | blasting | chewing | wasting |
| drinking | eating | washing | cleaning | brushing | crying |
| watching | cooking | lasting | dancing | starting | blasting |
| swinging | testing | reading | making | typing | resting |
| chopping | driving | hopping | stirring | fixing | shaking |
| bugging | sleeping | shopping | slipping | flinging | drying |
| speeding | toasting | grilling | poking | snowing | passing |
| striking | lightning | dating | splitting | naming | swimming |
| earning | calling | hiking | picking | finding | sleeping |
| reaching | pleasing | carving | coming | squirting | roasting |
| raining | starting | hurting | storming | riding | working |
| snoring | bursting | searching | cheering | forcing | spoiling |
| forming | sharing | hearing | clearing | learning | climbing |
| changing | knowing | shouting | surfing | racing | raising |
| grinding | drawing | waving | climbing | standing | pointing |
| repairing | noticing | erasing | beginning | targeting | ignoring |

# Practice the Common -er ending

| writer | taller | shorter | wider | reader | teacher |
| toaster | player | dancer | caller | speller | sprayer |
| softer | harder | cleaner | waiter | longer | tester |
| timer | cooler | cutter | pester | shopper | jumper |
| nicer | faster | heater | thicker | greater | grower |
| singer | helper | quicker | poster | hunter | baker |
| bigger | herder | marker | neater | zipper | rocker |
| slower | farmer | layer | sticker | swimmer | server |
| stranger | fighter | binder | logger | braver | farther |
| explorer | divider | enforcer | computer | forester | comforter |

# Practice the Common -ly ending

| nicely | quickly | shortly | gently | quietly | loudly |
| kindly | yearly | brightly | rudely | sweetly | clearly |
| sadly | thickly | bravely | wisely | hardly | partly |
| firmly | sternly | shortly | worldly | warmly | proudly |
| safely | closely | harshly | smoothly | plainly | barely |
| blindly | fully | poorly | worldly | largely | fairly |
| dearly | thinly | earthly | nearly | timely | wrongly |
| promptly | lastly | neatly | lightly | bravely | nearly |
| calmly | costly | friendly | freely | slowly | squarely |
| hopefully | finally | willingly | endlessly | unfairly | alertly |
| suddenly | randomly | joyfully | painlessly | happily | cleverly |
| carelessly | formerly | rapidly | currently | openly | frequently |
| timidly | tenderly | mannerly | politely | quarterly | annually |

# Lesson 62: Overview & Practice Reading Plural Endings

This lesson reviews the common plural endings of -s, -es, and -ies that are added to the ending of words to indicate more than one. Plural endings are very common making up approximately 31% of all suffixed words. Although these endings are phonetic, it is helpful to practice them. When plural words are written, usually an **s** or **es** is just added to the end of the word.

**Practice the Common plural -s ending...** **When reading you just add the /s/ or /z/ sound**

| | | | | | |
|---|---|---|---|---|---|
| sprints | spits | meets | writes | draws | leaps |
| eats | floors | keys | cleans | walks | blasts |
| drinks | cooks | tests | stirs | chops | trees |
| swings | reads | crawls | makes | pies | sleeps |
| slips | spells | toys | plays | ways | streets |
| fights | books | snakes | files | friends | news |
| dusts | phones | knows | spikes | shoots | paws |
| inspects | sisters | obeys | listens | complains | instructs |
| enjoys | dinners | wallets | binders | papers | carpets |

**Practice the Common plural -es ending...** **When reading you just add the /es/ sound.** Note: You add -es sound when word ends with s, ch, sh, x, z, the /s/ sound ('s' or 'ce') e, or the /j/ sound ('ge' or 'dge'). Instead of memorizing the list, just *listen* to determine when you need to use the 'es' plural spelling. Basically you use 'es' spelling when the word ends in a sound where you can NOT verbally add a /s/ sound to without putting in the /e/. Try it! You can hear the /e/+/s/.

| | | | |
|---|---|---|---|
| wish--wishes | fish--fishes | crunch--crunches | wash--washes |
| catch--catches | hiss--hisses | place--places | watch--watches |
| inch--inches | fix--fixes | box--boxes | dress-dresses |
| lunch--lunches | ranch--ranches | hush--hushes | miss--misses |
| horse--horses | bus--busses | page--pages | price--prices |
| leash--leashes | brush--brushes | pinch--pinches | edge--edges |

**Practice the Common plural -ies ending….** You read these by just adding the /z/ sound to the word. **The -ies ending is found in words that end in consonant-y.** Note: In words ending in consonant-y you change the y to i and add es. The pronunciation keeps either the /ee/ or /ie/ sound that the y represented in the original base word and add the /z/ sound.

(consonant-y words with the /ee/ sound… ….. the plural sound is /eez/)

| baby--babies | city--cities | candy--candies | story--stories |
|---|---|---|---|
| lady--ladies | party--parties | carry--carries | hurry--hurries |
| duty--duties | puppy--puppies | penny--pennies | kitty--kitties |

(consonant-y words with the /ie/ sound… ….. the plural sound is /iez/)

| fly--flies | try--tries | cry--cries | dry--dries |
|---|---|---|---|

# Lesson 63: Past Tense -ed Endings

The past tense **-ed** ending (suffix) used for verbs is extremely common, making up approximately 20% of all suffixed words. (This is the **-ed** past tense suffix for verbs not /e//d/ as in bed, red or shed.) The **-ed** past tense ending is pronounced three different ways, /id/ /d/ or /t/, depending on the ending sound of the base word. Once again we usually say and read these **-ed** endings without even noticing the difference in sounds. However, it is helpful to recognize different pronunciations of the **-ed** past tense ending for spelling. The past tense **-ed** ending is always spelled 'ed' regardless of the /id/ /d/ or /t/ pronunciation. Specifically notice the different pronunciations as you read the following words with the **-ed** past tense suffix.

**Practice the Common past tense -ed ending with the /id/ sound:**
(whenever a word ends in **d** or **t** the -ed ending is pronounced /id/)

| ended | lasted | started | painted | petted |
|---|---|---|---|---|
| landed | melted | petted | seated | dusted |
| pointed | threaded | slanted | printed | bended |
| baited | speeded | netted | rested | blasted |

| drifted | faded | darted | hunted | pouted |
| granted | handed | sprouted | lifted | toasted |
| grinded | tempted | pouted | reminded | corrected |

## Practice the Common past tense -ed ending with the /d/ sound:

| grabbed | tanned | tagged | sailed | sprayed |
| logged | slammed | played | filled | closed |
| poured | spooned | smoothed | timed | waved |
| loved | smiled | grinned | pleased | pinned |
| cleaned | called | learned | failed | dived |
| used | planned | dreamed | caused | paused |
| grabbed | boiled | saved | cooled | charged |
| fooled | crawled | carved | stirred | cried |
| stewed | called | mailed | amazed | carried |

## Practice the Common past tense -ed ending with the /t/ sound:

| snacked | cooked | kissed | missed | raced |
| marched | wished | jumped | poked | typed |
| raked | joked | leaped | tapped | blessed |
| mopped | flashed | placed | danced | flipped |
| bluffed | gripped | poked | dripped | laced |
| scratched | mixed | washed | kicked | rushed |
| asked | baked | masked | voiced | blocked |
| forced | walked | braced | striped | dressed |
| zipped | boxed | mashed | barked | thanked |
| finished | escaped | practiced | erased | famished |

**\*Note:** Our wonderful English language also contains irregular past tense verbs such as ride-rode, drive-drove, eat-ate, fly-flew, speak-spoke, run-ran, and sing-sang that do *not* apply the expected past tense -ed suffix. Luckily, the majority of these words can be read and spelled phonetically according to how we say the words in oral language.

# Reading Practice With a Mixed List of –ed past tense endings:

| | | | | |
|---|---|---|---|---|
| rested | flashed | jumped | poured | spooned |
| placed | danced | tracked | started | clapped |
| mended | knitted | pressed | cheered | cleared |
| poked | raked | sailed | speeded | shouted |
| shopped | grated | chopped | cooked | sliced |
| leaped | wished | smiled | saved | founded |
| cleaned | dusted | worked | missed | called |
| parted | placed | helped | lasted | asked |
| sounded | wanted | schooled | landed | headed |
| needed | handed | wished | neared | changed |
| turned | planted | learned | lived | added |
| rested | stated | voiced | fined | minded |
| watched | shipped | snowed | fetched | mailed |
| rained | missed | stayed | copied | acted |
| quilted | rubbed | parted | strained | heated |
| packed | chained | traded | blinked | counted |
| reached | yawned | pointed | toasted | charged |
| praised | traded | charted | painted | printed |
| waited | needed | called | smiled | marched |
| reported | completed | repaired | finished | ordered |
| practiced | mattered | followed | replaced | surfaced |
| noticed | remained | erased | hurried | paraded |
| whispered | answered | ordered | connected | expanded |
| explained | insisted | engaged | completed | inspected |
| carried | studied | behaved | packaged | gathered |
| enforced | informed | unchanged | connected | repaired |

# Lesson 64: Practice Reading -ve endings

English words can NOT end in the letter v so 'e' is always added to make the word not end in 'v'. Therefore, sometimes the 'e' is not acting as part of the vowel-v-e combination but simply there so the word does not end in 'v'. This 'e' does not contribute phonetically to the word. The -ive ending (suffix -ive that means likely to do or connected with) is the most frequent -ve ending.

**Practice the following words that end in the -ve /v/ sound where the 'e' is only preventing the word from ending in 'v' and does not influence the other sounds in the word.**

| | | | | |
|---|---|---|---|---|
| have | give | love | solve | live |
| valve | shove | weave | sleeve | dove |
| serve | active | native | captive | above |
| passive | motive | involve | forgive | resolve |
| revolve | festive | massive | positive | negative |
| expensive | relative | directive | expansive | effective |
| descriptive | detective | sensitive | relative | informative |
| attentive | impressive | directive | offensive | defensive |
| suggestive | protective | elective | aggressive | productive |
| corrective | supportive | abrasive | effective | alternative |

**Of course you still do have -ve endings where the 'e' is part of the vowel-v-e combination and this partner 'e' makes the first vowel have a long sound.**

| | | | | |
|---|---|---|---|---|
| save | gave | grave | Steve | dive |
| pave | hive | drove | grove | brave |
| drive | stove | slave | thrive | forgave |
| behave | survive | concave | | |

# Lesson 65: Review and Practice

**Reading Words:** The student reads the following words, sounding out with physical tracking and proper blending. Correct any errors immediately.

| | | | | |
|---|---|---|---|---|
| have | give | come | love | year |
| would | they | save | gnat | phase |
| graph | school | any | were | store |
| one | wrong | high | know | their |
| wrote | knee | edge | climb | fire |
| write | dodge | there | peas | would |
| give | could | come | words | great |
| warm | floor | bright | bruise | touch |
| screw | two | snake | please | page |
| have | change | faith | gave | phase |
| bridge | youth | learn | reach | small |
| place | worth | tiles | chore | fourth |
| growth | juice | north | squirt | from |
| search | front | tense | wild | talk |
| must | smile | wage | should | raft |
| straight | caught | bound | strange | might |
| harder | active | away | cleaned | marched |
| dances | running | longest | repair | spooned |
| practice | stories | always | artist | forgive |
| shared | border | thirty | sharp | spelling |
| church | forced | thunder | washes | longest |
| about | alarm | counting | always | faster |
| member | able | shortly | ignore | sharpen |
| color | slowly | summer | target | river |

| | | | | |
|---|---|---|---|---|
| going | teacher | shorter | follow | became |
| ridden | ended | cleaned | ladies | played |
| before | request | highest | fewer | include |
| famous | instead | tardy | drawing | afraid |
| behind | unless | normal | report | only |
| prayer | letter | indoor | nicely | parent |
| enforce | gather | power | return | total |
| oldest | refresh | behind | called | watched |
| belong | almost | respect | beyond | empty |
| program | handed | shortly | drawing | writer |
| nephew | contest | normal | falsehood | secret |
| respond | gather | major | control | hopeless |
| mindful | sharpen | speaker | darken | dancer |
| unreal | outline | spreading | older | errand |
| subject | coldly | entire | harvest | worked |
| believe | blacksmith | shelter | smaller | turned |
| waited | above | softer | instant | stranger |
| wisdom | quickly | manner | certain | better |
| needed | final | rapid | upper | collect |
| hardly | ahead | leaving | beside | anger |
| avoid | double | passage | emerge | current |
| event | observe | floated | declare | walnut |
| common | toward | exchange | welcome | process |
| shrugged | lower | forty | raised | elbow |
| correct | falter | insist | standing | warning |
| peered | leather | finish | leaving | clutched |
| something | darkness | blanket | poorly | tilted |
| partner | retire | keeping | retreat | afloat |

| | | | | |
|---|---|---|---|---|
| screamed | barely | rescue | promise | squinted |
| leaning | vacant | swallow | pencil | report |
| chapter | abridge | unknown | writeup | transfer |
| happen | coffee | hover | neatly | knocking |
| growled | distant | confine | ladder | package |
| foremost | outfit | fearful | mindful | Midwest |
| uptight | sprained | forgive | recruit | software |
| consume | arose | fortress | windy | domain |
| absent | sunroof | profile | constraint | athlete |
| keynote | footbridge | terror | reflect | report |
| deplete | sincere | foresight | author | acquire |
| confirm | disgrace | prepare | scoreboard | insane |
| cursive | unscrew | nearby | passport | seafloor |
| typical | uneven | together | encounter | possible |
| eventful | suddenly | establish | terrible | history |
| overhead | disaster | gathered | evidence | belonged |

This ends the program of direct instruction in the phonemic code and foundational skills necessary for phonologic processing. However, this is NOT the end of reading instruction. This structured direct systematic phonics program provides the foundation for proficient decoding. It is important to continue direct instruction to help the student acquire the advanced skills necessary for skilled reading. The student needs to learn to easily handle multisyllable words, build fluency, expand vocabulary, develop comprehension and enhance other advanced skills. A program of daily guided reading (student reads outloud to an adult with feedback and instruction) is essential for developing the skills for proficient reading. Do not skip this critically important and highly effective instructional tool!

# BEGIN DAILY GUIDED READING

See Section 7 for complete directions on conducting guided reading.

# Section 6: Reading Multisyllable Words

## Multisyllable Words - General Information

The multisyllable words *are* harder to read than short words. To read multisyllable words the student needs to apply a more advanced strategy. Some students automatically develop the proper strategies for reading multisyllable words but many do not and struggle with these longer words. Direct instruction and guided practice helps the student learn how to handle these 'long' words. The majority of English words are multisyllable so it is critical to read them effectively. This section provides direct instruction and practice in handling these 'long' multisyllable words.

Syllables are simply the hunks of sound within a spoken word that are said with a single puff of air. Every syllable has at least one vowel sound with or without the surrounding consonant sounds. Multisyllable words are made up of a combination of these distinct sound hunks. In these multisyllable words it is impossible to combine all the sounds together in one puff. To read multisyllable words the student has to not only process the print phonetically but he needs to learn how to distinguish and group the appropriate sounds together to form the correct syllables and then smoothly combine these correct sound hunks with all the adjacent syllables into one fluid word. The student needs to capture *all* the appropriate sound hunks in the word without missing one or without adding one that should not be there. The syllables need to be smoothly and quickly joined into one fluid word that is accented and pronounced correctly. Reading multisyllable words is a more complex process and absolutely takes practice.

The following lessons provide direct practice in this complex skill of handling multisyllable words. This instruction is designed for students who have already acquired knowledge of the phonemic code and established correct phonologic processing. If the student is not able to decode words they first will need to complete the initial sections of this program (Lessons 1-65). If the student is processing print phonetically and only lacking skills in easily handling multisyllable words instruction can begin with this section.

These lessons directly teach strategies and develop skills in handling multisyllable words. Activities are designed to help the student learn how to break words down into appropriate syllables, pay attention to detail, pick up all sounds and smoothly blend sound hunks. Common patterns, including the most frequently encountered affixes, are practiced. Direct guided instruction in handling multisyllable words develops necessary skills.

It is important to realize that distinguishing appropriate syllable breaks for reading instruction is based on the sound structure of the word. In other words base 'sound hunks' on how you say the word. This is NOT necessarily the official dictionary syllable splits. For example, in the word "effect" the split based on how we say the word is e-fect not the ef-fect official dictionary split. Don't get too picky about where the word is exactly split. *Base it on sound*! Sometimes we say words differently. (i.e. for puppy you can say either pup-ee or pup-pee…either split is fine for handling the multisyllable reading of the word). This is *not* learning the rules and making the official correct written syllable splits found in a dictionary but rather hearing and handling sound hunks within a word for reading.

**Explain to the Student:**

-- This section provides direct instruction in how to handle multisyllable words. You will learn and practice techniques for reading these longer multisyllable words.

--Syllables are hunks of sound within a word that we say in a single puff of air. ***If the student does not yet understand syllables, you MUST spend time with some oral exercises where the student says longer words and learns to hear and orally break the word into syllables. Accomplish this by orally saying a word (any multisyllable word) and having them repeat the word and then orally break it down into the syllables or sound hunks. Make sure the student can orally distinguish syllables. For example: running (run - ing), understand (un - der - stand), Washington (Wash - ing - ton), basketball (bas- ket -ball)

--To handle reading these "long" words you need to learn how to distinguish, or "see", the appropriate syllables or sound chunks within a word and then rapidly capture all sounds and smoothly put these sound chunks together. It is a more advanced skill than simply knowing and blending the individual sounds of single syllable words together. You need to combine the sounds into appropriate 'hunks', capture all these syllables which usually do not have a meaning on their own and join them rapidly and smoothly with the adjacent syllables to form the word. It is almost like reading 3, 4 or more separate nonsense words and smoothly combining them into one fluid word. Plus to top it off, you need to get the correct pronunciation and accent. This section will help you learn how to easily handle these longer words.

## Directions for Activities in the Multisyllable Word Lessons:

**Reading Words**: Each lesson includes guided reading of lists of multisyllable words. The student reads all the words in the list. The word lists, by design, require the student to develop correct skills. As the student reads the words to you, have your pencil ready. If the student has problems with breaking words into appropriate syllables help the student by placing little light pencil mark slashes in the appropriate syllable breaks so he can better 'see' the syllables. For example:

inconsistent → add the light pencil marks to indicate → in/con/sis/tent
combination → add the light pencil slashes to indicate → com/bi/na/tion
protective → → add the light pencil slashes to indicate → pro/tec/tive

This light pencil slash through the appropriate breaks and maybe a comment such as 'take another look' helps the student learn how to break words. Before long the student begins to 'see' the appropriate breaks on his own. Remember to only make the slash marks *when* the student needs help. The slash marks help the student learn how to handle these longer words.

Once again, as with all guided reading, make sure the student reads each word accurately. Often when students tackle multisyllable words they leave out parts, add sounds that are not there or change sounds. Stop any of these errors and have the student take another look. Make immediate corrections for any error. At this point, the correction technique of tapping the pencil on the word to signal 'stop and look again' is often all that is necessary. Correction is critical to developing the attention to detail and ability to pick up all sounds within a multisyllable word that is important to accurate fluent reading. Remember to help the student by making slash marks *when* needed. Direct instruction with correction helps the student learn how to capture all the hunks and smoothly combine them into a fluid word.

In addition, you may need to help the student with pronunciation. With multisyllable words placing the accent on the correct syllable adds another level of complexity to correctly pronouncing the word. Not only does the student need to accurately sound out the word but they need to accent it correctly. If the word is familiar to the student, they usually 'get' the correct accenting and pronunciation. If the word is unfamiliar you may need to provide the correct pronunciation. Help the student with correct pronunciation whenever they need assistance. With improper pronunciation, you can just say something similar to "Close, but we actually pronounce the word this way _____" . Then make sure the student re-reads the word pronouncing it correctly. This correct pronunciation is part of the 'fluent' neural model of the word so by all means help the student learn and practice correct pronunciation of new vocabulary. Guided practice reading multisyllable words is essential for developing necessary skills. If the student is not fluently reading the words in a list have them re-read the list of words at least once before moving on. If necessary, have the student practice reading previous lists. Fluency is built by practice. It is exciting to observe and note how with practice the student develops fluency on specific words.

**Writing /Spelling Words:** The student writes multisyllable words in each lesson. Printing orally presented multisyllable words effectively helps students learn how to tackle and proficiently read multisyllable words. Not only does printing words phonetically by syllable directly establish and develop necessary phonologic processing but it also builds understanding of the syllable structure of words. The student learns how long words break apart into smaller sound 'chunks' and gains knowledge of common patterns and affixes. Writing spoken multisyllable words by syllable directly strengthens the converse skill of breaking words into appropriate syllables for reading.

Select some of the listed multisyllable words and read the words out-loud to the student. Have the student write the word by syllable *as they say the sound hunk or syllable*. The student should write at least 20 words for each lesson (or affix group within the lesson). In the beginning, they can leave a small gap between the syllables to help them 'see' the syllable splits. Use words from any the lists in the lesson or previous lesson. You may also make your own multisyllable word writing lists. The word writing should be given to the student with specific affix or spelling patterns grouped together to help him learn and recognize common patterns in our language. Usually the writing itself is easy for older students allowing word writing to be used as a simple highly effective tool. If the physical printing process is difficult, you may need to give the student fewer words to write and instead provide additional direct reading practice.

The word writing activity is an exercise in handling and processing multisyllable words NOT a spelling test. *However*, you do not want a student to practice spelling a word incorrectly. Help the student learn the correct spelling patterns. Help the student build skills by grouping common patterns and providing direction. Help teach correct spelling by saying "these next words are going to use the ___ spelling for the ___ sound". As they write, help with spelling hints such as the /ow/ sound in this word is spelled with "ou", or "in this word the /s/ sound is spelled with 'c'". If you give a word with a 'tricky' spelling, teach the 'unexpected' portion so the student learns correctly. The following are some examples of spelling/word writing lists designed to help the student develop skills:

List 1: "These words have the -ment ending (remind the student that the e in ment sounds like an i but we spell it -ment)" and give…. placement, pavement, statement, refreshment, adjustment, equipment, banishment, enjoyment, employment, enrichment

List 2: "These words all start with the re- prefix" and give him…….renew, replace, return, recheck, review, repay, refill, reflect, reprint, revisit, rewind, remind, restore

List 3: "These words have the -able ending" and give him…..washable, bendable, moveable, readable, fixable, comfortable, agreeable, mixable, breakable, employable, changeable, punishable, questionable (don't mix -ible endings in the list when the student is practicing the -able ending)

List 4: "These words all start with the dis- prefix" and give him …..discover, display, discharge, disturb, discredit, disrespect, dispatch, distrust, disband, disagree, discount (if the student spells dispatch incorrectly with 'ch' instead of 'tch' give a reminder of the correct 'tch' spelling pattern).

List 5: "These words have the 'tion' spelling for the /shun/ ending" and give him…. nation, station, action, injection, tradition, rejection, motion, creation, lotion, migration, reflection, direction, formation (don't mix in words such as confession with the -sion endings on this word writing list)

Remember, fluency is built by practice. If a specific word is difficult for the student, have them write that word several times saying the sounds as they print the word. This repetition of correct phonologic processing in 'word writing' is an excellent tool for developing fluency on a specific word.

# Lesson 66: Practice Reading Multisyllable Words

This lesson provides practice reading multisyllable words. Remember learning and practicing how to handle these multisyllable words greatly improves your reading. *If* you need help breaking the words down into syllables, I will make a light pencil mark to help you 'see' the proper syllable breaks. You have already been reading numerous two and some three syllable words. Remember syllables are chunks of sound and every syllable has a vowel sound.

*As the student reads, have a pencil ready and make slashmarks to indicate syllable breaks *only* if and when the student needs assistance with a word.

## Practice with 2 syllable words

| | | | | |
|---|---|---|---|---|
| statement | canvas | carpet | cartoon | divide |
| children | notice | impress | reject | install |
| around | number | between | almost | inside |
| surface | within | sudden | himself | learning |
| outside | always | careful | became | prevent |
| morning | sentence | today | behind | problem |
| relax | adapt | after | recess | public |
| raccoon | neglect | pencil | refrain | afraid |
| contain | receive | complete | service | inspect |
| magnet | mustang | extend | hidden | entrance |
| canteen | hundred | hostage | outside | softly |
| plenty | gossip | ending | frequent | include |
| concrete | freedom | canteen | reflect | program |
| safely | explode | morning | hungry | captive |
| remote | silver | detour | discard | native |
| respond | around | beside | broken | given |
| vintage | yearly | regain | mushroom | laundry |
| graphic | flavor | confront | banish | confirm |
| confine | conflict | baptize | complex | divine |
| expense | forbid | glamour | forgave | helpless |

| invite | observe | obtain | engage | complain |
| lumber | mitten | unless | slander | static |
| temper | teaching | vessel | charcoal | follow |
| chapter | bandage | beaver | basement | artist |
| appear | account | simply | corrupt | decent |
| famous | hunter | inspect | insist | intense |
| lightning | manner | market | skipping | higher |
| enjoy | prepare | contact | antler | batter |
| report | events | suggest | river | worker |
| impeach | bundle | compress | county | danger |
| peanut | something | nasty | swimming | common |
| walrus | corner | detail | complaint | deadline |
| rainbow | lizard | tadpole | printer | finger |
| respond | closely | return | sharpen | plenty |
| amaze | money | express | control | equate |
| update | ahead | rattle | propane | lawless |

## Practice with 3 syllable words

| diligent | celebrate | testify | incomplete | impassive |
| terminate | similar | terminal | capital | appointment |
| expected | develop | disinfect | calculate | hesitate |
| vitamin | hospital | simplify | reported | carnival |
| tornado | circulate | quality | qualify | relative |
| fantasy | argument | adhesive | president | adequate |
| centipede | victory | classify | sediment | fantastic |
| tabulate | enjoyed | dedicate | inhabit | accident |
| balcony | capital | important | devastate | electron |
| obligate | expansive | obsolete | department | destiny |

| | | | | |
|---|---|---|---|---|
| determine | disappoint | average | primitive | principal |
| tangible | unfriendly | penetrate | indicate | latitude |
| compensate | obstacle | camera | agenda | electric |
| literal | multiple | objective | pelican | secretive |
| sensitive | vertical | charity | clarity | addictive |
| accomplish | memory | investment | diminish | dishonest |
| document | edible | engagement | entertain | exclusive |
| family | fascinate | festival | fortify | gentleman |
| history | honestly | horizon | inspector | internal |
| interval | invalid | innocent | isolate | justify |
| minister | minimize | modify | nonprofit | powerless |
| rejected | animal | important | multiply | hesitate |
| wonderful | resistant | assistant | adjustment | monitor |
| constantly | reminded | difficult | enormous | published |
| repeated | steadily | vertical | secretly | amazement |
| wondered | forgotten | employer | returned | contacted |
| completely | interest | expected | embarrass | interview |
| gratefully | evidence | wallpaper | numerous | astonish |
| tattered | frequently | extremely | amplify | abrasive |
| inspecting | ordering | effortless | company | practicing |
| popular | interrupt | continue | inventive | introduce |
| recover | adjusting | tremendous | fabulous | incorrect |
| preventive | comprehend | remember | understand | isolate |
| contrasted | correlate | unfaithful | different | opposite |
| forever | encounter | discover | however | whenever |
| medical | objective | refresher | oppressive | particle |
| unequal | establish | continue | resident | populate |

**Writing/Spelling Words:** Write some of the listed words.

# Lesson 67: Reading Multisyllable Words - Compound Words

In this lesson you practice reading compound words, a special type of multisyllable word. Compound words are usually easier to read because they are made up by joining other complete words.

| laptop | landmark | overflow | mainland | sideways |
|---|---|---|---|---|
| runway | horseback | playground | bedroom | bathroom |
| tablecloth | baseball | basketball | outdoor | doghouse |
| underground | schoolhouse | railway | railroad | mailbox |
| groundhog | typewriter | flashlight | bookcase | ladybug |
| placemat | football | backup | hotdog | doorbell |
| weekend | download | copycat | waterfall | highway |
| highchair | expressway | hamburger | birthday | backpack |
| sweatshirt | starfish | makeup | jailbird | jackknife |
| catfish | craftsman | cowgirl | cowboy | dugout |
| dumbbell | downstairs | seaweed | downtown | drainpipe |
| seafood | online | roundup | overgrow | outline |
| overhead | outsmart | overall | overcast | undergo |
| within | windmill | underdog | windfall | bookmark |
| bullfrog | wingspan | bluegrass | blindfold | blacktop |
| blueprint | blackmail | bighorn | blackout | bedrock |
| billboard | bathrobe | battleship | bareback | ballgame |
| backbone | armpit | dogwood | outside | armchair |
| spacecraft | thunderstorm | toolbox | toothpaste | weekday |
| toothpick | touchdown | upstairs | videotape | warehouse |
| wasteland | wheelchair | whirlwind | whitewash | wildcat |
| playpen | hairbrush | earring | shoelace | bookmark |
| manhole | bathtub | eyelash | notebook | offshore |
| nutcracker | outfield | outhouse | overcame | outgrow |
| outlaw | outline | desktop | fireman | lighthouse |

| | | | | |
|---|---|---|---|---|
| lifetime | junkyard | stopwatch | lifeboat | lightbulb |
| screwdriver | hacksaw | crosscut | crossroad | clockwise |
| crossword | crowbar | hotshot | crossbow | cookout |
| firefighter | crosswalk | handwriting | handbook | handshake |
| oatmeal | haircut | halfway | gentleman | gateway |
| sidewalk | overcoat | driveway | pickup | inkpad |
| underwear | chalkboard | headache | headline | into |
| fingernail | handshake | roadway | eyeglass | newborn |
| candlestick | nightgown | newspaper | checkup | anyone |
| bloodshed | anything | aircraft | anyplace | airstrip |
| drumstick | downstream | driftwood | driveway | drugstore |
| homeland | horseshoe | hubcap | household | paycheck |
| footsteps | earthquake | clipboard | sunrise | sunset |
| bluebird | toothbrush | landlord | yardstick | moonlight |
| campsite | hallway | brainstorm | buttermilk | dishpan |
| shortstop | pitchfork | doorbell | blackberry | workshop |
| haystack | cardboard | headlight | sandpaper | loophole |
| sunflower | shoelace | candlestick | coastline | jellyfish |
| snowshoe | toolbox | wallpaper | bookcase | handbag |
| teammate | lunchroom | barnyard | seashell | grandson |
| fishhook | birdhouse | battlefield | whenever | cookbook |
| paperback | cupcake | bedtime | proofread | footstep |
| shortbread | gingerbread | greenhouse | dragonfly | keyhole |
| steamboat | swordfish | blackbird | handmade | railway |
| afternoon | Thanksgiving | eyesight | moonlight | sunshine |
| grasshopper | blueprint | birthplace | fingernails | eyelid |
| grandstand | overboard | shipwreck | newspaper | hallway |
| waterproof | daredevil | underground | overhead | bulldog |

| | | | | |
|---|---|---|---|---|
| courthouse | snowflake | keyboard | touchdown | sometime |
| bedside | tugboat | textbook | nighttime | daytime |
| stoplight | firewood | worldwide | headboard | fullback |
| headlong | sunbeam | underway | breakaway | manpower |
| backboard | wildland | firehall | crackdown | daybreak |
| homeland | nearby | roadside | spokesman | cutthroat |
| taxpayer | walkway | overstretch | dashboard | breakaway |
| buttonhole | greenhouse | cheesecloth | clockwise | cookout |
| earplug | faraway | flashlight | homework | firestorm |
| spacewalk | campsite | household | earmark | watchdog |
| outpost | crackdown | notepad | catwalk | handcuff |
| checkout | cloudburst | copycat | cutback | flagpole |
| footbridge | rattlesnake | meanwhile | junkyard | worldwide |
| lawmaker | buyout | viewpoint | storewide | buttermilk |
| chairman | classmate | clubhouse | counterpart | freehand |
| grandfather | deadline | folklore | sunrise | outbuilding |
| slashmark | cookbook | copyright | cutoff | daylight |
| downhill | driftwood | dropout | highlight | homestretch |
| everyone | keynote | mixup | lifesaver | necktie |
| layout | wayside | matchbook | pipeline | kneecap |
| newborn | landslide | workbook | offshore | patchwork |
| lockout | parkway | troubleshoot | payroll | ponytail |
| lookout | nowhere | makeshift | penknife | sawdust |
| stairway | wildlife | sunflower | slipknot | timekeeper |
| warpath | soapbox | teaspoon | upstart | waistline |
| withstand | latecomer | woodland | lifeguard | workout |
| meanwhile | worldwide | birdhouse | jackknife | toothpaste |

**Writing/Spelling Words:** Write some of the listed words.

# Lesson 68: Common Prefixes and Suffixes

**Prefixes** are syllables or word parts with their own meaning that are added to the **beginning** of a base or root word that change the meaning of the word. **Suffixes** are syllables or word parts with their own meaning that are added to the **end** of a base or root word that changes the meaning.

Although most of the common prefixes and suffixes are phonetic it helps to quickly identify the appropriate 'chunks' of these common affixes. Direct practice in reading these common affixes helps the student quickly identify, group, and process appropriate sounds. The repeated practice builds fluency in these common affixes and greatly improves reading fluency of other words that contain the same common affixes. In addition, knowing the meaning of the common prefixes and suffixes helps students understand the word and expand their vocabulary knowledge.

There are hundreds of possible prefixes and suffixes the student will eventually need to learn. However, it is best to first focus efforts on those prefixes and suffixes that are most commonly encountered. Twenty prefixes account for approximately 97% of the prefixed words. Teaching the most frequent prefixes helps in both reading fluency and in vocabulary. A good list of common affixes is found in the Texas Education Agency publication number GE01-105-04 . On page 28, this publication contains a table "The Most Frequent Affixes in Printed School English". (www.tea.state.tx.us/reading/practices/redbk5.pdf).

| RANK | PREFIX | % of all prefixed words | SUFFIX | % of all suffixed words |
| --- | --- | --- | --- | --- |
| 1 | un- | 26% | -s, -es | 31% |
| 2 | re- | 14% | -ed | 20% |
| 3 | in-, im-, il-, ir- | 11% | -ing | 14% |
| 4 | dis- | 7% | -ly | 7% |
| 5 | en-, em- | 4% | -er -or (agent) | 4% |
| 6 | non- | 4% | -ion, -tion, -ation | 4% |
| 7 | in-, im- | 3% | -able, -ible | 2% |
| 8 | over- | 3% | -al, -ial | 1% |
| 9 | mis- | 3% | -y | 1% |
| 10 | sub- | 3% | -ness | 1% |
| 11 | pre- | 3% | -ity, -ty | 1% |
| 12 | inter- | 3% | -ment | 1% |
| 13 | fore- | 3% | -ic | 1% |
| 14 | de- | 2% | -ous, -eous, -ious | 1% |
| 15 | trans- | 2% | -en | 1% |
| 16 | super- | 1% | -er (comparative) | 1% |
| 17 | semi- | 1% | -ive, -ative, -tive | 1% |
| 18 | anti- | 1% | -ful | 1% |
| 19 | mid- | 1% | -less | 1% |
| 20 | under- | 1% | -est | 1% |

To assist reading fluency, it is also helpful to look at the length of the affix. The longer affixes (such as inter- ) are more difficult to read quickly than the shorter ones. The next lessons provide practice with the more common as well as the longer prefixes and suffixes. There are numerous other prefixes and suffixes the student will encounter as he reads. With practice the student will also begin to build fluency and quickly identify and rapidly process these common "hunks".

# Lesson 69: Reading Multisyllable Words - Common Prefixes

Although most of these common prefixes are phonetic it helps in reading to quickly process them. Practice reading and writing these common prefixes helps the student master the complex task of reading multi-syllable words. In addition, learning the meaning of the prefixes develops vocabulary.

This lesson is long and usually should be worked on over several days. Work through reading and writing one prefix group at a time. For each prefix, have the student read the listed words. Make syllable breaks only if the student needs help. Next have them write/spell 10-20 words from *each* prefix listing. If the student is not fluent in the words have them re-read the list of words at least once before moving to the next prefix. If necessary, include review where the student reads previous lists. Remember, fluency is built by practice. If specific words are difficult, have the student write those word several times.

## un- (not or opposed to)

| | | | | |
|---|---|---|---|---|
| unpack | unclean | unlike | unbolt | unglue |
| unfold | unbound | unclear | unearth | unknown |
| unload | unreal | unseen | untrue | unfit |
| uncap | unrest | unfurl | unhook | unjust |
| unwell | unsafe | uncoil | undress | unwise |
| unclench | unwind | unfed | uncurl | uncut |
| unfair | unpaid | unclasp | unscrew | unburnt |
| unsure | unwrap | untold | untried | unclog |
| uncertain | unconcern | uncover | uneven | unable |
| unarmed | unbeaten | unchosen | uneaten | unfasten |
| unfriendly | ungrateful | unhappy | unselfish | untangle |
| untimely | unwilling | unlikely | unequal | unbroken |
| unwritten | unworthy | uncorrupt | uncalled | unceasing |
| unending | ungodly | unhealthy | unbending | unbiased |
| uncanny | unfearing | unfeeling | unscramble | uncaring |
| uncommon | unfounded | unsightly | unselfish | unwrapped |
| untidy | unfenced | unplanned | unfaithful | unabashed |
| unchained | unspoken | unhelpful | unclogged | unafraid |
| unfinished | unwilling | unworthy | unloaded | unbuckle |
| unchanging | uncouple | unbalanced | unadjusted | unashamed |

| | | | | |
|---|---|---|---|---|
| unappetizing | unavailable | unheroic | unconcealed | undecided |
| unprofitable | unsuccessful | unemployed | unpopular | unprepared |
| unbalanced | unconcerned | undisturbed | undisputable | unbelieving |
| unconstricted | uncontrolled | unexciting | undamaged | unlimited |
| unexplained | unseasoned | unaffected | unfamiliar | uninvited |

## re- (again or back)

| | | | | |
|---|---|---|---|---|
| renew | replace | redo | return | restore |
| repeat | remind | rebuild | recheck | regroup |
| remove | reload | relay | rename | reshape |
| rebound | recall | recede | reclaim | redeem |
| reflect | remit | react | reprint | retain |
| retrieve | review | revive | revise | rehire |
| rewrite | repay | refill | restate | retie |
| rewind | recount | return | reheat | respond |
| remake | report | reread | restart | retake |
| reuse | revolt | revolve | resolve | refrain |
| retype | rework | remade | reroute | restrain |
| reword | resend | rehire | retest | recoil |
| retraced | refreshing | refilled | reenter | renumber |
| recopy | relocate | reinvent | rekindle | reoccur |
| remember | recover | redirect | revisit | reinsert |
| reinspect | reaffirm | reappoint | reattach | rekindle |
| reconfirm | redefine | redivide | refurnish | repeated |
| reinfect | reconstruct | resharpen | readjust | rearrange |
| reappear | reenter | reinvest | reprocess | reinforce |
| redirected | repopulate | recovery | reflective | reprocess |
| retranslate | reevaluate | reignite | recirculate | reconfirmed |

# in- (not, without)

| | | | | |
|---|---|---|---|---|
| insane | inept | incorrect | infinite | incomplete |
| inexact | incorrupt | inactive | informal | inhuman |
| injustice | indistinct | indirect | indecent | infidel |
| infamous | insanity | inedible | ineffective | infrequent |
| incompetent | inequity | incapable | inability | inadequate |
| inconsistent | incredible | independent | inorganic | invisible |
| inconvenient | inaudible | inaccurate | inarticulate | incoherent |
| incombustible | incompatible | indifferent | inconclusive | inconsiderate |
| incurable | insecurity | indecisive | indefinite | inoperable |
| inequality | inconsolable | incomparable | inescapable | inflexible |
| intolerant | inflammable | indestructible | inapproachable | |

## the prefix *in-* (not, without) has spelling variations including im-, ir- & il-

**im-** this spelling variation is often used with base words starting with 'p' and 'm'

| | | | | |
|---|---|---|---|---|
| impart | impure | immoral | immense | imperfect |
| immobile | immortal | immodest | imperfect | improper |
| impolite | impassive | immigrate | immovable | impersonal |
| impassible | immobilize | immediate | impossible | immorality |
| immodestly | immaterial | immaterialize | imperishable | improperly |
| imbalance | immigrant | implausible | improbable | |

**ir-** this spelling variation is often used with base words starting with 'r'.

| | | | | |
|---|---|---|---|---|
| irregular | irreplaceable | irrecoverable | irrelevant | irresponsible |
| irresistible | irretrievable | irreverence | irreversible | irrefutable |
| irradiant | irritable | irreducible | irrevocable | |

**il-** this spelling variation isn't as common and is often used with base words starting with 'l'.

| | | | | |
|---|---|---|---|---|
| illegal | illiterate | illegitimate | illicit | illogical |

## in- (in, into, within)

| | | | | |
|---|---|---|---|---|
| include | increase | induce | induct | indulge |
| infect | inflate | inflict | inflow | influx |
| inform | infuse | inhale | inlay | inscribe |
| inspect | inspire | install | instill | instruct |
| intend | institute | inherit | increasing | included |
| incumbent | incubate | inclusive | incorporate | incriminate |

## dis- (away from, apart, or the reverse of)

| | | | | |
|---|---|---|---|---|
| distract | discount | disband | discard | discharge |
| disturb | distrust | disgrace | dislike | disprove |
| displace | dispatch | distort | discreet | disbar |
| dismount | disown | disdain | dispense | display |
| disarm | displease | disguise | disclaim | disband |
| dissent | distance | disservice | disaffirm | disarray |
| disobey | disembark | disable | disenchant | disfavor |
| discover | disagree | discolor | discomfort | discredit |
| disfigure | dishonor | disorder | disregard | disrespect |
| disconnect | disappoint | disrepair | disorder | disgruntle |
| displacement | disloyal | disavow | discontent | distribute |
| disclaimer | disinfect | dislocate | disappear | disapprove |
| disengage | disrespect | distribute | discharged | disconnected |
| discontinue | disobedient | disorganize | disqualify | dissatisfy |
| discovered | disadvantage | disagreement | disgraceful | disorderly |
| discriminate | disdainful | discouraged | disinterested | disregarded |
| disruptive | disrespectful | dissimilar | distributive | disappointed |

## en- (to place into, to cover or surround)

| | | | | |
|---|---|---|---|---|
| enclose | enforce | engage | endure | enact |
| encamp | enchant | encode | enroll | enclasp |
| enclave | enshrine | engrave | engross | engulf |
| enhance | enjoy | enlarge | enlist | enrich |
| entrench | ensnare | enslave | entrust | enrage |
| engrain | endear | enfold | encode | ensnarl |
| enliven | enrichment | envelope | enforced | encroach |
| enable | endanger | endeavor | enfeeble | encircle |
| encompass | encumber | encourage | entangle | envelop |
| enjoyment | enclosure | encounter | endowment | enduring |
| engagement | enhanced | enlargement | enlighten | encampment |

## em- (to place into, to cover or surround) this spelling variation of en- is often used with base words starting with 'b' or with 'p'.

| | | | | |
|---|---|---|---|---|
| employ | embalm | embank | embark | embody |
| emblaze | embrace | embarrass | embattle | embellish |
| embitter | empower | employed | empathy | embankment |
| embargo | embraced | employment | embarked | embedded |

## non- (not)

| | | | | |
|---|---|---|---|---|
| nonuse | nonsense | nonstop | nonprofit | nonliving |
| nonmetal | nonbasic | nonburnable | nonlethal | nonnative |
| nondescript | nonstandard | nonequal | nonrigid | nonverbal |
| nonvisual | nonfestive | nonfatal | noncorrosive | nonbeliever |
| nonviolent | noncontrolling | noncompliant | noninvasive | nonmember |
| nonconforming | nonreactive | nonproductive | nonvocal | nontoxic |
| nonresident | nonheroic | nonexistence | nonflowering | nonlinear |

| nonacademic | nondurable | noncombatant | nonflammable | nonobjective |
| nonexempt | nonlicensed | nonmineral | nonrestrictive | nonproductive |

## over- (excessive or above/on top of)

| overall | overtake | overtime | overwork | overstep |
| overlay | overland | oversight | overboil | overcame |
| overdrive | overkill | overrun | overblown | overboard |
| overcast | overcome | overdo | overhand | overwrite |
| overhang | overwhelm | overhear | overlap | overturn |
| overthrow | overlook | overpass | overspend | overreach |
| overheat | overdose | overeat | overhead | overseas |
| overcharge | overhaul | overprice | overrate | overpay |
| overview | overpower | overshadow | overruled | overextend |
| overeager | overexpose | oversimplify | overactive | overestimate |
| overprotective | overcrowded | overdeveloped | overdramatize | overcharged |

## mis- (bad, amiss, wrongly, not)

| misshape | misfit | miscall | misfire | misdeed |
| mismatch | mislay | mislead | mistreat | misuse |
| misguide | mishear | misplace | misread | misjudge |
| miscount | misdate | misrule | misspoke | misspell |
| mislabel | mistrial | misprint | misquote | mistake |
| misdirect | misguided | misnomer | mistaken | misconduct |
| misbehave | mismanage | mispronounce | misapply | misjudgment |
| misclassify | misunderstand | misinformed | misappropriate | misprinted |
| misrepresent | miscalculate | misinterpret | misquoted | misdirected |

195

## sub- (under, beneath or below)

| | | | | |
|---|---|---|---|---|
| **sub**way | **sub**floor | **sub**mit | **sub**due | **sub**text |
| **sub**scribe | **sub**side | **sub**ject | **sub**lease | **sub**merge |
| **sub**group | **sub**script | **sub**set | **sub**let | **sub**tract |
| **sub**sequent | **sub**sidy | **sub**tropics | **sub**divide | **sub**compact |
| **sub**alpine | **sub**develop | **sub**sample | **sub**zero | **sub**total |
| **sub**contract | **sub**surface | **sub**arctic | **sub**standard | **sub**stitute |
| **sub**marine | **sub**atomic | **sub**continent | **sub**classify | **sub**ordinate |

## pre- (before or in front of)

| | | | | |
|---|---|---|---|---|
| **pre**cede | **pre**cook | **pre**dict | **pre**face | **pre**set |
| **pre**fer | **pre**fix | **pre**flight | **pre**scribe | **pre**vent |
| **pre**view | **pre**date | **pre**clude | **pre**warn | **pre**heat |
| **pre**paid | **pre**school | **pre**test | **pre**judge | **pre**sume |
| **pre**dawn | **pre**soak | **pre**pay | **pre**plan | **pre**sale |
| **pre**scribed | **pre**arrange | **pre**amble | **pre**dispose | **pre**figure |
| **pre**liminary | **pre**occupy | **pre**register | **pre**program | **pre**destined |
| **pre**dominate | **pre**fabricate | **pre**historic | **pre**liminary | **pre**designate |
| **pre**determine | **pre**occupied | **pre**medical | **pre**requisite | **pre**ventive |

## inter- (together, with each other, or between two things)

| | | | | |
|---|---|---|---|---|
| **inter**act | **inter**cede | **inter**cept | **inter**change | **inter**view |
| **inter**lock | **inter**mix | **inter**sect | **inter**sperse | **inter**state |
| **inter**com | **inter**link | **inter**cede | **inter**change | **inter**dict |
| **inter**fere | **inter**ject | **inter**lay | **inter**lude | **inter**rupt |
| **inter**val | **inter**vene | **inter**link | **inter**twine | **inter**lace |
| **inter**net | **inter**connect | **inter**office | **inter**mingle | **inter**agency |
| **inter**coastal | **inter**dependent | **inter**planetary | **inter**locked | **inter**cepted |

## fore- (earlier in time or place; or at or near the front)

| | | | | |
|---|---|---|---|---|
| forecast | foresight | forehand | foreword | foreclose |
| forearm | foretold | forewarn | foreground | foreseen |
| foretell | forenoon | foregone | foremost | foresee |
| foreman | foreleg | foregone | forehead | forerunner |
| forecaster | forefather | foreshadow | foreboding | |

## de- (away from; off; down; or sometimes to undo or reverse an action)

| | | | | |
|---|---|---|---|---|
| depart | decode | deflate | defrost | deplete |
| detach | decrease | default | destruct | debug |
| debrief | decant | defend | demount | defense |
| debone | declaw | delist | debrief | deform |
| describe | defame | debase | defraud | deflect |
| depress | descend | decongest | demerit | devalue |
| demolish | decompress | deforest | depressed | depolarize |
| dehydrate | deactivate | deglorify | deodorize | decentralize |
| degenerate | defoliate | declassify | | |

## trans- (across, over, through)

| | | | | |
|---|---|---|---|---|
| transport | transect | transmit | transcribe | transfer |
| translate | transfix | transform | transfuse | transgress |
| transpire | transplant | transverse | transit | transpose |
| transcript | transarctic | translated | transpire | transported |
| transfigure | transparent | transcontinental | transient | transmitter |

## super- (above, beyond, more than)

| | | | | |
|---|---|---|---|---|
| **super**heat | **super**script | **super**busy | **super**charge | **super**sede |
| **super**power | **super**vise | **super**market | **super**sonic | **super**highway |
| **super**impose | **super**lative | **super**difficult | **super**critical | **super**important |
| **super**script | **super**visor | **super**sensible | **super**abundant | **super**alloy |

## semi- (partly, exactly half)

| | | | | |
|---|---|---|---|---|
| **semi**round | **semi**circle | **semi**annual | **semi**arid | **semi**final |
| **semi**lunar | **semi**weekly | **semi**monthly | **semi**private | **semi**rigid |
| **semi**automatic | **semi**conductor | **semi**tropical | **semi**skilled | **semi**perfect |
| **semi**comas | **semi**darkness | **semi**classic | **semi**desert | **semi**civilized |

## anti- (against, opposed to)

| | | | | |
|---|---|---|---|---|
| **anti**freeze | **anti**war | **anti**virus | **anti**dote | **anti**aircraft |
| **anti**biotic | **anti**bacterial | **anti**political | **anti**personnel | **anti**perspirant |
| **anti**slavery | **anti**oxidant | **anti**tobacco | **anti**climax | **anti**septic |
| **anti**venom | **anti**trust | **anti**depressant | **anti**histamine | |

## mid (middle, amid)

| | | | | |
|---|---|---|---|---|
| **mid**way | **mid**night | **mid**land | **mid**point | **mid**west |
| **mid**rib | **mid**riff | **mid**ship | **mid**year | **mid**term |
| **mid**town | **mid**story | **mid**week | **mid**wife | **mid**stream |
| **mid**air | **mid**field | **mid**range | **mid**sole | **mid**day |
| **mid**summer | **mid**shipmen | **mid**winter | **mid**morning | **mid**afternoon |

## under- (below in position, beneath)

| | | | | |
|---|---|---|---|---|
| underhand | underact | underdog | underage | undercoat |
| understand | understate | underarm | underclass | underwrite |
| underdone | underfeed | undergrowth | underrate | undertake |
| underfoot | underbreath | underscore | undertone | undergo |
| underground | underpay | underneath | undermine | underlay |
| underside | undertone | underripe | underlie | underbid |
| underarm | undercut | underwent | underfund | underpass |
| underway | underpin | undersea | undersign | undertow |
| undertheme | understood | undergrowth | undercount | underline |
| undercoat | underrun | undersized | undernourished | underpowered |
| underachieve | underwater | underclassmen | underrated | undervalue |
| underexpose | undercover | undercurrent | understudy | underestimate |
| understanding | underhanded | undertaking | underutilize | underscored |

**Writing/Spelling Words:** Write words from each of the prefix groups.

# Lesson 70: Reading Multisyllable Words - Common Suffixes

Although most of these common suffixes are phonetic it helps in reading to quickly process them. Practice reading and writing these common suffixes helps the student master the complex task of reading multi-syllable words. In addition, learning the meaning of the common suffixes helps the student understand the word's meaning and develop vocabulary knowledge.

As mentioned before, **-s & -es** (the plural endings), **-ed** (the past tense ending), and **-ing** are the most common suffixes (65% of all suffixed words). These suffixes have already been practiced in previous lessons as well as in much of the vocabulary encountered in the student's other reading. In addition, even young children regularly use these endings in their oral language, making them easier to read.

This lesson is long and usually should be worked on over several days. Work through reading and writing one suffix group at a time. For each suffix, have the student read the listed words. Make syllable breaks only if the student needs help. Next have them write 10-20 words from each suffix listing. If the student is not fluent in the words have them re-read the list of words at least once before moving to the next suffix. If necessary, include review where the student reads previous lists. Remember, fluency is built by practice. If specific words are difficult, have the student write those word several times.

## -ly (suffix of adjectives & adverbs meaning like or pertaining to)

| | | | | |
|---|---|---|---|---|
| kindly | yearly | brightly | rudely | sweetly |
| tiredly | quickly | slowly | loudly | thinly |
| nicely | thickly | sadly | safely | lately |
| lonely | smoothly | calmly | cheaply | bluntly |
| blindly | neatly | partly | lowly | nearly |
| lastly | plainly | lately | smartly | lightly |
| deeply | boldly | costly | merely | bravely |
| softly | nightly | strongly | lively | richly |
| likely | mostly | rightly | wisely | newly |
| proudly | promptly | freely | fairly | timely |
| sickly | gladly | strictly | friendly | portly |
| silently | quietly | actively | rapidly | secretly |
| suddenly | easily | normally | finally | directly |
| brotherly | absently | hopefully | motherly | locally |
| mannerly | overly | quarterly | precisely | modestly |
| cleverly | politely | foolishly | sisterly | tenderly |

| | | | | |
|---|---|---|---|---|
| unjustly | forcefully | mortally | positively | vertically |
| evenly | formerly | abruptly | admittedly | formally |
| amazingly | concisely | refreshingly | unselfishly | absolutely |
| nervously | alternately | perfectly | astoundingly | currently |

## -er with noun (person or thing that performs the action; agent)

| | | | | |
|---|---|---|---|---|
| maker | teacher | worker | mover | reader |
| writer | caller | speller | poster | farmer |
| sprayer | timer | hunter | hiker | pointer |
| herder | shopper | singer | grower | marker |
| binder | elder | driver | player | jumper |
| zipper | burner | toaster | sticker | swimmer |
| dancer | camper | logger | rocker | mixer |
| explorer | computer | stapler | manager | eraser |
| fighter | stranger | recharger | divider | officer |
| comforter | enforcer | employer | transporter | forester |

## -er with adjective or adverb (comparative)

| | | | | |
|---|---|---|---|---|
| harder | wider | nicer | darker | taller |
| longer | bigger | softer | cooler | cleaner |
| clever | later | rounder | shorter | faster |
| slower | braver | faster | farther | greater |
| smoother | richer | smarter | nearer | quicker |
| quieter | older | kinder | brighter | higher |
| later | calmer | deeper | prouder | lower |
| sweeter | stronger | sharper | stricter | clumsier |

# -able (capable of; likely to; tending to)

| | | | | |
|---|---|---|---|---|
| washable | bendable | readable | workable | moveable |
| loveable | solvable | fixable | peaceable | mixable |
| breakable | suitable | curable | changeable | teachable |
| payable | treatable | learnable | changeable | valuable |
| adjustable | achievable | adorable | presentable | predictable |
| reasonable | questionable | honorable | favorable | agreeable |
| comfortable | employable | noticeable | manageable | preventable |
| punishable | exchangeable | avoidable | enjoyable | excusable |
| excitable | supportable | serviceable | respectable | perishable |
| returnable | invaluable | remarkable | chargeable | transportable |
| repairable | unnoticeable | disagreeable | considerable | durable |
| allowable | justifiable | knowledgeable | acceptable | deliverable |
| forgettable | identifiable | indisputable | inseparable | invaluable |
| available | preventable | adaptable | untreatable | attainable |

# -ible (capable of; likely to; tending to)

| | | | | |
|---|---|---|---|---|
| sensible | visible | possible | terrible | tangible |
| edible | credible | audible | forcible | feasible |
| defensible | detectible | reducible | digestible | collapsible |
| collectible | convertible | impossible | expressible | destructible |
| constructible | suggestible | accessible | digestible | reversible |
| transmissible | impossible | irreversible | plausible | indefensible |

# -ness (condition of; state or quality of being)

| | | | | |
|---|---|---|---|---|
| thick**ness** | weak**ness** | mad**ness** | sick**ness** | quick**ness** |
| pale**ness** | good**ness** | well**ness** | ill**ness** | dark**ness** |
| kind**ness** | blind**ness** | calm**ness** | smooth**ness** | dim**ness** |
| soft**ness** | like**ness** | neat**ness** | new**ness** | bright**ness** |
| faint**ness** | great**ness** | fresh**ness** | fair**ness** | sad**ness** |
| gentle**ness** | clever**ness** | wilder**ness** | happi**ness** | foolish**ness** |
| bitter**ness** | lazi**ness** | thankful**ness** | useful**ness** | playful**ness** |
| alert**ness** | unhappi**ness** | clumsi**ness** | bitter**ness** | forgive**ness** |

# -ment (the product or result of; the means of; the result of)

| | | | | |
|---|---|---|---|---|
| place**ment** | vest**ment** | state**ment** | base**ment** | treat**ment** |
| pave**ment** | oint**ment** | parch**ment** | fig**ment** | tor**ment** |
| ease**ment** | pay**ment** | abate**ment** | detach**ment** | deploy**ment** |
| install**ment** | argu**ment** | experi**ment** | equip**ment** | fila**ment** |
| adorn**ment** | escarp**ment** | engage**ment** | enforce**ment** | amaze**ment** |
| comple**ment** | govern**ment** | excite**ment** | supple**ment** | orna**ment** |
| employ**ment** | agree**ment** | replace**ment** | announce**ment** | refresh**ment** |
| punish**ment** | enjoy**ment** | enrich**ment** | endorse**ment** | banish**ment** |
| adjust**ment** | fulfill**ment** | astonish**ment** | develop**ment** | appoint**ment** |
| confine**ment** | docu**ment** | entice**ment** | amuse**ment** | achieve**ment** |
| settle**ment** | content**ment** | environ**ment** | advertise**ment** | require**ment** |
| apart**ment** | commit**ment** | embarrass**ment** | assign**ment** | sacra**ment** |
| nourish**ment** | parlia**ment** | assort**ment** | disburse**ment** | contain**ment** |
| astonish**ment** | compli**ment** | retire**ment** | tourna**ment** | testa**ment** |
| allot**ment** | displace**ment** | encamp**ment** | amuse**ment** | align**ment** |

# -ive  -ative  -tive  (having a tendency to; having the nature, character or quality of)

| massive | motive | passive | captive | festive |
| expensive | offensive | descriptive | expansive | attentive |
| detective | supportive | impressive | suggestive | directive |
| relative | protective | elective | informative | defensive |
| negative | aggressive | effective | positive | affirmative |
| corrective | restrictive | combative | tentative | creative |
| representative | conservative | sensitive | alternative | ineffective |

# -ful (full of) *note that the -ful suffix is spelled with only one l

| fruitful | gainful | frightful | gleeful | handful |
| hopeful | armful | useful | playful | painful |
| harmful | careful | helpful | thankful | truthful |
| faithful | fearful | joyful | peaceful | dreadful |
| armful | skilful | watchful | cheerful | youthful |
| restful | wasteful | mindful | forceful | mouthful |
| grateful | cupful | hateful | trustful | blissful |
| frightful | prideful | flavorful | colorful | forgetful |
| wonderful | powerful | delightful | meaningful | merciful |
| sorrowful | suspenseful | successful | prayerful | respectful |
| delightful | plentiful | disgraceful | resentful | disrespectful |
| unfaithful | unmindful | neglectful | eventful | effortful |

## -less (without)

| | | | | |
|---|---|---|---|---|
| sleepless | needless | timeless | pointless | baseless |
| aimless | flawless | soundless | tasteless | thornless |
| wordless | voiceless | stainless | boneless | classless |
| nameless | homeless | restless | hopeless | priceless |
| harmless | helpless | reckless | endless | worthless |
| faultless | useless | fruitless | countless | sightless |
| fearless | careless | speechless | painless | cloudless |
| meaningless | defenseless | blameless | ageless | childless |
| rainless | breathless | groundless | numberless | irregardless |
| sleeveless | sugarless | noiseless | carelessly | needlessly |

## -est (superlative degree of adjective)

| | | | | |
|---|---|---|---|---|
| hardest | strongest | tallest | shortest | neatest |
| loudest | fastest | quickest | cleanest | smartest |
| softest | longest | darkest | neatest | tallest |
| wettest | brownest | deepest | smoothest | fondest |
| fastest | greatest | softest | nicest | widest |
| safest | quietest | farthest | coldest | slowest |
| rudest | wildest | coolest | oldest | cheapest |
| youngest | highest | largest | tightest | bounciest |
| cloudiest | craziest | earliest | friendliest | rockiest |

**Writing/Spelling Words:** Write words from each suffix group.

# Lesson 71: Practice Reading Multisyllable Words

This lesson provides additional direct instruction and practice with multisyllable words. Remember learning and practicing how to handle these multisyllable words greatly improves your reading. I will add a light pencil mark if you need help breaking a word apart. As the student reads, have a pencil ready. Make a slashmark to indicate syllable breaks *only* if and when they need some assistance with a word.

## Practice with mixed 2 and 3 syllable words

| | | | | |
|---|---|---|---|---|
| evergreen | notice | reject | neglect | victory |
| refrain | contain | receive | complete | electric |
| inspect | extend | hidden | entrance | hundred |
| softly | frequent | included | celebrate | testify |
| understand | suddenly | behind | remember | anything |
| around | number | between | almost | inside |
| surface | within | sudden | himself | learning |
| outside | always | careful | became | prevent |
| morning | sentence | laptop | behind | problem |
| complete | concrete | terminate | terminal | purpose |
| capital | hostage | freedom | entrance | adequate |
| disinfect | reflect | calculate | hesitate | vitamin |
| hospital | simplify | whatever | capital | carnival |
| tornado | circulate | ordinary | relative | sediment |
| argument | adhesive | president | victory | circulate |
| dedicate | accident | balcony | explode | malignant |
| prudent | excellent | proclaim | increase | insist |
| endure | general | introduce | combine | careful |
| devastate | electron | obligate | expansive | captive |
| obsolete | documents | destiny | determine | discarded |
| disappoint | average | native | primitive | remotely |
| similar | unfriendly | vintage | yearly | penetrate |
| mushroom | laundry | indicate | impassive | consider |

| | | | | |
|---|---|---|---|---|
| graphic | flavor | fantastic | develop | confront |
| confirm | confine | conflict | baptize | amplify |
| abrasive | observe | pelican | secretive | temper |
| obstacle | complain | compensate | complex | camera |
| agenda | expensive | glamour | helplessness | charcoal |
| lumber | multiple | objective | sensitive | vertical |
| chapter | bandage | artist | artistic | appear |
| appointment | addictive | adaptable | leather | corrupt |
| accomplish | accident | constructed | diminish | dishonest |
| displacement | document | enrichment | entertain | exceed |
| exclusive | extreme | internet | fascinate | festival |
| finance | finger | forbid | forecast | fortify |
| gentleman | handful | fragile | frustrate | furnish |
| history | honestly | horizon | inspecting | women |
| inspector | intense | internal | interval | invalid |
| investment | isolate | justify | lightning | monitor |
| elapse | minister | minimize | incentive | introduce |
| medium | dedicate | incomplete | published | recorded |
| replenish | perform | pattern | enormous | canopy |
| forbidden | assignment | wonderful | interrupt | victory |
| continue | centipede | adequate | carpenter | harmony |
| orphanage | tornado | circumstance | circulate | carpeted |
| neglected | attacking | celebrate | circumvent | halibut |
| hurricane | illustrate | sacrifice | inhabited | hospital |
| mineral | detective | reflective | episode | avoiding |
| statistic | adjustment | extend | forbidden | classical |
| satisfy | fearfully | refueling | ownership | repaired |

| proceeding | generally | disturbed | distribute | rewarding |
| converted | migrating | sheltered | excitement | excited |
| exciting | excitable | monument | delighted | replaced |
| replacement | retirement | internal | arrangement | adjusted |
| respectful | minimal | benefit | vitamins | retailer |
| maintaining | difference | different | differing | related |
| envelope | companion | expected | informed | element |
| professor | dentist | exclusive | sponsored | explain |
| concrete | freedom | complex | balance | reflect |
| bottle | morning | shipment | remote | clearly |
| discord | exploring | narrow | regain | conflict |
| pretend | meaning | difficult | banish | confirm |
| prohibit | diplomat | prolific | migrate | sideways |
| address | disconnect | virus | discount | provided |

## Practice with 4 & 5 syllable words

| unseasoned | emergency | material | accumulate | ordinary |
| centimeter | harmonica | certificate | humanity | intensify |
| capitalism | personality | unexpected | confidently | academic |
| consequently | development | accordingly | disconnecting | identify |
| companionship | disadvantage | affirmative | disappointment | astronomy |
| accomplishment | fertilizer | unexpected | elementary | particular |
| enormously | universal | administer | vocabulary | equivalent |
| apparently | ornamental | replenishing | indirectly | participate |
| particular | accordingly | consolidate | considerable | environment |
| considering | successfully | fundamental | permanently | unhappiness |
| independence | indestructible | informative | understanding | increasingly |

**Writing/Spelling Words:** Write some of the listed words.

# Lesson 72: /shun/ Suffixes  -tion -sion -cian -cion

These special /shun/ suffixes are found in the second or subsequent syllable of a multisyllable word. These suffixes mean the action or process of, a condition or state of being, or result of. There are 4 ways to spell the /shun/ ending of a multisyllable word; -tion, -sion , -cian, and -cion. Of these, -tion and -sion are the most frequently encountered. By far, the most common spelling for the /shun/ suffix is -tion. The -sion is the alternate spelling. The use of -tion or -sion is often determined by the spelling of the root word (For example for direct--direction, vacate--vacation, tense--tension, confess-confession). The --cion spelling is used for an occupation such as electrician. The unexpected -cion suffix is rarely used.

## -tion  (this is the most frequently encountered /shun/ ending)

| | | | | |
|---|---|---|---|---|
| nation | traction | station | motion | notion |
| action | option | function | portion | section |
| lotion | ration | portion | caution | junction |
| fraction | fiction | edition | flotation | question |
| rational | national | infection | subtraction | exception |
| adoption | eviction | eruption | fraction | solution |
| donation | hydration | vacation | relation | deletion |
| correction | convention | emotion | inspection | transition |
| direction | reaction | addition | prescription | invention |
| emotion | vibration | ignition | tuition | duration |
| intention | election | tradition | foundation | attraction |
| condition | affection | instruction | migration | attention |
| reflection | completion | tradition | promotion | location |
| position | formation | collection | digestion | construction |
| destruction | injection | vocation | objection | protection |
| rotation | suggestion | pollution | selection | projection |
| expedition | expectation | fascination | conversation | aggravation |
| obligation | organization | circulation | abbreviation | orientation |
| isolation | adaptation | redirection | observation | condensation |
| federation | application | institution | installation | identification |
| occupation | inspiration | confrontation | intuition | explanation |

| | | | | |
|---|---|---|---|---|
| confirma**tion** | investiga**tion** | activa**tion** | condensa**tion** | ammuni**tion** |
| contradic**tion** | invita**tion** | observa**tion** | illustra**tion** | interven**tion** |
| satura**tion** | recrea**tion** | prepara**tion** | conversa**tion** | popula**tion** |
| infla**tion** | planta**tion** | transla**tion** | agita**tion** | amputa**tion** |
| capitaliza**tion** | concentra**tion** | conforma**tion** | contempla**tion** | frustra**tion** |
| celebra**tion** | communica**tion** | decora**tion** | opera**tion** | viola**tion** |
| salva**tion** | starva**tion** | situa**tion** | produc**tion** | interna**tion**al |
| filtra**tion** | sanita**tion** | incep**tion** | litiga**tion** | viola**tion** |
| alloca**tion** | notifica**tion** | considera**tion** | delega**tion** | consolida**tion** |

## -sion (this is the alternate spelling of /shun/ or /zhun/)

| | | | | |
|---|---|---|---|---|
| vi**sion** | disper**sion** | confes**sion** | aver**sion** | mis**sion** |
| aggres**sion** | occa**sion** | explo**sion** | conver**sion** | pen**sion** |
| confu**sion** | expan**sion** | inva**sion** | ver**sion** | omis**sion** |
| inver**sion** | expres**sion** | depres**sion** | admis**sion** | divi**sion** |
| exten**sion** | permis**sion** | colli**sion** | delu**sion** | abra**sion** |
| dimen**sion** | suspen**sion** | deci**sion** | transgres**sion** | pen**sion** |
| ten**sion** | illu**sion** | intermis**sion** | transmis**sion** | confes**sion** |
| confu**sion** | ero**sion** | explo**sion** | deci**sion** | pen**sion** |
| pas**sion** | ses**sion** | compas**sion** | televi**sion** | adhe**sion** |
| proces**sion** | submis**sion** | conclu**sion** | succes**sion** | transfu**sion** |

## -cian  (this /shun/ ending is used for an occupation)

| | | | | |
|---|---|---|---|---|
| electri**cian** | magi**cian** | musi**cian** | physi**cian** | politi**cian** |
| techni**cian** | pediatri**cian** | mathemati**cian** | | |

## -cion  (this 'unexpected' spelling of /shun/ is rarely used)
suspi**cion**     coer**cion**

**Writing/Spelling Words:** Write some of the listed words for each group.

# Lesson 73: Other "Special" Endings to learn

**There are 2 ways to spell the /shul/ ending of multisyllable words; -cial or -tial.** Once again the root word usually determines the spelling of the ending (race--racial  part--partial  face---facial  finance--financial)

## -cial and -tial

| special | artificial | facial | financial | social |
|---|---|---|---|---|
| racial | glacial | commercial | official | superficial |
| beneficial | crucial | partial | nuptial | potential |
| glacial | judicial | provincial | sacrificial | unofficial |

**There are 2 ways to spell /shus/ ending of multisyllable words; -tious -cious**

## -tious and -cious

| cautious | infectious | contentious | nutritious | ambitious |
|---|---|---|---|---|
| fictitious | atrocious | audacious | spacious | vicious |
| ferocious | conscious | gracious | delicious | suspicious |
| precious | pretentious | | | |

**The /zhur/ ending of multisyllable word is spelled  - sure.**

| measure | pleasure | treasure | leisure | closure |
|---|---|---|---|---|

**The /chur/ ending of multisyllable words is spelled   -ture**

| fracture | picture | nature | sculpture | future |
|---|---|---|---|---|
| mixture | overture | feature | denture | fixture |
| moisture | scripture | creature | culture | capture |
| posture | structure | texture | lecture | pasture |
| feature | departure | denture | mature | torture |
| vulture | indenture | recapture | signature | aperture |
| adventure | agriculture | horticulture | furniture | |

**Writing/Spelling Words:** Write some of the listed words from each group.

# Lesson 74: Practice Reading Multisyllable Words

This lesson provides additional direct instruction and practice handling multisyllable words. As the student reads, have a pencil ready. Make a slashmark to indicate syllable breaks *only* if and when the student needs assistance with a word.

| | | | | |
|---|---|---|---|---|
| upset | amazing | wonderful | article | prepare |
| outline | direct | passive | interested | destroy |
| transform | nearly | distant | exceed | exclusive |
| understand | between | around | important | discover |
| almost | several | surface | within | sentence |
| simple | different | another | himself | outside |
| always | usually | possible | however | became |
| example | together | today | behind | second |
| recently | restore | working | believe | flexible |
| distress | shipment | number | message | litter |
| connect | cancel | explore | successful | advantage |
| conversation | similar | events | expands | rapidly |
| testing | destroy | standards | students | however |
| requirement | agreement | processing | improved | normal |
| missing | debate | according | appear | shortcut |
| increase | completed | address | displace | request |
| report | multiple | intercept | largest | support |
| provide | defending | system | crackers | represent |
| parents | interview | fighting | federal | assessment |
| nationwide | lifestyle | balanced | contributed | electrical |
| combination | involved | another | reported | develop |
| decided | winter | eliminate | ensure | offered |
| alternative | member | district | responsible | contract |
| vending | existing | published | triple | canceled |

| | | | | |
|---|---|---|---|---|
| section | delayed | southern | bitter | arctic |
| window | several | concerned | searched | anybody |
| halted | imports | expected | feeding | section |
| located | another | infected | problem | assume |
| remain | computer | history | options | delay |
| presented | placement | heater | weekend | salad |
| several | remark | announce | entire | transfer |
| consider | powerful | vicinity | money | member |
| northern | hospital | corrupt | standoff | suspect |
| undercover | outside | investigate | department | protest |
| reserve | rewritten | disturb | conflicts | assume |
| doctor | away | office | faded | trouble |
| return | available | temporary | waiting | better |
| decorate | uncommon | accept | compare | updated |
| identify | interview | aimed | preview | demand |
| discuss | programs | disputed | increase | mistrust |
| according | unlikely | interest | finalize | return |
| dental | urgent | searching | difficult | principle |
| hardship | alter | dislike | certainly | practice |
| snowpack | percent | operated | assist | several |
| feeling | progress | reverse | deployment | unfair |
| actions | compete | adding | appoint | compromise |
| again | duration | leaving | expanding | maintains |
| conflict | restrict | repaint | coldest | average |
| driven | jackets | allowed | alert | inflame |
| everything | predict | prevent | constrict | inhale |
| clinic | replace | sudden | episode | component |
| infect | direct | secure | afford | policy |

213

| | | | | |
|---|---|---|---|---|
| listen | twenty | afraid | enter | inside |
| wonder | material | daily | deliver | request |
| reward | product | thrifty | obligate | happened |
| monument | explain | infested | program | consult |
| shortest | external | camera | complete | recommend |
| release | become | focus | correct | select |
| continue | indicate | display | subject | confirm |
| enter | agreed | motion | activity | classroom |
| divide | specific | indirect | darkness | breaking |
| notice | practice | control | triple | powered |
| describe | basket | attention | example | border |
| purchase | supplies | affection | begins | details |
| presorted | paintbrush | finally | harmony | extend |
| establish | obvious | property | expansive | renewal |
| worshipped | traditions | government | descendents | answered |
| fortunately | enormous | frightening | vaulting | craftsmen |
| festivals | destroyed | convinced | mountains | completely |
| conquered | disgusting | unmerciful | tranquility | subpolar |
| explanations | gladiator | peaceful | approaching | notorious |
| admired | aqueducts | introduction | elementary | marvelous |
| civilization | victorious | triumphantly | conversion | senators |
| dictator | impossible | settlements | retreated | unfaithful |
| servant | invaluable | invention | property | dangerously |
| intensity | experienced | opportunity | endurance | individuals |
| unexpected | challenging | approaching | supervisor | resistant |
| meanwhile | demonstrate | frequently | achievement | kilometer |
| successfully | throughout | considered | miracle | discovered |
| ceremony | visitors | offerings | particular | appeared |

# Lesson 75: Practice Reading Multisyllable Words

This lesson provides additional direct instruction and practice with handling multisyllable words. As the student reads, have a pencil ready. Make a slashmark to indicate syllable breaks *only* if and when the student needs assistance with a word.

| | | | | |
|---|---|---|---|---|
| extending | entrance | oversee | maintain | distress |
| flexible | discipline | persistent | attacking | splendid |
| activity | speculated | prospective | shipment | excitement |
| purchase | disappoint | cultivated | perfectly | different |
| afternoon | persistent | discovered | ownership | difficult |
| observe | properly | equipment | information | unexpected |
| underneath | beneath | around | number | several |
| almost | understand | suddenly | morning | another |
| complete | common | voyage | nothing | careful |
| without | together | remember | everyone | treacherous |
| between | learning | flexible | exploring | covered |
| thousand | combined | literally | deepest | planet |
| countless | discover | certain | remaining | trusted |
| sometimes | confident | insult | careful | establish |
| underwater | farthest | predictable | finished | clockwise |
| surrounded | consisting | landscape | transmit | modify |
| frantic | provided | difficult | comforting | internet |
| attach | challenge | dangerous | improving | remembering |
| recently | exclusive | protect | wonderful | gathering |
| responsible | property | containing | participate | leadership |
| overcast | blindfold | unselfish | investment | enjoyment |
| support | continue | division | concentrate | appropriate |
| adjacent | adjoining | programmable | according | accordingly |
| encountering | competent | ultimately | untimely | researcher |

| | | | | |
|---|---|---|---|---|
| determine | overheard | troublesome | creative | wisdom |
| universal | corrective | foundation | meaningful | avoiding |
| handling | practice | practical | majority | effectively |
| automatic | developing | condition | advocate | unfamiliar |
| successful | sentence | realize | classroom | existing |
| extensive | inappropriate | centralize | illustrate | announcing |
| everything | possibility | requirement | attendance | absolutely |
| ignorant | indicator | moment | monument | inclination |
| analysis | contradict | internal | consequence | progress |
| publisher | consultant | segments | percentage | assessment |
| individual | fluently | informative | acquire | mastered |
| increasing | performance | introducing | difficulty | manipulate |
| subtract | substitute | activities | towards | undergoing |
| processing | probability | network | particular | frequent |
| ordering | mistakes | department | comments | commentator |
| commentary | workout | organization | instructing | computer |
| antelope | detection | pronounced | leaving | subscribe |
| nutrition | escape | scraping | certificate | waterproof |
| difference | dependable | opportunity | average | accomplish |
| following | participate | community | commute | processing |
| donated | anywhere | remember | promptly | following |
| talented | reflection | afternoon | delivering | monitoring |
| arrangement | blessings | deflect | inspect | introduce |
| available | abolish | progress | highlights | emergency |
| experiment | belong | prescribe | decision | expected |
| marketed | advertise | increased | restriction | annoyance |
| respected | witness | dexterity | description | continued |
| recruit | contract | contact | contain | conflict |

| insider | insist | insistent | reverse | reversal |
| reminder | separate | separately | beginnings | forested |
| escape | shimmered | protest | program | pretend |
| decided | counted | destructive | placement | committed |
| protective | prevention | coordinate | coordinator | implement |
| recommend | nationwide | progress | document | implement |
| environment | training | volunteer | compliance | result |
| policy | surrounding | celebrate | practices | practical |
| offering | attention | attentive | outstanding | involved |
| opportunity | particular | priority | declined | silence |
| commitment | migrant | explained | writing | listened |
| sketches | helpful | underneath | discovery | exchanged |
| discovering | interesting | necessary | challenges | positive |
| unlikely | framed | samples | recently | deadline |
| admire | activity | deliberate | remember | abandon |
| sensible | frustrate | participate | urgently | meaning |
| rightful | stepping | temporary | sending | formulate |
| throughout | forgotten | forgetful | shrinking | support |
| impact | relative | visited | centerpiece | generous |
| committed | proclaim | entertainment | material | assistance |
| quicken | recruit | plover | pilgrim | practical |
| primitive | nickname | restrictive | stampede | perfectly |
| monitor | percentage | performance | powerless | projectile |
| monopoly | popularity | octagon | restrictive | ornament |
| considerably | political | nativity | humidity | sacrifice |
| selective | tendency | tolerate | repeating | condensation |
| transpire | resourceful | prolific | unnoticeable | obligation |
| perfection | caregiver | information | community | invigorate |

# Lesson 76: Practice Reading Multisyllable Words

This lesson provides additional direct instruction and practice handling multisyllable words. As the student reads, have a pencil ready. Make a slashmark to indicate syllable breaks *only* if and when the student needs assistance with a word.

| | | | | |
|---|---|---|---|---|
| transformed | behavior | predicted | remarkable | alongside |
| comparative | incident | commander | evacuation | consolidate |
| expected | narrowly | boundary | legislation | establish |
| connecting | engineer | responsible | reconstruction | resident |
| tropical | vertical | confident | uncertain | platforms |
| documenting | respiratory | security | furthermore | moderate |
| necessary | interaction | certainty | organized | renovate |
| military | historical | reasonable | comprehension | incompetent |
| ointment | conversion | obligation | memories | injustice |
| fundamental | connections | prehistoric | dramatic | gentleness |
| amusement | destructive | majority | dedicate | principal |
| creativity | excitement | humorous | transportation | imaginary |
| elegant | capitalize | imperfect | ungracious | uniform |
| plastic | faithfulness | destruction | rumble | recognized |
| reconstruction | distant | unpublished | background | improperly |
| disgraceful | foreshadow | prearrange | overprotective | dealing |
| exchangeable | disqualify | unbelieving | irrelevant | underground |
| suggestible | ineffective | resharpen | independent | punishment |
| unadjusted | quarterly | preliminary | forerunner | interchange |
| avoidable | forgetful | countless | midshipmen | semiperfect |
| transcribe | antibacterial | decrease | inspiration | supervisor |
| underestimate | disagreeable | usefulness | retirement | disrespectful |
| meaningless | friendliest | primitive | sensitive | reformat |
| withdrew | appointment | interest | managing | customize |

| | | | | |
|---|---|---|---|---|
| boundless | creating | remarkable | documents | transporting |
| erosion | balanced | mineral | community | intensity |
| viewing | accomplished | navigating | behavior | security |
| expedition | experienced | visual | evacuation | troubleshoot |
| preview | assemble | renegade | online | underline |
| moderate | acquainted | multimedia | increased | urgently |
| technology | inexperienced | treacherous | international | incorrect |
| updates | multiple | velocity | underline | multiple |
| obligation | password | reliable | highlight | encouraged |
| alongside | digital | harness | connection | endurance |
| element | desirable | mixture | dissolve | confusion |
| delivers | performance | automatic | dependability | advanced |
| streamlined | frequently | taskbar | throughout | hazardous |
| progress | systems | desktop | warnings | professional |
| download | noticed | retailer | homemade | broadcasts |
| abilities | collections | network | scanner | independence |
| confusion | biologic | fundamental | security | reference |
| section | selection | subdivided | evaporate | identifies |
| characteristic | parallel | substances | chemicals | ingredient |
| inactive | destructive | pollinate | reptiles | percent |
| vertebrate | enclosed | reusable | interaction | invention |
| submerse | pressure | overtake | hurricane | granite |
| durable | contrasting | sediment | computer | compound |
| properties | turbine | rotation | backup | unbalanced |
| generate | friction | unequal | applying | bacteria |
| promptly | reinforce | earthquake | groundwater | forecast |
| disband | exchange | commerce | surrounded | unfamiliar |
| properly | resources | residence | ignorant | concentrate |

| preventive | correctly | returning | effective | fragmented |
| --- | --- | --- | --- | --- |
| assistance | competence | abbreviated | attractively | consultation |
| incredible | disembark | incentive | incompletely | complexity |
| application | unmistakable | automatic | nervously | presentable |
| haphazard | productive | replenish | excavation | conference |
| mobility | essentially | presorted | expressive | conferences |
| obstruction | liberty | asteroid | leadership | connection |
| unreasonable | avalanche | disdainfully | compartment | operating |
| arbitrary | interchangeable | unluckily | provided | infrequent |
| astrology | continuously | conservative | sponsoring | magnetic |
| notified | advocating | additionally | promise | barrier |
| bewilderment | rehearsal | opening | disposition | incorporate |
| transformation | softening | searched | encouragement | participants |
| preferences | frequently | spearheading | starved | satisfactory |
| comparative | technology | contemporary | snarled | upgradeable |
| barricade | reconnect | minority | enemies | suspect |
| carnivorous | unexpressive | compliment | confinement | memorials |
| internet | inconclusive | advertisement | yourself | opportunities |
| database | unexpected | holiday | international | supervision |
| logistical | digital | regretting | ordinary | continued |
| grooming | informed | observation | alongside | diversion |
| overboard | frightening | declaring | imagine | backward |
| attackers | abandon | slavery | remarking | mainland |
| dramatic | considerate | regained | volunteer | implement |
| lurched | indignant | absolutely | comical | interruption |
| courtyard | urgently | resourceful | bandaged | sustained |
| intently | momentarily | predictably | nonproductive | disrespectful |
| incompatible | overactive | mismanaged | forecaster | decentralize |

# Lesson 77: Continued Practice with Multisyllable Words

It is important to continue *guided* practice with multisyllable words until the student has mastered this complex skill. Repeated practice with multisyllable words helps the student not only build fluency on specific words but also develop awareness and knowledge of the common patterns in our language that will help them master reading other multisyllable words. The following are a few ideas for continued practice of multisyllable words:

**Reading Word Lists**: Continued practice with reading lists of multisyllable words helps develop skills. Once again word lists are effective because they force the student to use proper careful processing. They intentionally train the student to look carefully at all sounds. The student is not able to glance at portion of the word and 'guess' based on context. Word lists are a wonderful teaching tool for developing skills. Of course after the student has developed necessary skills, word lists are no longer necessary.

**Reading Dictionary Entries:** Another way to practice handling multisyllable words is to grab a dictionary and quickly read down the entries in the dictionary pages. The words already have the syllable breaks shown. This is not reading the entire dictionary but using the dictionary entries as an easily accessible list for practice reading multisyllable words. Some of the school/junior dictionaries (not young children editions) are preferable as the print is easier to see and also they contain fewer unusual words than a collegiate dictionary. Reading word lists with syllable breaks shown gives practice "seeing" the appropriate syllables in words and helps develop knowledge and recognition of common patterns.

**Marking the syllable breaks when necessary as the student reads**: Continue guided practice with reading multisyllable words. Use a combination of word lists and any printed text that contains multisyllable words. It is advantageous to have the student read material that you can write on (a copied page, newspaper, magazine or book that you can write on). As the student reads, you can help them by making light pencil marks or slashes in the appropriate break *when* they need help seeing the syllables. Or have them make their own pencil marks at the appropriate breaks when needed. Remember with guided reading it is important to have the student read the word correctly. Stop the student if they make an error. If they struggle with a word, indicate the syllable breaks for them with a pencil and have the student re-read the word. As they practice, the syllable breaks will become automatic and you will no longer need to indicate these with pencil slashes. The pencil marks are an intermediate step to assist learning how to read the multisyllable words by breaking them into appropriate hunks.

**Writing/spelling multisyllable words:** As discussed earlier, the process of having the student hear a multisyllable word and then write the word phonetically is a highly effective technique for learning how to read multisyllable words. Remember this is an exercise in handling multisyllable words not a spelling test. Teach the student and make sure they are writing the words phonetically. If a student has difficulty with a specific multisyllable word, have them write that word 5 to 10 times saying the sounds by syllable as they write it. This word writing helps build fluency on specific words.

**Review New Multisyllable Words Before Reading a Passage:** Another suggestion to help a student improve their handling of multisyllable words in their reading is to preview the new multisyllable words in isolation before reading the passage. Before the student reads a new chapter, go through the text and list the new vocabulary and more difficult multisyllable words. Have the student practice reading and writing these words in isolation before they tackle the entire passage. By practicing the new words in isolation ahead of time, they will be better prepared to read and comprehend the chapter. In addition to building fluency in reading multisyllable words, this method of previewing new words before reading text is also a terrific tool for improving vocabulary and enhancing reading comprehension.

# Section 7: Instructions for Using Guided Reading to Improve Reading Skills

**The validated research shows that guided out loud reading has significant beneficial impact on word recognition, fluency and comprehension across a range of grade levels.[7]**

*Guided reading* is reading out loud to an adult, or other proficient reader, with feedback. This is NOT independent silent reading. The key part to the effectiveness in developing skills is to provide 'guidance' to the student. Do not confuse this beneficial teaching tool with various independent reading programs some of which are labeled 'guided reading'. Correction and instruction are the *essential* elements to helping a student learn and improve skills.

In order to achieve the *significant* beneficial impact on word recognition, fluency and comprehension:
#1 The student must read out loud to an adult (or other proficient reader) and
#2 The adult must provide correction, feedback and instruction on specific skill development.

Guided reading benefits both good and struggling readers. In contrast, silent independent reading may *not* actually improve reading skills for beginning readers. Numerous studies show the best readers read the most and poor readers read the least. However, these studies are all correlational in nature and correlation does not imply causation. It may just be the good readers just choose to spend more time reading. Although it sounds like a good idea to have children read more alone, there is *no* research evidence that shows *independent silent reading* actually improves reading skills. Think about it. If a poor reader is just sitting there flipping pages or struggling with the reading and making errors, their skills will not improve, no matter how much time they sit there. In contrast, *guided* oral reading instruction is proven to help students improve reading skills. This is NOT saying students should not read on their own, or that there are no benefits for children sitting there looking at books, or that students do not need to read more. Rather, it demonstrates *to improve skills*, particularly in learning or remediation stages, the student needs to read *out loud with feedback*. At more advanced levels, silent reading does improve the higher skills of fluency, vocabulary acquisition and comprehension.

Guided reading has significant beneficial effects on helping student's develop reading skills. It is one of the most effective tools not only to improve a student's fundamental reading skills but also to help the student develop higher level comprehension skills.

With guided reading you can directly help the student:
- establish fundamental skills necessary for proficient reading
- identify weaknesses and strengthen specific skills
- improve attention to detail
- build fluency
- expand vocabulary knowledge
- develop reading comprehension skills

PLUS guided reading is enjoyable! This is where you sit down with your student and read. Guided reading offers a wonderful opportunity to share the joy of reading with your student.

---

[7] National Reading Panel's "Teaching Children to Read" Summary Report
www.nationalreadingpanel.org/publications/summary.htm

## Specific Instructions for Conducting Guided Reading:

- Conduct guided reading with the student a minimum of 20 minutes/day (more is better!).

- The student must read outloud to you.

- The parent/teacher/other proficient reader must be looking at the printed text and providing immediate feedback. This careful monitoring is particularly important in the learning and remedial stages. You MUST be looking at exactly what the student is reading so you can make immediate corrections. This careful monitoring of each and every word is necessary until the student has become skilled at accurate decoding. (The rule of thumb is when the student makes no more than 1 or 2 errors per page). Either sit directly next to the student where you can both see the print OR make a copy of the material so you can follow along. Having a separate copy is sometimes preferred if you are tutoring other students or if the student does not appreciate someone 'reading over their shoulder'.

- Require the student to read carefully. Teach the student to look carefully at the words instead of rushing through with 'fast & careless' reading. Stopping the student at every mistake is highly effective in slowing down the 'fast & careless' reading. Usually, the impatient students who like to 'rush' do not like to be stopped. Therefore, when you stop them at every mistake they begin to read more carefully. Like anything else, the careful reading is a habit. Help the student develop good habits.

- Require complete accuracy in all reading. Stop the student all errors, no matter how 'minor' they may appear. This includes skipped words as well as any mistake on accurately reading a word. Stopping the errors is critical for effective remediation as you must extinguish incorrect processing as well as develop proficient reader skills. With correction on errors, often all you need to do is tap the missed word with a pencil. This signals the student to 'look again'.
    - If the student skips a word, tap the word they missed and have the student reread it.
    - If the student reads a word inaccurately (says wrong word or misses detail of word) have him reread the word correctly. Point to the specific sound/error if necessary.
    - Do not let any errors slip by, no matter how 'small'. Make sure the student is paying close attention to all details.
    - If the student uses the wrong choice/alternate sound, tell them something similar to "Good try, however this word uses the __ sound" ( For example if the word was 'bestow' and the student uses the /ow/ sound for 'ow' instead of the correct /oa/ sound). Have the student re-read the word applying the correct sound.

- The student needs to correct their mistake. Frequently the student has the skill to accurately read the word but either they were not paying attention or slipped back into a previous incorrect strategy (such as word guessing or visual 'whole word' processing). Often by 'looking again' the student uses the correct process and is able to accurately read the word.

- If the student is lacking a skill then you need to teach them that skill so they are able to accurately read the word. Examples:
    - If the student does not know the correct sound (lacks knowledge of a sound within the word) tell them the sound and then have them read the word to you. This is not 'telling' the student the entire word where all he needs to do is orally repeat the word. In contrast, this is only giving the student the knowledge he is missing and then requiring him to apply this to his reading. This technique can also be used when student comes across code he has not yet learned For example reading 'vacation' before the student has learned 'tion'=/shun/ you would tell them something similar to "the 'tion' partner letters have the

/shun/ sound..try sounding that out again". In addition, if the student misses a sound several times you know the student needs to practice that specific sound in isolation so it becomes automatic
- Focus on building necessary skill. Help the student develop necessary skills. For example often students who have previously learned phonetically incorrect 'consonant clusters' will add sounds when they are not present. (strap as stramp, clap as clamp, sting as string, ) In this case you need to focus the student on looking carefully at the exact printed letters. You can say something similar to "look closely" and point at the specific sounds.

- Help the student with multisyllable words when necessary. Use a pencil to make light slash marks at the syllable breaks. If certain words are difficult, you can write these down for later practice in isolation. See Section 6 for specific instructions on handling multisyllable words.

- Help with proper pronunciation whenever necessary. New words, especially some of the multisyllable words with the 'lazy' schwa, pronunciation can be tricky. The decoding is correct but the word is mispronounced. By all means help the student learn the correct pronunciation. Tell them how the word is pronounced. Say something similar to "Good try, that was close, we actually pronounce the word _____". Have them repeat the word and then reread it with correct pronunciation while looking at the letters.

- Require physical tracking (with finger, pencil or other pointer) when reading UNTIL the student no longer makes tracking errors. If the student is making *any* tracking errors or whole word errors be sure they continue to physically track. Once again this kinetic motion helps direct correct processing of each letter/sound. The tracking also helps focus the student on the details of the word and improves attention to detail.

- Develop vocabulary as the student reads. When appropriate, stop the student at new words. If they do not understand the word, explain what the word means. Then have the student re-read the sentence so they will understand it. See Section 10 for more details on developing vocabulary.

- Work on developing specific comprehension skills. This often involves questions and discussing the material as they read along. The depth of comprehension skills increases as the student becomes older and their skills advance. Beginning comprehension is having the student simply pay attention to what they are reading. The higher level comprehension skills have the student thinking about deeper questions such as 'why did this happen', and inferring 'what do I think this means'. See Section 9 on Developing Reading Comprehension for more detailed instructions.

- Monitor the student's progress and modify the instruction to what the student needs. When the students decoding skills improve/advance to the point where he makes very few errors/page, the careful attention to accurate decoding is no longer necessary and the guided reading can shift primarily to the higher level skills. At this point, you no longer have to monitor each and every word. Instead you primarily focus on the vocabulary and reading comprehension skills. This level of guided reading where you shift from the 'technical skills' of decoding to the content of what you are reading is extremely enjoyable.

**Other tips and suggestions:**

- If the student is 'skipping lines' as they read or frequently losing their place, have the use a bookmark or index card to hold under the line. The student uses the index card to mark the line they are reading. This is especially helpful in books with small print where it is easier to accidentally miss lines.

- If the student reads 'run on' sentences help them learn to make the appropriate pause at the end of sentences. Have the student take a breath at each period. If necessary, place your pencil on or tap the period to remind the student to pause. While this intentional 'stop' and conscious breath slightly exaggerates the needed pause it helps the student begin to notice and react properly to periods. Guided reading of text is where the student develops this necessary skill of appropriate pauses and inflection.

- Help the student practice proper inflection and expression as part of the guided reading. Fiction is often the easiest material to help the student practice and develop skills in appropriate expression. Demonstrating and encouraging expressive reading helps students develop these skills. If the student reads an passage in a flat monotone voice, simply ask him to reread it with expression.

- Use high interest books for the guided reading. Have the student pick out a book that interests him or her. The high interest books help make the guided reading time something to look forward to. There is nothing like an engaging story or a fascinating subject to keep the student excited about the guided reading time.

- Increase the enjoyment by reading the book together. Share the reading by alternating chapters or pages. Not only is this shared reading enjoyable, it is useful in both demonstrating and building enthusiasm for reading.

- While you should definitely incorporate 'fun' 'exciting' reading of the students choice, some of the guided reading can and should be done with the students classroom reading material. This ability to 'kill two birds with one stone' of directly developing reading skills while studying for the next day's science test is helpful on the busy nights. The use of classroom reading material is also particularly useful with students in a classroom pullout situation. The guided reading of classroom material, whether it be the history textbook or the science unit not only directly develop reading skills but also helps the student gain knowledge in other subjects. From a time efficiency standpoint, many students prefer to do some guided reading with classroom material, especially if they have to read it anyways. It is also important to do some guided reading with textbooks so you can help the student develop comprehension skills with the textbook format.

# Section 8: Building Fluency

## What is fluency?

Fluency is 'fast' or 'automatic' reading. Fluent readers are able to read quickly and accurately without effort. By appearances, the student instantly recognizes words and reads the 'fast way' without slowly sounding out. It seems by simply 'knowing' the words the student is able to read easily and quickly.

We know fluency is critical to reading comprehension and skilled reading. However, it is important to realize appearances do **not** reveal the actual process involved in fluent reading. To help students become fluent readers, we need to learn specifically about the actual process of fluent reading and how fluent reading is developed. The necessary answers lie in the amazing field modern neuroscience.

The remarkable advances in neural imaging allow scientists to look closely at the process of fluent reading. Researchers have learned and discovered much about the neural processes involved with fluent reading and how fluent reading is developed. Neuroscientists learned fluent reading uses a 'fast reading area' different from the 'slow' phonologic processing pathways used by beginning readers. Fluent reading uses a neural 'expressway' to process the word. With fluent reading, a quick look at the word activates a stored neural model. This neural model allows not only 'fast' reading but also activates correct pronunciation and understanding of the word. These 'fast' pathways allow rapid, effortless reading.

## How is fluency developed?

Importantly, neuroscientists are learning how fluency is developed. Fluent reading is established after the individual reads the word at least four times using accurate phonologic processing (slow accurate sounding out). Fluency is build word by word and entirely dependent on repeated, accurate, slow sounding out of the specific word. Fluency is not established by 'memorizing' what words look like but rather by developing correct neural-phonologic models of the word. Repeated accurate phonologic processing is essential for developing fluency. In simplified terms, the repeated accurate phonologic processing literally engraves a neural model of the word. This neural model is then is stored in the 'fast reading area' available for rapid retrieval. An individual's storehouse of fluent 'fast' words is built word by word and is dependent on repeated accurate print to sound (phonologic) processing.

Neuroscientists also discovered dyslexic readers do not develop these fluent or 'fast reading' pathways. Struggling readers do not convert print to sound. Because the struggling readers are not accessing the initial phonologic processing pathways the neural models of the words are never made and fluent reading is not developed. Consequently struggling readers fail to develop fluent 'fast' reading pathways. Without these 'fast' reading pathways, reading remains slow and takes much effort. Students who fail to establish initial correct phonologic processing do not develop fluency.

In summary, 'fast' or fluent reading is different than slow sounding out. However, this rapid effortless reading is entirely dependent on initial phonologic processing. Individuals build fluency one word at a time by repeatedly sounding out individual words using correct phonologic processing pathways. Phonologic processing is key to developing fluency.

# How do I help a student become a fluent reader?

The critical information to keep in mind for effective reading instruction is fluency or effortless 'fast' reading is developed word-by-word based on repeated accurate phonologic processing of specific words. To develop fluency, the student FIRST has to be reading by correct, accurate phonologic processing. The student must be 'sounding out' the words correctly. THEN, the student needs to build their storehouse of fluent or 'fast' words by repeated accurate phonological processing of individual words. This expansion of fluent reading requires practice repeatedly reading individual words.

To help a student develop fluency:

- First you must ensure the student is **reading using proficient phonologic processing pathways.** The best way to ensure your student is reading with phonologic pathways is to teach him with an **effective direct systematic phonics program**. If the student is NOT using phonologic neural processing pathways to convert print to sound, he will be unable to develop the neural 'expressway' of fluent reading. The initial phonologic processing or 'slow sounding out' is essential to developing fluency.

- Teach the student the **complete phonetic code** (all the vowel combinations, r-controlled vowel combinations and other complexities). This gives the student the necessary knowledge to process print to sound proficiently and form accurate phonologic models of the word. If their code is incomplete they may not be processing the word accurately. Knowledge of the complete phonetic code is a necessary subskill of correct phonologic processing.

- Teach the student to pay **attention to details** as he reads. The details are critical to form accurate neural models of the word.

- Remember fluency is built one word at a time based on repeated phonologic reading. This requires repeated accurate reading. **Practice is essential**! Repeated practice reading correctly builds a student's 'storehouse' of 'fast reader neural models'. With practice the student adds word-by-word to their fluency. Obviously, the more the student reads the more words he will repeatedly read correctly and the quicker he will build fluency. Because fluency is build word-by-word, students do not develop fluency overnight.

- After fundamental skills are established, **guided oral reading** is the single most effective way to help your student develop and build fluency. The guided reading has significant positive impact on reading skills across all age and reading levels. Guided reading works! Note: Guided reading is NOT the same as silent independent reading. With guided reading, the student reads out loud to an adult *with* feedback and correction.

- Another highly effective tool for building fluency on individual words is phonologic writing/spelling of specific words. This is **spelling/writing the word by sound** (writing down as you say the sounds not spelling by letter name). For this to be effective in developing fluency, the student must repeatedly print the word by sound. Have the student print the word 5 to 10 times, saying the sounds as they print. Then have the student read the word a few times paying careful attention to the specific print=sound relationship. The repeated writing by sound helps the student form the 'fast' neural model of the word necessary for fluency on the specific word.

Remember, fluency is build word-by-word and entirely dependent on repeated, accurate phonologic processing of the specific word. Fluency is *not* established by visually 'memorizing' what words look like but rather by developing correct neural-phonologic models of the word. **Repeated accurate phonologic processing is essential for developing fluency and practice reading is essential for expanding fluency.**

# Section 9: Developing Reading Comprehension Skills

**Overview of Reading Comprehension:**

Comprehension is acquiring meaning from the text. Comprehension is a complex higher level skill. Obviously, comprehension is critically important to the development of a student's reading. Comprehension is an active process that requires an intentional and thoughtful interaction between the reader and the text. Vocabulary development is critical to comprehension.

While readers acquire some comprehension strategies informally, **explicit or formal instruction in the application of comprehension strategies has been shown to be highly effective in enhancing understanding** (from the Report of the National Reading Panel). In other words you *can* take specific actions to help a student develop comprehension skills.

Remember the student must *first* develop accurate phonological decoding skills and build fluency. This fluency that is critical to reading comprehension is accomplished word by word and is absolutely dependant on repeated accurate phonological processing. Comprehension strategies focus on teaching students to understand what they read NOT to build skills on how to read/decode. If the student struggles with accurate fluent decoding then comprehension will continue to be limited. Basically if decoding is not automatic and easy then the student has little energy left to devote to thinking about what they are reading. Remember, if the student has decoding difficulties you need to *first* establish the necessary fundamental decoding skills of proficient phonologic processing BEFORE you can develop the more advanced comprehension. This section addresses techniques for developing the higher level comprehension skills.

**Specific Actions You CAN Use To Help Readers Develop Comprehension:**

This summary gives some specific techniques you can use to help students develop comprehension skills. These strategies will help the student think about what he or she is reading, understand what he is reading, and remember what he read. These strategies are effective for non-impaired readers. The following reading comprehension strategies should be implemented as a part of the guided reading.

**Overview material BEFORE starting to read: Use various techniques to focus the student on the material before they begin reading. Basically, you help the student think about the material before they start reading.**
- Before the student begins reading, provide statements to direct the student toward what they will be reading. Quickly summarize previous text and overview the section/chapter they are about to read. Make statements such as: "In the last chapter you already learned about ___. This chapter is going to discuss ___". For example: "The last chapter was on invertebrates, now you will be reading about vertebrates." or "You just finished learning about the Roman Empire. Now you are going to read about the fall of the Roman Empire". "You are continuing to learn about energy. This section discusses thermal or heat energy."
- Before they start reading, ask questions to ensure the student is actually on target. Ask questions such as: "What will this chapter be about?" "What will this chapter discuss?" "What are you learning about now?" Make questions specific to the material such as: "Which region of the country does this chapter cover?" "What form of energy is this chapter discussing?"
- In non-fiction, preview the titles and headings of the sections before starting to read the chapter. This overview of the chapter outline is especially helpful with textbooks. This preview helps the student understand the overall intention of the chapter or section.
- Review key vocabulary before reading the chapter. Some textbooks highlight key words, and important new vocabulary terms. Defining the keywords before reading is especially critical with

subject terminology. For example, knowing the definition of the term 'Axis Powers' is important before reading about WWII history. Knowing the difference between exothermic and endothermic reactions is important to understanding text discussions on chemical reactions. To comprehend the basic physics of motion the student needs to understand the difference between the terms speed, velocity and acceleration.

- With fiction, you can summarize the previous chapters and ask the student to briefly review key events. Ask specific questions on the plot or key events to 'set the stage' for reading such as: "So what is going on in the story?", "What happened so far?" "Where are they at?".
- With fiction, in addition to having the student give you the quick overview of key events ask the student what they think may happen next. Ask questions along the lines of "What do you think will happen now?" Make questions as specific as possible: " How do you think Sarah will be able to help her grandmother?" "Do you think the old man will be able to land the fish?"

**Help the student understand the structure and organization of writing**:   By recognizing important fundamentals about the structure and organization of writing, the student is better able to extract the important material and achieve comprehension.

- Specifically point out the structure of paragraphs, sections and chapters. In informative writing most sections should have a main idea and supporting details. Most paragraphs have an opening, a middle and an end. The opening sentence usually outlines the main idea of the paragraph. The supporting points and details should be in the body of the paragraph and the concluding sentence at the end. Awareness of the structure of paragraphs, sections and chapters helps the student better understand material.
- Non-fiction can be organized differently. For example, stories usually contain a conflict with the typical plot structure of exposition, rising action, climax and conclusion or catastrophe. Awareness of elements including the point of view or voice the author uses to tell the story, situation, setting, and characterization all contribute to overall comprehension.  Help the student understand key writing elements.

**Help the Student Learn to Identify and Extract the Main Ideas**: The ability to find, identify, extract and understand main ideas is critical to not just reading comprehension but to educational objectives. Much of the reading students do is to acquire specific information.  Some students have high comprehension on fictional stories yet have difficulty extracting necessary information from textbooks and other non-fictional informational reading. These students need direct instruction on how to identify and extract necessary information. Many of the new textbooks contain a style of writing that many students need to learn how to read. The short paragraphs, numerous interruptions, interesting but irrelevant trivia, and tidbits of boxed information at various locations can sometimes make it more difficult to locate, identify and extract pertinent information. For example, if the student is reading a chapter on United States expansion, the photo of a grizzly bear and sentences about how Thomas Jefferson had a grizzly bear in a cage on the White House grounds may distract the student from the main point. For content comprehension, the student can't just relate the trivia of the grizzly bear in the cage. The student needs to understand Thomas Jefferson made the Louisiana Purchase and sent the Corps of Discovery expedition to explore this new territory. They need to understand how Lewis and Clark mapped this new region and recorded information not just on many new plants and animals but also on the peoples that lived there. Help the student learn how to look for and identify the main idea both before reading and during the reading process.

- As discussed in the 'overview materials' techniques, introductory statements and questions can point the student in the right direction before they start reading.
- Review the main headings and overall outline of the chapter.
- As the student reads, help them identify and focus on main ideas by asking specific questions. Stop the student at appropriate paragraphs or sections and ask targeted questions that direct the student

to important information. "What was the Lewis and Clark expedition?" "What were the primary missions of the Corps of Discovery?" "What important information did Lewis and Clark gather during their expedition?" "Explain the process of oxidation?" "What happens in an exothermic chemical reaction and how is it different from an endothermic reaction?" "Why did the Greeks begin the first Olympic Games? "What weakened the Greek civilization and made is susceptible to defeat?" Help the student learn how to focus on important information. Ask specific questions that help the student identify and understand the key concepts.

- By asking questions you can help target the student toward the key concepts that they do not recognize or understand. For example if you ask the student to explain complete metamorphosis and he gives you the answer 'a frog', then you would ask the student a follow up question such as "Yes, a frog is an example of an animal that undergoes complete metamorphosis, but can you explain the primary difference between complete and incomplete metamorphosis?". You do not want to 'give' the answers to the student, but rather help direct them toward locating and understanding the main ideas.
- If the student can not answer questions or is missing pertinent details, then have them re-read the paragraph or section. Not only does this allow the student to find necessary information but it teaches the student the essential skill of looking back and re-reading text to find necessary information.
- Outlining can be a highly effective tool for helping students identify main points. Show the student how to make an outline. Outlining does not have to be detailed. Short bullet statements are often effective in identifying main ideas. The student can then orally explain the bullet points.

**Stop or pause the student during the reading to think about and process the material. Directly encourage and develop the student's skills in processing and understanding text as they read.** These techniques help the student develop the interaction between the reader and the text that is important to comprehension. Encourage and develop skill in actively processing the material. Help the student think about what they are reading.

- Stop at appropriate paragraphs or sections and ask specific questions that make the student think about what they are reading. Once again design questions to help the student think about specific aspects of the text. Ask both direct informational as well as more advanced interpretative questions.
- As the student comes across unknown vocabulary or expressions, stop and see if they understand what they are reading. Explain or define the word or expression and then have the student re-read the paragraph or section. For example, the reader comes across the phrase "take the bull by the horns" make sure they understand the phrase means "to tackle tough issues head on with direct action". The English language is full of many sayings and phrases that do not make sense if read literally. The student needs to not just read the phrase correctly but understand what that phrase means to comprehend the overall meaning of the text.
- Once again, if the student can not answer a question or is missing pertinent details, have him go back and re-read the section.
- Begin helping the student develop the higher level processing skills of interpretation and inference. Ask both 'what do you think' and 'why do you think' type questions. The process of explaining "why" helps the student think through and back up their answers with reasoning.

**Help Reader Learn to Summarize:** Help the student learn to summarize material as they read. In other words, teach the reader how to integrate all the various aspects of the material and give the 'nuts and bolts' of a short and quick summary of the text. This ability to summarize is a more advanced skill than simply pulling out the main points. Summarizing main points can be harder for some students because they need to understand the material well enough to be able to explain the key points in their own words.

- Have the student practice this essential skill by asking "What was that about?" or "How would you summarize that in your own words?" If the student is unable to 'pull out' and summarize important information, give guidance that teaches him how to do this. Sometimes students will remember small details but are unable to summarize the important points. Once again questions and discussions are effective in helping the student learn this important skill of understanding and summarizing important points.

**Specifically Develop Vocabulary Knowledge:** Vocabulary instruction leads to gains in comprehension. Please see Section 10 for further details and specific techniques to expand vocabulary.

**Develop Comprehension Monitoring:** Self-monitoring is where the reader checks themselves and recognizes if they understand the material. The goal is for the student to develop self awareness of his or her comprehension.
- The student needs to ask themselves at the end of each paragraph or section "Do I understand this material?". To develop this essential skill, have the student ask themselves outloud, "What was that about?" By asking and answering this question outloud, the student learns to check himself. The outloud self questioning is a temporary tool. When the student learns to automatically check and monitor their own comprehension, the outloud self questioning is no longer necessary.
- Another technique for developing self comprehension monitoring is for the student to generate questions about various aspects of the content. By coming up with their own key questions, it allows them to review their understanding of the material. The student answers these questions himself or asks you the questions.
- If the student does not understand what they read, they need to learn to go back on their own and re-read the section. This self-directed 'going back' and re-reading is critical to comprehension. Be sure and compliment the student when you notice them going back on their own.
- Point out this self-monitoring of comprehension is a characteristic of skilled readers.

**Use of Graphic Organizers:** Organizers where the student makes various graphic representations of the material such as story maps, outlines and timelines can effectively enhance comprehension. The key with graphic organizers is to ensure these tools are carefully targeted to achieve comprehension goals and the tools are appropriate for the content areas.
- Maps are virtually mandatory when studying content areas dealing with geography. Maps are also critical in understanding history. For example: It is difficulty to understand the importance of the Panama Canal without looking at a map, and understanding the ancient Egyptian civilization is dependent on understanding the influence of the Nile river and the geography of the region.
- Timelines are a highly useful tool. The timelines allow students to 'see' the progression of events chronologically. Once again history is a prime candidate for timelines. The timelines are also useful in other subjects that relate to chronologic progression such as medicine, scientific discoveries, and advancement in technology.
- Sketches, illustrations, diagrams and other visual representations can be highly effective when they are properly applied. For example, sketches of the various landforms helps students define and understand geography terms. Diagrams are important in describing and understanding the physical structure and function of item such as atoms, molecules, cells, and life cycles.
- Story maps are a tool for visually outlining fiction.
- Outlining is a highly effective tool across a wide range of subjects and material context.
- Once again, all these tools need to be properly targeted to develop the necessary content objectives. It is important to realize that not all 'projects' or 'visual representations will enhance comprehension. For example spending time making a paper pirate ship mobile is unlikely to improve comprehension of 'Treasure Island'. Building a model of a pyramid out of sugar cubes is unlikely to help the student learn the importance of the ancient Egyptian civilization. Remember to target and focus graphic organizers to what the student needs to learn.

**Cooperative Learning:** Cooperative learning is where students learn and discuss material with others. As can be expected, effectiveness of 'cooperative learning' strategies varies greatly. These cooperative learning strategies need to be properly applied and carefully monitored.

- Discussions guided or facilitated by a knowledgeable instructor are more effective than unguided discussions. Even if the instructor does not direct the details of the discussions, facilitation is important. Students who start off discussing their thoughts about "The Old Man and the Sea" can easily drift off into a series of unrelated fishing stories. Facilitation is important for keeping students on target.
- The open discussions between students are usually more appropriate for fictional text than for non-fictional informational reading. Students can learn from each other when discussing elements such as 'what do you think will happen? "Why did this character do this?" "Why do you think…" etc. These types of discussions can bring out elements of the story that the student had not previously thought of.
- Common sense dictates the effectiveness of these 'cooperative' discussion strategies with factual informational text. Obviously, it does not help students' comprehension if the 'cooperators' share incorrect or inaccurate information. Particular care and careful monitoring is essential so that uninformed students do not share misinformation with other students. The 'cooperative' discussions among students often have limited benefit when students are learning new concepts and information. While question generation from students is helpful, the answers and factual information need to be provided by knowledgeable sources.
- Cooperative learning with knowledgeable individuals or subject experts can be highly beneficial. For example, if my son discusses military history with his grandfather the cooperative discussions between them provide incredible opportunities for him to expand his comprehension and knowledge base. Obviously he would not achieve this enhanced comprehension if he discussed the same topic with his buddy whose knowledge of WWII history was limited to a fictional TV show.
- Monitoring is always important with cooperative learning to ensure accurate information is shared and the students remain on target.

In summary, comprehension is the essential higher level skill of actually understanding the material being read. Obviously, comprehension is the goal of proficient reading. You can help students develop these critical comprehension skills with various direct instruction strategies. Most of these activities that develop comprehension skills can be effectively applied as a part of guided reading.

# Section 10: Expanding Vocabulary Knowledge

## Overview of Vocabulary Development:

As can be expected, vocabulary knowledge is critical to reading development. Vocabulary is beyond correct decoding. Vocabulary is understanding the meaning of the word. Expanding the student's knowledge bank of vocabulary words is important to comprehension. The greater the student's vocabulary the easier it is to make sense of and understand text. Vocabulary is generally related to understanding individual words where comprehension generally refers to understanding larger parts of the text. Vocabulary and overall comprehension are closely related.

Vocabulary knowledge is distinct from the skill of decoding print. A student can fully understand words that he is not able to read. For example a five year old has a much larger speaking and understanding vocabulary than a printed reading vocabulary. He may not be able to read the printed words 'gorilla', 'vacation' or 'chocolate' but knows exactly what the words mean. He has the necessary vocabulary knowledge even though he can't read the print. In contrast a student may be able to correctly decode a word perfectly and still now know what it means. This would be a vocabulary knowledge issue. Of course for comprehension, the student needs to both accurately decode the word *and* know what the word means.

Expanding a student's vocabulary knowledge is important to reading development. Vocabulary instruction leads to gains in comprehension (noted by the National Reading Panel). A comprehensive reading program needs to include vocabulary development. The student can learn vocabulary both incidentally and through direct instruction. Various techniques designed to directly build vocabulary are effective in expanding vocabulary knowledge and improving reading comprehension. Optimal learning occurs when vocabulary instruction involves a combination of different techniques.

## Specific Actions You CAN Use To Help Readers Develop Vocabulary:

Vocabulary is enhanced by both direct instruction and incidental exposure. Techniques you can use to help your student expand their vocabulary knowledge include:

- Directly teach new vocabulary to the student. To maximize effectiveness the student should learn and practice new words both in isolation and in context. The student can practice the meaning of the words in isolation (word lists with definitions) and in context (using the word in a sentence). In other words, the old-school English teacher method of presenting a list of new vocabulary words and having students write both the full definition and writing a complete sentence using the word is highly effective in helping students learn new vocabulary. These direct methods of expanding vocabulary have beneficial impacts on reading comprehension.

- Highlight and define key words before having the student read a passage. Comprehension is improved when students to learn new vocabulary words before reading text. This strategy is especially beneficial with subject terminology that is critical for overall comprehension. Acquiring the vocabulary knowledge prior to reading the text enhances overall understanding of the material. (For example before reading a science chapter on energy, highlight and learn the meanings of kinetic energy, potential energy, thermal energy, conduction, convection and radiation.)

- As a part of guided reading, have the student stop if he does not know the meaning of the word. You can verbally explain the word and then have the student re-read the sentence. As they read, the student will also 'figure out' the meaning of many new vocabulary words simply from context.

- Help the student learn to use a dictionary as a resource. You want to help the student learn how wonderful and informative a good dictionary is. The goal is to help the student to progress from the stage where they need direct orders to 'go look it up' to where they voluntarily reach for the dictionary to determine word meanings. Directly practice looking up new words in a dictionary.

- Help the student learn to notice new unknown vocabulary words. The student can then either look up the word as they are reading or they can write down the word for later. It is helpful for the student keep a small notepad to record new words. The student can then look up and learn these unknown words at a later time. My daughter prefers the 'write down for later' method, because she does not have to stop reading a good book to look up a definition. To encourage the student, you can even come up with a system of rewarding a certain number of new vocabulary words.

- Repetition and multiple exposures to new vocabulary enhance vocabulary knowledge. In other words, teach words more than one time and have the student practice words more than once.

- Vocabulary can also be learned indirectly/incidentally through exposure. Vocabulary knowledge can be acquired through oral conversations, discussions and other verbal presentations. In general, written language contains a higher level of vocabulary than oral language.

- Because vocabulary is acquired through exposure, books on tape can be an excellent supplemental tool for exposing students not only to expanded vocabulary but also the benefits of a wide variety of literature and information. A collection of fiction and non-fiction audio books are found at most libraries. While these audio books should not replace reading, they offer an opportunity to expose your family vast wealth of literature at times where sitting down and reading a book is not feasible. These audio books can be listened to while driving in a car, preparing dinner, conducting chores or while engaged in other activities. For example, my son loves to listen to audio books while playing basketball in the driveway.

- Students can also learn new vocabulary from various word games. Fun vocabulary games, such as crossword puzzles and the vocabulary quizzes found in Reader's Digest magazine, can be used to expand vocabulary in an entertaining manner. You can also make your own games where members of the family find, learn and quiz each other on their 'new' words.

- Direct instruction in the most common affixes helps students expand their vocabulary knowledge. Learning the meaning of these common 'building blocks' helps students understand many new words. The definitions of common prefixes and suffixes are included in Section 6 (Multisyllable Words). The definitions of other prefixes and suffixes can be found in dictionaries, other lists and vocabulary programs.

- Direct instruction in the common Latin and Greek root words is highly beneficial in expanding vocabulary knowledge. Study of the Greek and Latin root words provides a strong foundation for vocabulary development. For example if the student knows the Latin root script=write they can better understand the meaning of the words scribe; transcribe, manuscript, prescription, inscription, describe, transcript.

Lists of root words are readily available through internet searches for 'common root words'. Many sources can be found on organization (.org) and education (.edu) websites. In addition, complete structured root word programs such as "English from the Roots Up" by Joegil Lundquist are also available.

A partial list of common Greek and Latin root words is included on the next pages.

**Greek Roots:**

astron - star (astronaut, astronomy, astrology, astronomical)

auto - self (automobile, automatic, autobiography, autograph, automate, autonomy)

biblio - book (bibliography, Bible, bibliomania)

bio - life (biology, biodegradable, biography, biosphere, antibiotic)

chron - time (chronology, chronic, synchronize, chronological)

demos - people (democracy, demography, democratic)

dia - across or through (diameter, diagonal, diagnosis, diagram, dialect)

geo - earth (geology, geometric, geography, geopolitical, )

graph - to write or draw (graph, telegraph, graphic, autograph, homograph)

hemi - half (hemisphere)

homo - same (homograph, homogeny, homonym, homophone)

hydro - water (hydrant, hydrate, hydroelectric, hydrology)

logos - word study (logic, -ology = the study of biology, geology)

mega - large or great (megaphone, megapod)

meter - measure (thermometer, barometer, diameter, optometry, altimeter)

micro - small (microscope, microbe, micron, microfilm)

mono - single (monorail, monologue, monarch, monopoly)

para - beside (parallel, parable, parenthesis, paragraph, parachute)

pathos - feeling (pathetic, apathy, sympathy)

philia - love friendship (Philadelphia= city of brotherly love, philosophy, philanthropist)

phobia - fear (claustrophobia, hydrophobia)

phone - sound (phonics, telephone, symphony, microphone, phonological, homophone)

photo - light (photograph, phototropic, photocopy, photosynthesis)

poly - many (polygon, polymer, polynomial, polygamy, polyhedron)

psych - mind, soul (psychology, psychic, physics, psyche

scope - to look at inspect (scope, microscope, telescope, periscope)

sphere - ball (hemisphere, sphere, spherical, atmosphere)

syn/sym -together or with (synonym, symphony, synchronize, synthesis, symmetry)

techne - skill or art (technology, technical, technician)

tele - distant, far away (telephone, telegraph, telescope, television)

therm - heat (thermometer, thermostat, thermodynamics, thermos)

thesis - place position (thesis, theme, synthesis)

tropic -turning (tropics, phototropic)

**Latin Roots:**

annus - year (annual, anniversary, perennial, annuity)

aqua - water (aquarium, aquifer, aqueduct)

audio - hear (audible, auditory, audience, auditorium)

bene - well, good (beneficial, benefit)

bi - two (bisect, bicycle, bipartisan, biped, binary, binocular bicentennial, bifocal)

capitis - head (capital, captain, cabbage, capitalism)

centum - hundred (centimeter, cent, percent, century, centipede)

circum - around (circumvent, circumference, circulate)

contra - against (contrary, contradict, contraband, contrast)

dict/dictum - say or speak (dictate, dictionary, contradict, dictation, predict, verdict)

duct - lead (conduct, aqueduct, conductor)

duo - two (dual, duet, duel, duplex)

equi - equal (equitable, equator, equal)

finis - end (finish, final, finite, infinite)

fix - fix or attach (fix, affix, prefix, suffix)

fract - break (fracture, fraction, infraction, refract)

ignis - fire (ignite, igneous)

ject - throw (reject, interject, object, project)

junct or join - join or connect (join, joint, junction, rejoin)

manus - hand (manuscript, manufacture, manual, manipulate, manicure)

migrat - move (migrate, migrant, migratory)

ped - foot (pedal, pedestrian, pedestal, centipede)

populus - people (people, popular, population, republic, publish)

port - carry (portable, porter, deport, transport, import, airport, portage)

pre - before (predict, prepare, predawn, preset, preamble)

quartus/quad - fourth (quart, quadrant, quarter, quadrilateral)

scribe/script - write (script, transcribe, prescribe, scribble, inscribe, describe, manuscript)

spect - look (inspect, speculate, spectacle, perspective, introspect)

struct - build (construct, structure, destruction, instruction)

tempor - time (temporary, contemporary, temporal, tempo)

trans - across (transfer, transcript, transplant, transparent, transaction, transmit)

verb - word (verb, verbiage, proverb, verbal, verbose)

vid/vis - see (video, visible, evident, visual, visit, visitor)

# SPELLING

## A. General Information for the Parent or Teacher

This section helps you teach a student how to spell (correct written representation of our language). Common patterns should be taught from the beginning as a part of the direct systematic phonics instruction. In addition it is beneficial to specifically teach spelling guidelines to students. Although there are exceptions, guidelines are very useful in learning to spell correctly. While the spelling of individual words in our English language can be "goofy" at times, for the most part it is not complete chaos. It is always much easier to learn a few general guidelines than try and memorize a vocabulary of 50,000+ words individually with no overall guidance or direction.

First and foremost, always **emphasize the phonetic nature of spelling**. Teaching a student how to read using a direct, systematic phonics approach, will already greatly improve their spelling ability. Help them learn to listen to the sounds in the word. Practice spelling with common patterns. Although there is overlap with the code (more than one way that a sound can be written) and irregular and unexpected spellings, spelling is not a matter of memorizing random letters in tens of thousands of individual words. Learning accurate spelling is trickier than reading. Good phonetic knowledge is essential to proficient spelling. A strong phonetic base, awareness of frequency patterns and knowledge of spelling 'guidelines' are very useful tools in learning common and expected spelling patterns in our language.

The spelling 'guidelines' listed in this section are not a list of rules meant to be memorized but rather a tool to **teach common spelling patterns**. Teaching how and why certain patterns are used and then practicing these common patterns is more effective than memorizing a list of rules. A table summarizing expected spelling patterns for the sounds is located in Appendix E.

I will make a comment on the use of "invented spelling" that is contrary to some of the prevalent educational theory. **Do *NOT* use 'invented spelling'** where the student is allowed to 'discover' and write words however he would like to. Although the student will obviously make spelling errors and perfection should not be expected, do *not* allow and encourage the continued, repeated use of improper spelling. Instead of letting the student continuously repeat errors, simply teach them the correct way to spell the word. This is not just a minor problem with spelling a few words wrong. The use of "invented" or "self-discovery" spelling allows the student to learn and repeatedly reinforce incorrect patterns and form improper 'neural models' of the words. You witness this in the many perfectly bright older students who continue to spell they as 'thay'. Repeated writing of 'thay' for years engrained the incorrect 'thay' representation in their brain. It is a disservice to the student to let them learn incorrectly. I strongly believe as parents and teachers it is our job to teach students the correct representation of our language. There are numerous things that are wonderful and necessary for students to discover on their own. However accurate representation of our written language is not one of them. Once again the corrections and teaching can and should be done in a positive manner. Acknowledging and even encouraging their phonetic spelling attempts should not preclude teaching correct spelling. ("You wrote that word how it sounds. That's a great try. But let me show you the way that we actually spell it"). It is always better to learn correctly!

Accurate spelling is not an isolated skill limited to a student's weekly spelling test or for competing in a spelling bee. Spelling is one of the fundamental subskills of effective written communication. The vast majority of spelling occurs in real life applications to achieve communication objectives. The goal of spelling instruction should not be temporary memorization of words but rather the development of skills to be able to correctly represent our written language. Help the student learn how to accurately represent our written language.

## B. Specific Recommendations for Teaching Spelling: (For the parent or teacher)

**Use the following tips to help your student develop successful spelling skills.**

1. Directly teach phonetic spelling. Base spelling on 'writing' the sounds *not* on memorizing letter names.

2. In the beginning, teach spelling as a part of the reading instruction. Start with basic phonetic spelling and include only the sounds and phonetic code the student has already learned. For example do not ask a student to spell the word 'rain' if they have not learned 'ai'=/ay/. Do not have them spell 'time' if you have not yet directly taught them the i-consonant-e vowel combination. Include 'reach' and 'east' only after you have directly taught them the 'ea' vowel combination. Teach spelling in a systematic, phonetic based manner to establish strong foundational spelling skills.

3. As the student masters the basic sounds and skills, add the complexities in a systematic manner. Teach one spelling pattern at a time. Directly and systematically teach specific vowel combinations, r-controlled vowel combinations and other complexities. Structure spelling instruction so that is makes as much sense as possible. *Give word lists by groups of common spelling patterns.* Teaching spelling of specific patterns and groups is much more effective than 'testing' mixed lists or phonetically unrelated words.

4. Directly teach and practice the common spelling guidelines. By learning these common spelling patterns, the student is better able to understand the structure of our spelling. Knowing the patterns, guidelines and expected frequency of occurrence helps children (and adults) learn how to spell. This program includes helpful spelling guidelines.

5. The most effective and efficient way to have the student learn spelling words is to have the student write the word 5 to 10 times while saying the sounds. It is simple; all you need is paper and pencil. It's efficient because it directly teaches the necessary print to sound and you are not wasting time on processes that have nothing to do with spelling. It is highly effective because it directly builds knowledge in the correct printed representation of the word using multisensory processes (kinetic-forming the letters), visual (seeing the correct print), oral/auditory (saying and hearing the word). Writing the word 5-10 times provides the repetition that enhances learning. Simple, effective and efficient.

6. Directly teach the 'irregular' words and 'unexpected' patterns. Teach these irregular words in a systematic manner, including them where appropriate. For example, teach the unexpected /ay/ sound in 'great', 'steak', and 'break' as part of your instruction in the 'ea' words. Have the student specifically notice these 'unexpected' spelling patterns.

7. Advance skills in a systematic manner. Add complexities and multisyllable words after basic foundational skills are established.

8. For multisyllable words, teach the student to sound out and spell by syllable. Writing the word by syllable helps prevent the common problem of leaving out parts of the word.

You can easily create a spelling program by selecting words from the systematic word lists in the *Right Track Reading Lessons* program. Use these lists in combination with the specific lessons on spelling guidelines to create a highly effective spelling program. Remember, teaching in a direct systematic manner helps the student learn.

When making spelling lists, remember it is best to teach spelling in common patterns. After the student has mastered and learned the common patterns you can then test for 'spelling' knowledge. In the learning stages it is important to teach by grouping spelling patterns. The following examples demonstrate how to make spelling list that teach specific spelling patterns.

>If you are teaching the student to spell /ay/ words, group by spelling pattern. List 1 would have the 'ai' words (rain, bait, brain, wait, grain…). List 2 would give the 'ay' words (play, away, stay, pay, pray…). List 3 would give the a-consonant-e spelling pattern (gate, trade, game, make, grade…). List 4 would contain the single vowel 'a' spellings (rang, bank, thank, sang…). List 5 would contain the 'unexpected' spellings of /ay/ (eight, weigh, great, …).

>If you are teaching the student to spell the /er/ sound, group by common spelling pattern to help the student learn. List 1 would contain the words are spelled with 'er': (verb, river, under, stern, sister, hunter….). List 2 would give the /er/ words spelled with 'ur'(hurt, burn, church, curl, burst….). List 3 would give the /er/ words spelled with 'ir' (bird, firm, stir, dirt…). List 4 would give the words spelled with the more unusual 'ear' spelling (early, earn, earth, learn..) When teaching specifically point out the spelling pattern. Also teach that the 'er' is the most common spelling pattern for the /er/ sound.

It is preferable to give students lists of common spelling patterns grouped together because this systematic grouping helps the student *learn* how to spell. This can be contrasted to using lists of mixed spellings. Using a list of mixed spellings for a sound, especially before the student has learned all the individual patterns, contributes to confusion. The mixed lists not only make spelling difficult but they often prevent students from even recognizing the common patterns. For example if you use a mixed "long-a" list (wait, space, great, game, bang, play, they, eight) it is difficult for the student to recognize and learn the individual ways we spell /ay/. Similarly, 'theme' based spelling lists are frequently very poor tools for teaching spelling. For example a 'summer' theme that contains the words; summer, swimming, dive, pool, vacation, hot, ice cream, beach, picnic. This type of mixed list makes recognizing and learning patterns difficult. At the younger level, these lists frequently contain patterns the student had not yet learned. As a result, the student often spells by memorizing random letters instead of learning how to correctly write our phonetic language. While students eventually need to learn all the spelling patterns and know which spelling pattern to use for what word, foundational spelling skills are most effectively taught in a systematic manner grouped by common phonetic spelling patterns.

It is best to avoid all worksheet and activities that show words spelled incorrectly. You do NOT want the student to read incorrect spelling. Repeated exposure to incorrect spelling allows the student to build incorrect neural models of specific words and to actually learn combinations and patterns that do not exist in English. Check carefully! Many spelling worksheets and programs provide exposure to repeated incorrect spelling. While students do need to learn how to proofread and identify spelling errors, repeated exposure to incorrect spelling *in the learning stages* can be detrimental. If the student continually sees misspelled words they develop incorrect models of the words. In contrast, if the student learns the correct representation he is then better able to recognize incorrect spelling.

In addition, many spelling programs use inefficient activities to teach spelling. While puzzles and games such as solving codes, searching through word finds, unscrambling letters, and answering riddles, can be entertaining and provide other benefits these activities tend to be time consuming and often have limited value *in directly developing spelling skills*. Some of these activities such as jumbled letter arrangements can possibly confuse the development of correct spelling skills. At best these activities frequently consume large quantities of time on the activity itself (such as the searching process in a word find) instead of on developing a necessary skill (learning the correct written representation of words). In contrast, the highly effective and extremely efficient activity for directly developing spelling skills is to have the student repeatedly print the word correctly while saying the sound.

# C. Specific Recommendations for Learning Spelling Words (For the Student)

The following tips will help you develop effective spelling skills and study spelling words.

**Learn expected spelling patterns and helpful guidelines. Practice spelling by common patterns.**

**When learning how to spell specific words:**

1. First look at the written word and say the word, looking at how the sounds are written. This should be done *phonetically* NOT by letter name (for example: bird is /b//ir//d/ not the letter names B..I...R..D which is said /bee/ /ie/ /ar/ /dee/). Read the word once or twice paying attention to the sounds and how they are written.

2. Next write the word at least 5 times (10 times is better), taking care to *write* the letters *as you say the sound* that they make. Look at which letters are making what sounds. Pay close attention to the 'partner' letter combinations. For example when writing the word "bird" you write 'b' as you say /b/ and write 'ir' as you say the /er/ sound and write 'd' as you say the /d/ sound. Notice specifically which letters are representing the sound. This is especially critical for sounds that have multiple spellings (specifically note that in bird, the /er/ sound is made by the 'ir'). Be sure to practice by sounds not letter names.

3. For any multisyllable word, be sure and say and write the word by syllables. Example for the word 'consistent' you would write 'con' as you said /kun/, write 'sis' as you say /sis/, and write 'tent' as you say /tent/.

4. A helpful hint for learning how to spell a word is to pronounce all the sounds in the word, even if that is not how you actually say the word. We often speak 'lazy' English. This is fine in speaking and reading but it creates problems with accurate spelling. When you practice spelling completely pronounce all the sounds in the word. This often gives you a silly sounding 'proper' version of the word. Although we don't really say the word that way, it helps greatly when practicing spelling to say all the sounds. This is especially important with the 'schwa' pronunciation of many unstressed short vowels in multisyllable words where a 'proper' complete pronunciation of the short vowel sound greatly aids spelling. For example:
    - for 'clothes' say /clo**th**z/ not the usual lazy /cloze/
    - for 'family' say /fam- i -lee/ not the usual lazy /fam-lee/
    - for 'listen' say /lis-**t**en/ emphasizing the /t/ that is normally silent
    - for 'aunt' say /**aw**nt/ even if you usually pronounce it /ant/
    - for 'manual' say /man-yoo-**al**/ emphasizing the /a/ of the -al ending
    - for 'environment' say /en-vi-ron-ment/ instead of the usual /en-vi-ru-ment/
    - for 'magazine' say /mag-**a**-z**i**ne/ emphasizing the /ay/ sound for the a and saying the /ie/ sound for the 'i' in the last syllable instead of the actual /ee/ pronunciation

In summary, the most effective and efficient way to learn spelling words is write each word 5 to 10 times while saying the sounds. It is simple; all you need is paper and pencil. It's efficient because it you are not wasting time on processes that have nothing to do with spelling. It is highly effective because it directly builds knowledge in the correct printed representation of the word using multisensory processes of forming the letters(kinetic), seeing the correct print(visual), and saying/hearing the word (oral/auditory). Writing the word 5 to10 times provides the repetition that enhances learning. Simple! Effective! Efficient!

# Spelling Lessons
# Helpful Spelling Guidelines and Patterns

The following spelling lessons directly teach helpful spelling guidelines and patterns. Each lesson presents and explains a guideline and includes a list of applicable words (or reference to the reading lesson the words are located in). Read the guideline, look at the words, notice the specific spelling pattern. Have the student practice writing/spelling words meeting the guideline. Writing/spelling these words allows the student to 'see' and practice the expected patterns. The majority of these lessons are not memorizing a rule but rather learning the guideline or pattern and understanding how and why it works.

## Spelling Lesson 1:

### Every syllable has a vowel

Syllables are simply the hunks of sound within a spoken word that we say with a single puff of air. It is important to know **every syllable has a vowel.** Knowing that every syllable has a vowel is a fundamental element of spelling English words.

- Knowing every syllable has a vowel helps in spelling words where the final e is silent.

    Practice Words: little  sparkle  struggle  handle  angle  apple  article  triple  principle  flexible  possible  table  tumble  riddle  puzzle  fiddle  single  grumble  tumble  saddle  raffle  simple  bubble  terrible  brittle  cattle  jungle  stable  dazzle  dribble  candle  scribble

- Knowing every syllable has a vowel also helps the student look at a word and 'see' if it 'looks right'. If a syllable doesn't have a vowel then something is missing.


## Spelling Lesson 2:

### 'Silent e': Learning the 5 types of 'silent e' and knowing when to use the 'silent e'.

"Silent-e" is found at the end of many words. It is important to realize in most cases this 'silent-e' is *not* randomly added to the end of words. Although the 'e' is 'silent', it has very important purposes. There are five ways the 'silent-e' occurs. Spelling is easier when you understand the important functions of this 'silent e'. The five primary functions of 'silent-e' are:

1. In the vowel-consonant-e combinations the 'e' is needed to make the first vowel say its name. This is the most common occurrence of 'silent e' when the 'e' is acting as a necessary partner of the other vowel. It is not 'magic'. This 'e' has a specific function. The final, silent 'e' is the hardworking partner for the vowel in the vowel-consonant-e combination. (tim-time, bit-bite, at-ate, not-note, rob-robe, cod-code, home, strike, graze, flute)
Practice Words: See Reading Lessons # 22 - 26.

2. In words with 'ce' and 'ge' where the 'e' is necessary to make the 'c' have the /s/ sound (as in dance, chance, fence, justice, sentence, prance, prince, peace) or the 'g' have the /j/ sound (large, charge, manage, change, edge, fridge). This 'silent-e' is necessary to make the 'soft c' /s/ or 'soft g' /j/ sound.
Practice Words: See Reading Lesson # 27.

3. In words ending in **ve**: In the English language words do *not* end in **v**. Therefore, the '**e**' is added to the end simply to prevent the word from ending in 'v'. This 'e' often does not change the sound of other letters in the word.
   Practice Words: have, give, love, above, live, active, native, captive, passive, massive, active, negative, motive, relative, expensive, aggressive, descriptive, detective, sensitive, informative
   See Reading Lesson #64 for additional words.

4. In words with ending consonant blend and **le** ending, the 'e' is necessary because every syllable needs a vowel. This was explained in Spelling Lesson 1.
   Practice Words: See words listed in Spelling Lesson #1 on the preceding page.

5. And of course, some words have a final '**silent-e**' for no apparent phonetic reason. Maybe it is just to make spelling difficult and confusing! Although the 'e' is not needed phonetically, a spelling pattern does exist for many of these words. Notice most of the 'no-reason' silent-e words end in the /s/ or /z/ sound spelled with the letter 's'. These 'no-reason' silent-e words do need to be practiced and learned. Grouping by similar spelling patterns helps the student learn these words.
   Practice Words: (house, mouse, grouse, louse);(please, crease, lease, tease, grease, decrease, increase, release); (geese, cheese); (cruise, bruise); (cause, pause, because, clause); (loose, choose, goose); (some, come, done), horse, promise, noise.

# Spelling Lesson 3:

## No English words end with the letter i

No *English* words end with the letter 'i'. It is very helpful to remember this in spelling because **you must spell the word in a pattern that does NOT end in 'i'.**
- The /oy/ sound at the *end* of words is always spelled with 'oy' (boy, toy, ploy, destroy) as 'oi' can never be used at the end of a word. See Reading Lesson 30 for practice words.
- In the same way the /ay/ sound at the end of a word cannot be spelled with 'ai'. It must be 'ay' (play, away, stay) or another pattern (sleigh, they). See Lesson 20 for practice words.
- In spelling the 'ie' ending of words such as brownie, collie, cookie, rookie, and auntie you know the 'i' must come first as 'e' must end the word. See Lesson 38 for practice words.

Exceptions are words from *other* languages and proper names.
- taxi (short for taxicab);
- macaroni, manicotti, rigatoni, (The Italian 'noodle' words)
- radii, nuclei, (the plurals of some Latin words found mostly in math and science)
- alkali (French from an Arabic word); zucchini (Italian); chili (Spanish); kiwi (Maori)
- lei, Maui, Hawaii, Molokai (You guessed it; these are Hawaiian words.)
- Proper names can always provide exceptions. For example: location names (Cincinnati, Missouri, Mississippi… ), personal names (Jeni, Heidi, Toni…), and numerous surnames. There are also a few common nouns originating from proper names ending in 'i'. For example the wildland firefighting tool, 'pulaski' was named after Edward Pulaski, a US Forest Service Ranger and firefighter hero of the 'Big Burn' that raged though Idaho and western Montana in 1910.

While this trivia on word origination and search for exceptions may be interesting, the guideline "No English words end in the letter i" remains a very useful spelling guideline.

# Spelling Lesson 4:

## No English words end with the letter v

As previously discussed in the 'silent e' section, no English words end with the letter 'v'. If a word ends in the /v/ sound, you *must* add the 'silent e' to the end just so that the word does *not* end in 'v'. This is most common in the -tive and -ive suffixes.

Practice Words: See Spelling Lesson #2 "Silent e" words ending in -ve and Reading Lesson #64.

# Spelling Lesson 5:

## No English words end in the letter j

No English words end in the letter 'j'. Therefore if a word ends in the /j/ sound, you must spell the /j/ ending with either the 'ge' or 'dge' ending.

Practice Words: charge, barge, rage, strange, range, edge, ledge, pledge, stage, page, fridge, change, large, cottage, savage, engage, package and words from Reading Lesson 27 and 57.

# Spelling Lesson 6:

## If g= /j/ then it must be spelled 'g+e', 'g+i' or 'g+y'

To have the /j/ sound, g *must* be followed by 'e', 'i' or 'y'. Remember 'g' can keep the /g/ sound if 'e', 'i' or 'y' comes after it (get, give, girl, gift, gear, shaggy). However, *if* the 'g' has the /j/ sound an 'e', 'i' or 'y' must come immediately after the 'g'. This guideline is extremely helpful when accurately spelling words that contain the g=/j/ sounds.

- This helps to know when you must add the 'silent e' to some words that end in the g=/j/ sound (change, range, charge, large, savage, package, manage, voltage) See Spelling Lesson #2
- This helps you remember how to spell words such as 'angle' and 'angel' that can be easily confused.
- This helps when adding suffixes to words ending in 'ge'. For example to add 'able' to 'change' you must retain the 'e' ('changeable') to keep the /g/ sound. (More on suffixes in later spelling lessons)

Practice Words: gym, ginger, gentle, gyroscope, giant, giraffe, geometry, general, gender, energy, gypsy, biology, ecology, other -ology endings, Spelling Lesson #5 and Reading Lesson # 27 and #57

# Spelling Lesson 7

## The /j/ sound: Is the /j/ sound spelled with j, g or dge?

The /j/ sound can be made by either 1) the **j**, 2) the **g+e, g+i, or g+y**, or 3) the **dge** combination.

- The 'j' is *only* found at the beginning of syllables. (joy, juniper, jungle, reject, enjoy, rejoice, inject) Note: The 'j' spelling beginning syllables is not exclusive as 'g'=/j/ also begins syllables.

- For the letter 'g' to have the /j/ sound, the 'g' *must* be immediately followed by either 'e', 'i' or 'y'. See Spelling Lesson 6. Therefore if the /j/ sound is followed by any other vowel (a, u, or o) the 'j' spelling *must* be used. Practice Words: jam, jail, jacket, jade, jagged, jacks, jab, jaguar, join, joint, journal, jog, joke, journey, enjoy, just, juniper, jump, junk, jungle, judge, juvenile, justify).

- English words do not end in 'j'. Therefore, the /j/ sound at the *end* of a word needs to be spelled with 'ge' or 'dge'. See Spelling Lesson #5.

- The 'dge' spelling is used when the extra consonant 'd' is needed to retain the short vowel sound. The 'd' is necessary for 'blocking out' and preventing the 'e' after the 'g' from making the first vowel "say its name". Notice 'dge' is found at the end of words with the single short vowel sounds /a/, /e/ /i/ /o/ and /u/. (bridge, edge, wedge, ledge, badge, dodge, fudge, lodge, fridge, budge). The 'd' is necessary and added so there is a double consonant to prevent the 'e' from changing the short vowel sound to a long vowel sound. Without the silent 'd' the 'e' would act as a partner with the first vowel and change the vowel sound to a long sound (vowel-consonant-e combination). For example in 'page' notice how the 'e' both gives the 'a' the /ay/ sound in the vowel-consonant-e combination and also modifies 'g' to the /j/ sound. But the 'd' in 'badge' prevents the 'e' from changing the /a/ sound to /ay/ and retains the short /a/ sound. Badge without the 'd', 'bage' would be pronounced /b//ay//j/.

Practice Words: See Reading Lessons # 5, 27 and 57.

# Spelling Lesson 8

### If c = /s/ then it must be spelled c + e, i or y
c+e    c+i    c+y  =  /s/

The important fact that '**c always has the /s/ sound whenever e, i or y comes after it**' is extremely helpful when accurately spelling words that contain the c=/s/ sounds. This dictates the spelling guideline that to have the /s/ sound the 'c' *must* be followed by an e, i or y.
- This often tells us if a word with the /k/ sound is spelled with 'c' or 'k'. (kitten could not be spelled 'citten' as the c would have the /s/ sound and it would become /s//i//t//e//n/; rake has to be spelled with 'k' or else it would be 'race' /r//ay//s/).
- This helps in knowing when you must add the 'silent e' to some words that end in the c=/s/ sound. See Spelling Lesson #2. Practice Words: dance, trance, prince, practice, glance, since, entrance, notice, furnace, balance, distance, violence, justice, juice, allowance, and Reading Lesson # 27.
- This helps to correctly add suffixes to words that end in -ce. For example: change-changing-changeable and notice-noticeable-noticing. (More on suffixes in later Spelling Lessons)

# Spelling Lesson 9

**Spelling the /k/ sound:** The following guidelines help you accurately spell the /k/ sound. This lesson explains when to use 'c', 'k' and 'ck'. Additionally, the Greek 'ch'=/k/ and the /k/ sound within 'qu'=/kw/ are addressed.

**1. The beginning /k/ sound must be 'c' or 'k' (or sometimes 'ch' or 'qu'). The 'ck' spelling NEVER starts words.**

**2. \*\*Always remember c+e, c+i, c+y = the /s/ sound.** This guideline dictates when you must spell a word with 'k' to maintain the /k/ sound. Understanding this guideline helps you accurately spell the /k/ sound in many words. (See Spelling Lesson #8)

## 3. If the /k/ sound is immediately followed by e  i  or y, the 'k' spelling must be used.

The 'k' spelling is necessary to maintain the hard /k/ sound. If you spell the /k/ sound with 'c', the 'e', 'i' or 'y' would make the 'c' have the /s/ sound. Look at the spelling of rake-race, fake-face, brake-brace to demonstrate why the 'k' must be used to maintain the /k/ sound. Carefully look at the following words to see WHY the 'k' spelling *must* be used.

| kid | kind | king | keg | kitten | kite | kill |
|-----|------|------|-----|--------|------|------|
| kiss | kick | kitchen | kerosene | like | rake | brake |
| strike | basket | parakeet | kept | keep | kennel | poke |
| stroke | choke | skin | skip | skirmish | skirt | sky |
| pumpkin | markers | snake | ketchup | key | monkey | basket |

## 4. If the /k/ sound is followed by any other letter (NOT 'e', 'i', or 'y') the /k/ sound is usually spelled with 'c'.

**The /k/ sound followed by other vowels (a, o, u) is USUALLY spelled with 'c':**

| cot | camp | call | cut | cover | capitol |
|-----|------|------|-----|-------|---------|
| cast | come | cap | color | computer | cart |
| camel | can | car | carry | cash | cat |
| cave | cove | collect | code | cow | coin |
| count | confess | cone | curl | curve | coil |
| contest | cure | cover | consider | coat | copy |

**ALMOST ALL consonant blends when /k/ is FOLLOWED by another consonant sound, the /k/ sound is spelled with 'c':** (the 'cr' and 'cl' are commonly encountered k+consonant blends)

| clip | clasp | clue | crisp | class | clank |
|------|-------|------|-------|-------|-------|
| clam | clear | cloak | club | crunch | crazy |
| script | scream | cross | cramp | crumble | crown |
| clover | classic | scroll | screw | scratch | screen |
| scrub | scribe | act | insect | respect | inspect |
| strict | deflect | reject | obstruct | destruct | object |
| product | predict | perfect | | | |

There are exceptions to this expected pattern of spelling the /k/ sound with 'c' when it is followed by letters other than 'e', 'i' or 'y'. The exceptions are primarily proper nouns and unusual words.

-Some exceptions to the /k/ + a, o, u include: kangaroo, koala, kayak, kudos, karate, kazoo, skunk, skull, and skate. Other exceptions are primarily proper nouns (Kansas, Koran, Kodiak, Korea, Karachi, Kabul) or unusual words (karyoplasms, kumiss, kumquat, kurbash, kapok, kana, kolinsky) Most exceptions are not everyday words unless you happen to be studying advanced cell microbiology or learning about fermented mare's milk drunk by the nomads of central Asia.

-Exceptions to the expected 'c' for /k/ + consonant words are a few proper nouns (Klondike, Klamath, Klein, Kremlin…) or uncommon (klystron, klaxon, krait, krona, kloof). There are only a few 'k+consonant words that would likely be read by most students (krill, kleptomaniac). The vast majority of blends where /k/ is followed by a consonant ARE spelled with 'c'.

## 5. WORDS with the /kw/ sound (/k/+/w/) ARE SPELLED with 'qu';
There are NO 'cw' spellings and NO 'kw' spellings in English. The only exceptions are a few Chinese provinces such as Kwangtung and Kweichow, and words such as kwacha, the monetary unit of Zambia. Therefore it is very helpful to teach students the /k+w/ sound IS spelled with 'qu'.

## 6. The ending 'k' sounds a slightly more complex:

**The 'ck' is ONLY used at the END OF A SYLLABLE with a SINGLE SHORT VOWEL SOUND.** *Most* 'ck' words are one syllable single short vowel words or these one-syllable base words with a prefix or suffix. (pack-unpack-packing; back-backed-backing; luck-unlucky-lucked). A few other words use the 'ck' spelling to maintain the /k/ spelling. Once again this 'ck' spelling occurs *only* at the end of a single, short vowel syllable ending with the /k/ sound. Look and you can see why the 'ck' spelling is necessary to maintain both the short vowel sound and the ending /k/ sound. (locket, picket, ticket, rocket, package, racket). Note this 'ck' spelling is only used ending single short vowel syllables. It is not used with vowel combinations, long vowel sounds, r-controlled vowel combinations or blended consonant endings.

| sick | back | stick | black | rack | chuck |
|------|------|-------|-------|------|-------|
| sock | stuck | rock | flick | deck | duck |
| muck | lick | track | stack | pack | crack |
| slick | shack | kick | pick | block | fleck |
| packet | rocket | sticking | packing | chucked | rocking |
| flicking | racket | locket | truck | unpack | package |

**Most SINGLE SYLLABLE words with vowel combinations or consonant clusters ENDING in the /k/ sound are spelled with 'k':** Words with any combination except the single short vowel word/syllable endings.

| folk | ask | walk | milk | silk | elk |
|------|-----|------|------|------|-----|
| balk | talk | bulk | risk | mask | task |
| bank | tank | thank | pink | bunk | hawk |
| rink | caulk | peek | beak | break | steak |
| pork | disc | shark | hook | look | dark |
| book | spark | pork | mark | peak | frisk |
| task | work | | | | |

**The final /k/ sound in MULTISYLLABLE WORDS is USUALLY spelled with a 'c'**

| picnic | plastic | panic | stoic | economic | metric |
|--------|---------|-------|-------|----------|--------|
| periodic | politic | basic | medic | acidic | terrific |
| domestic | public | pediatric | frolic | historic | automatic |
| classic | clinic | patriotic | prolific | graphic | topic |

Also note the pattern: When a prefix or suffix is added to a base word, the same 'ck' or 'k' spelling is usually maintained. (pack-repack-unpack-packed-packing; hook-unhook-hooking-hooked; mark-marked-marking-remark; walk-walking; public-republic). There are a few exceptions when the spelling of the base word is changed when suffixes beginning with 'e', 'i' or 'y' are added and would alter the sound of the word. This occurs with some of the multisyllable words ending in the 'c' spelling such as picnic and frolic. In these words the spelling of the ending is changed from 'c' to 'ck' when the suffix is added in order to maintain the /k/ sound and the short vowel sound (picnic - picnicking, frolic - frolicking, panic-panicking-panicked)

## 7. *To keep things interesting, a few Greek words use 'ch' spelling for the /k/ sound:
You just need to learn these!

| Christ | school | scheme | ache | chronic | chromosome |
|--------|--------|--------|------|---------|------------|
| character | chlorine | chorus | chronicle | Christmas | Christian |

See Reading Lesson # 59 for additional words.

(The 'kn' spelling is NOT covered in this lesson as the 'kn'=/n/ and is not a spelling for the /k/ sound.)

# Spelling Lesson 10

## The /ch/ sound: Is the /ch/ spelled with ch or tch?

**The 'ch' spelling for /ch/:**
- **ch** is by far the most frequent spelling of the /ch/ sound
- **ch** is *always* used at the beginning of a word or syllable (chest, chimp, check, chum, chat, chip, chin, chess, chap, chant, chop, chick, chug, champ, choice, change, cheap, checkers, cheer)
- **ch** is used when there is a consonant sound immediately preceding the /ch/ sound (lunch, pinch, ranch, branch, hunch, crunch, inch, pinch, flinch, crunch, bunch, brunch, belch, mulch, trench)
- **ch** is used for the /ch/ sound following all vowel combinations (roach, reach, coach, preach, pouch, teach, touch, crouch, speech ) and r-controlled vowel combinations (march, birch, church, porch, starch, larch, torch, parched)

**The 'tch' spelling for /ch:**
- The **'tch'** spelling is **only** used when the /ch/ sound is the end of a word or syllable immediately following a single short vowel sound. (batch, itch, fetch, match, notch, catch, ditch, latch, patch, hutch, stitch, pitch, catching, pitching, and hatchet) The 'tch' spelling pattern is limited to this syllable ending /ch/ for single short vowel words. Also note, these are primarily one-syllable words or variations of these base words with affixes added (fetch-fetching, latch-unlatch).
- NOTE: such, much and rich are exceptions (these are spelled with the 'ch' spelling)

In summary, the **'ch'** spelling is used for the /ch/ sound except for the final /ch/ in a syllable with a single short vowel sound when the 'tch' is used. Practice Words: See Reading Lesson # 6

# Spelling Lesson 11

## Doubling consonants at end of one syllable words (f, l , s )

Sometimes consonants are doubled at the end of a word. The letters most frequently doubled are **f, l & s**. With **one syllable** words with **one vowel** that end in f, l s or z, the final letter is *usually* doubled.
Practice words:
   **ff:** puff, gruff, stuff, off, stiff, staff, fluff, bluff
   **ll:** ill, pill, dill, cell, tell, well, yell, still, doll, bell, tall, shell, fell, hill, grill, frill, chill, drill, ball, all, fall, hall, mall, wall, pull, full, kill
   **ss:** dress, mess, miss, pass, toss, less, glass, mass, chess, bass, class, bliss, gloss, press, cross, stress

# Spelling Lesson 12

## These consonants are not doubled (j, k, w, v, x )

In English, the consonants j, k, w, v and x are never doubled. The only exceptions are a few compound words such as 'bookkeeper', 'jackknife' whose parts happen to end and begin with the same letter and a few slang words ('savvy' and 'divvy'). It is not necessary to memorize this guideline. However, through reading and writing the student should recognize these letters doubled 'look wrong'. (One of the reasons the student should not practice spelling incorrectly or be exposed to repeated incorrect spelling.)

# Spelling Lesson 13

## Is the word spelled with 'ie' or 'ei'?

Remember **"i before e, except after c, or sounding as /ay/ in neighbor and sleigh" and a few exceptions.** I am not a big proponent of memorizing rules but it is very useful to memorize this one. To this day I still use this 'i before e' rhyme my mom taught me years ago to correctly spell many 'ei'/'ie' words. This 'guideline' as well as knowing that English words do NOT end in 'i' is very helpful in spelling the often confusing 'ie'/'ei' words. You also need to learn the common exceptions.

- **"i before e"**:
  belief, believe, thief, brief, grief, chief, yield, relief, shield, field, friend, priest, niece, shriek
- **"except after c"**
  receive, receipt, ceiling, conceive, deceive, perceive, deceit
- **"or sounding as 'ay' in neighbor and sleigh**:
  eight, sleigh, freight, neighbor, weigh, weight
- **"and the common exceptions"**
  either, neither, height, seize, weird (As in "Spelling is so weird at times!")
- **And don't forget….words can not end in 'i'**
  collie, brownie, cookie, rookie

# Spelling Lesson 14

## "When 2 vowels go walking the first usually does the talking (but not always!)"
*****This is an essential vowel 'guideline' to know and understand !!!!!*****

*It is important to know and understand that usually when vowels are together (BOTH when they are standing right next to each other and also often when they are separated by only one consonant) the first vowel will usually 'talk' or 'say its name'* (make the long vowel sound). Although there are exceptions, this basic knowledge helps greatly with spelling many words.

- This helps with remembering how to spell the basic vowel combination words. (For example: boat is spelled 'oa' not 'ao' because the first vowel does the talking.)
- This helps in spelling the vowel-consonant-e words in understanding when to add the 'silent e' (for 'time' you add the e to make the 'i' say /ie/, without the 'silent e' the word would be /tim/).
- This knowledge helps in accurately adding suffixes. Many of the lists of 'rules' and directions for handling the addition of suffixes to words can be explained and understood with this single fundamental 'when two vowels go walking' guideline. For example, this explains why you must add the 2$^{nd}$ 'p' to 'hop' when you add the '-ing' suffix to correctly spell 'hopping'.
- This knowledge helps you understand when you must spell words with the 'dge' ending to maintain the short vowel sound (ledge, badge, fridge) or spell words such as 'package' with the correct 'ck'.

It is critical for the student to understand this fundamental concept of two vowels working together. It is not memorizing the little 'when two vowels go walking' rhyme in isolation, but fully understanding how vowels impact each other. The way I explain the concept to younger students is to make an analogy between the 2 vowels and 2 buddies poking each other in class. When the buddies poke each other, one of them will squawk. For vowel buddies, the first vowel usually 'says' its name or the long sound when its buddy 'pokes' it. I use this analogy because it is helpful not only with reading but also in explaining how to handle consonants with spelling. When the two students are in line 'poking' each other and making noise, the teacher splits them apart. If the teacher splits them with only one other student they can still reach around and poke each other. This is why the vowels in the vowel-consonant-e combinations can still impact each other. They can still 'reach around' the single consonant and poke their buddy. To keep the students or vowels 'quiet' the teacher must split the troublemakers by 2 people. Or in the case of vowels, you need to split the vowels by 2 consonants so they are too far apart to reach around and 'poke' each other. Use your own explanation, but insure the student fully understands this important concept.

**Lesson 15 - 21 give the detailed explanations of adding suffixes under certain situations. Don't try to memorize all the variations. Simply look at and try to understand how they work and practice the patterns.**

# Spelling Lesson 15

**Adding Plural Endings: How do you spell words with plural endings?**

- For **most words** just **add s.** (cat-cats, tiger-tigers, table-tables, tree-trees, train-trains, storm-storms)

- If the words **end in s, ch, sh or x,** you need to **add es.** These are the words that you can *not* verbally add or say the /s/ sound without adding the /es/ syllable. You do not need to memorize this guideline. Simply, *listen* to how you say the word! (class-classes, watch-watches, dish-dishes, tax-taxes, fix--fixes)

- If the words **end in vowel-y combination** (ay, oy, uy) just **add s.** These are the same as most regular words. (boy-boys, toy-toys, play-plays, key-keys)

- If the words **end in consonant-y** need to **change the y to i and add es.** (city--cities, fly-flies, pony--ponies, party--parties, cry--cries)

- In *some* words that **end in f** you need to **change the f to v and add es.** (leaf-leaves, shelf--shelves, calf--calves, half--halves)

- There are exceptions with irregular words that have their unique plural form (mouse-mice, goose-geese, child-children, foot-feet, man-men, ox-oxen). These irregular words just need to be learned. Luckily once you verbally know the correct plural form of the word, most are spelled phonetically.

Practice Words: See Reading Lesson #62.

# Spelling Lesson 16

**Adding the -ed past tense ending to verbs: How do you spell past tense verbs?**

- The past tense suffix for verbs is spelled **'-ed'**. This '-ed' suffix is pronounced three different ways depending on the ending sound of the base word. It is pronounced either: 1) /id/ (graded, blasted) 2) /d/ (loved, climbed) or 3) /t/ (baked, hopped, wrecked). In reading and speaking we usually say the word without noticing these variances. However, in spelling it is important to realize the past tense verb ending is spelled '-ed' regardless of the pronunciation.

- Notice when words end in **'silent e'** you drop the original 'silent-e' when adding '-ed' as the 'e' in the '-ed' ending takes over the 'silent-e' duty. Or you use the existing 'e' and just add 'd' to the make the '-ed' ending. Either explanation results in only one 'e' for the '-ed' suffix. (Don't create a double 'ee' in the word (create--created, waste--wasted, bake--baked, race--raced).

- With the words that end in **consonant-y** (cry, try, spy, baby, party, hurry)… **change the y to i and add -ed** (cried, tried, spied, babied, partied, hurried..). This still keeps the '-ed' spelling of the past tense, except you must first change the y to i before adding the -ed.

- With 'short vowel' words you often need to double the final consonant so that the 'e' in the 'ed' ending does not change the sound of the first vowel (hop--hopped, bat-batted, grab--grabbed, grip-gripped). More on this in the next guideline!

- English contains irregular words that have their unique past-tense form. These must be learned. The good news is that most of these are commonly used in oral language and once you verbally know the accurate past tense form, most are spelled phonetically. (run-ran, fall-fell, write-wrote, fly-flew, grow-grew, make- made, ride-rode, eat-ate, fly-flew, speak-spoke, sing-sang, draw-drew…)

Practice words: See Reading Lesson 63.

# Spelling Lesson 17

**General patterns for adding suffixes to words that have a short vowel sound and one consonant at the end:**

When you add suffixes that begin with vowels (such as -ed, -ing, -y, -er, -ous, -ish,) to the end of words that have a short vowel sound and end with only one consonant, you need to take care to ensure the sound of that short vowel is NOT changed by the addition of the suffix. (Remember your understanding of "when 2 vowels go walking"). How you handle this *depends* on if it is a one-syllable or multisyllable words. If it is a multisyllable word, the syllable accent determines how you handle adding the suffix.

When you add suffixes that begin with vowels (such as -ed, -ing, -y, -er, -ous, -ish) to **one-syllable words** with short vowel sounds that end in single consonants (run, hop, drop, kid, bug, sun, hit) you first need to double the consonant so that the short vowel sound is maintained (running, hopped, dropping, kidding, sunny, hitter). With this understanding you will realize that if the one-syllable word already ends in two consonants, then simply add the suffix (fast--fastest, gift-gifted, grant-granting).

Of course it can't be too simple. So with **multi-syllable words** that have the short vowel sound, the consonants are ONLY doubled when you add suffixes that begin with vowels **if** the last syllable short vowel sound is the accented syllable. If last syllable is *not* accented no doubling is necessary (as in… exit --exiting; visit--visited; profit--profiting; happen--happening) If the last syllable *is* accented then the doubling of the consonant is necessary to maintain the short vowel sound (forgot--forgotten, permit--permitted, admit--admitting). This takes listening to the word, practice and yes, some memorization and checking with a dictionary.

# Spelling Lesson 18

**General Patterns for adding suffixes to words with "silent e' at the end:**

When suffixes that begin with a vowel (-es, -ed, -ing, -er, -y , -ity, ) are added to words with a 'silent e' at the end, the silent e is often dropped because the vowel in the suffix provides the 'partner' vowel to maintain the proper sound in the first vowel. Check to see if you are maintaining the proper sounds. (rake-raking, bake-baking, save-saving, vote-voter, smoke-smoker, dance-dancer-dancing, give--giving, replace--replacing, grade--grading, safe--safer--safest, trade--trader--trading, brave--bravest).

# Spelling Lesson 19

## General Patterns for adding suffixes to words that end consonant-y:

When you add suffixes that begin with a vowel (-es, -er, -ing, -ed, -ish, -est ) to the end of words that end in the consonant-y:

- Most often you change the 'y' to 'i' and add the suffix the same as was previously discussed in spelling past tense -ed and plural endings. For example cry-cried-cries, dry-dried-dries, baby-babied-babies, fly-flies-flier, candy-candies, silly-silliest, foggy-foggiest, hungry-hungriest-hungrier, happy-happiest-happier.
- However, you can *not* have a double 'i' (ii). So in the suffixes that begin with 'i' (such as -ing and -ish) you just add the suffix without changing the y. (dry-drying, baby-babyish, fly-flying, cry-crying, try-trying, carry-carrying)

# Spelling Lesson 20

## General Patterns for adding suffixes to words ending in -ce /s/ or -ge /j/ sounds:

Remember the c+e, c+i, or c+y is necessary in order to create the c=/s/ sound. (Spelling Lesson 8)
Remember that g+e, g+i, or g+y is necessary in order to have the g=/j/ sound. (Spelling Lesson 6)

When adding suffixes to the end of words that have the -ce /s/ sound or the -ge /j/ sound, just remember the important fact that for 'c' to have the /s/ sound or for the 'g' to have the /j/ sound it MUST be followed by 'e', 'i' or 'y'. Knowing and understanding this important guideline helps explain many spelling patterns with suffixes:

**If the suffix does NOT begin with 'e', 'i', or 'y', you must keep the -e before adding the suffix in order to maintain the soft /s/ or /j/ sound.** This is often with the -ous, -able suffixes because the 'a' or 'o' would not keep the 'soft' /j/ or /s/ sound. In the following examples notice how the 'e' is necessary to maintain the /j/ or /s/ sound:

    change---changeable    courage-courageous    notice--noticeable
    outrage--outrageous    embrace--embraceable    enforce-enforceable-enforcing
    service--serviceable    knowledge--knowledgeable    replace--replaceable

**If the suffix begins with 'e', 'i' or 'y', you usually drop the 'e' because the 'e', 'i' or 'y' in the suffix maintains either the /s/ or /j/ sound.** In suffixes such as '-ing', '-y', '-ed', and '-er' the leading 'e', 'i' or 'y' vowel in the suffix maintains the /s/ or /j/ sound. Notice how dropping the 'e' does not alter the sound.

    change--changing--changed    replace--replacing--replaced    dance--dancing--dancer
    fleece--fleecy    place--placing--placed    practice--practicing-practiced
    race--racing--racer--raced    service--servicing-served-server

# Spelling Lesson 21

## Adding Suffixes to many other words

When you add many suffixes to most other words (words that do not contain short vowel sounds in the last syllable, do not end with the ge/j/ or ce/s/ sound, or do not end in 'silent e') or when adding suffixes that start with consonants (such as -ly, -ness, -ment, -ful, -less) you usually add the suffix with no changes to the base word. For example:
>join-joining; park-parking; punish-punishable; deep-deeper; disagree-disagreeable; short-shortest; lone-lonely; quiet-quietly, year-yearly, bright-brightly, pay-payment, place-placement, rest-restless; fear-fearless; speech-speechless; grow-growing; perfect-perfectly; high-higher; strict-stricter

Practice Words: Reading Lesson #70 contains word lists grouped by common suffix.

# Spelling Lesson 22

## Spelling the -ful suffix

The word "full" is spelled with two ll's. *However* when the "full" is used in multisyllable words as a suffix to mean full of or characterized by, the suffix is spelled -ful with only one l.
Practice words: See Reading Lesson # 70

# Spelling Lesson 23

## Spelling with -able or -ible suffix

The -able and -ible suffixes (which both mean capable of or likely to) often sound the same. So which one do you use to correctly spell a word? There are a couple of patterns that can help. First, based on frequency, the '-able' is used more often than the '-ible'. Secondly, although this does not always work, often **if the base word is complete or when the only change is dropping the 'silent e'** before you add the -able you spell the suffix '-able' (bendable, agreeable, favorable, manageable, readable, punishable, notable, desirable, escapable, comfortable, profitable, reasonable, laughable). If the base word is **incomplete (Hint: i=incomplete)** without the suffix then often the "-ible" spelling is used (terrible, edible, reducible, visible, tangible, horrible, possible, visible, reducible, accessible, sensible, plausible, feasible, divisible). Also notice the pattern with the '-ible' spelling: many of the base words that are spelled with '-ible' end in the /s/ or /z/ sound.

Practice Words: See Reading Lesson # 70 for a list of words with the '-able' and '-ible' endings.

# Spelling Lesson 24

## Spelling with the suffix -ist or -est

The suffix -ist and -est sound the same when saying a word. How do you know which one to use to correctly spell the word?

The **-est** spelling is by far the more common and **means the superlative degree** (longest, quickest, fastest, highest, greatest, slowest, tallest). A list of words is found in Reading Lesson #70.

The **-ist** is **someone who does something** (druggist, artist, pianist, typist).

# Spelling Lesson 25

## Spelling with 'ant-ance-ancy' OR the 'ent-ence-ency' endings

The suffixes -ant & -ent; -ance & -ence; -ancy & -ency sound the same. So which one is the 'correct' spelling?

- Frequently by looking at the spelling of the base word you can determine which suffix to use. Although it does not always work, the following examples show the usual pattern:

**ent-ence-ency**:

| | | |
|---|---|---|
| absent - absence | adhere - adherence | affluent - affluence |
| confident - confidence | confluent - confluence | decent - decency |
| delinquent - delinquency | different - difference | fluent - fluency |
| independent - independence | frequent - frequency | negligent - negligence |
| potent - potency | resident - residency | solvent - solvency |
| turbulent - turbulence | urgent - urgency | violent - violence |

**ant-ance-ancy**:

| | | |
|---|---|---|
| abundant - abundance | brilliant - brilliance | distant - distance |
| expectant - expectance | fragrant - fragrance | jubilant - jubilance |
| ignorant - ignorance | observance - observant | reluctant - reluctance - reluctancy |
| redundant - redundancy | significant - significance | truant - truancy |
| tolerant - tolerance | vagrant - vagrancy - vagrancy | variant - variance |
| vibrant - vibrancy | vigilant - vigilance | |

- Another tool for determining the correct spelling is to apply the guidelines for 'g' = /j/ and 'c'=/s/. If the base word ends in the 'g' = /j/ or 'c' = /s/ the '-ence or -ency' spelling must be used so the 'e' maintains the /s/ or /j/ sound. (See Spelling Lessons # 6 and #8). For example:

| | | |
|---|---|---|
| agent - agency | converge - convergence | emerge - emergent - emergence |
| intelligent - intelligence | translucent - translucence | insurgent - insurgence - insurgency |

- Finally, if you know how to spell one variation of the word you can often determine the correct spelling of the other endings. For example, if you know how to spell 'tolerant' you could correctly spell 'tolerance' by applying the consistent 'ant-ance' pattern.


# Spelling Lesson 26

## Spelling the /tion/ endings:

There are 4 ways to spell /shun/ at ending of a multisyllable word (-tion, -sion, -cian, -cion). These special suffixes are found in the second or subsequent syllables of a multisyllable word. There are a few patterns that help you spell these words.

- First, consider frequency of occurrence. The **-tion** spelling is by far the most common spelling of the /shun/ ending. The **-sion** spelling is next in frequency. This frequency pattern is helpful because thousands of words use the '-tion' spelling compared to only about 200 words that use the -sion spelling. The **-cian** occurs only in a limited number of words referring to a person or occupation. The unexpected **'-cion'** spelling is rarely used, found only in two words (suspicion and coercion).

- Although it does not always work, often the use of **-tion** or **-sion** can be determined by the spelling of the root word.

  **Root word spelled with 't', use -tion**:
  create--creation   direct--direction   decorate--decoration   pollute -- pollution
  edit -- edition   promote--promotion   violate--violation   frustrate--frustration

  **Root word spelled with 's', use -sion:**
  tense--tension   confess--confession   express--expression   televise--television
  confuse--confusion   process--procession   transgress--transgression

- The **-cian** is limited to words for person or occupation: electri**cian**  physi**cian**  musi**cian**  techni**cian**

- The **-cion** is *rarely* used. This unexpected spelling is only found in 'suspicion' and 'coercion'. You just need to learn these!

Practice Words: See Reading Lesson # 72.

# Spelling Lesson 27

## Spelling the /shal/ and /shus/ endings:

- **-cial or -tial:** There are 2 ways to spell /shal/ at ending of multisyllable word, **-cial** or **-tial**. The -cial is more common and often can be determined by the spelling of the root word,
  **cial:** race--racial   finance--financial   glacier-- glacial   office-official
  **tial:** part -- partial

- **-tious or -cious**: There are two ways to spell the /shus/ ending, **-tious** or **-cious**. The spelling of the root word often helps you spell these words.
  **tious:** infect-infectious
  **cious:** grace - gracious   space-spacious

- Knowledge of how other variations of the word are spelled helps in spelling these unusual /shal/ and /shus/ endings: For example: If you know 'caution' it helps you spell 'cautious' correctly. If you know 'ambition' it helps you spell 'ambitious'.

Practice Words: See Reading Lesson #73.

# Spelling Lesson 28

Spelling Words When Adding Prefixes:

Prefixes are usually just added to the base word with no change.

dis + appear = disappear, dis + continue = discontinue, dis + agree = disagree
un + happy = unhappy;  un + clear = unclear;
re + turn = return, re + place = replace, re + make = remake,
pre + arrange = prearrange, pre + test = pretest, pre+school=preschool, pre + historic = prehistoric

Practice Words: See the lists of common prefixes in Reading Lesson #69.

# Spelling Lesson 29

Spelling "all" when it is used as part of other words:

The word "all" (the entire substance or every) is spelled with two l's. However, when "all" is used as a part of another word, it usually is spelled with only one l.

Practice Words: almost, always, almighty, altogether, already, although

# Spelling Lesson 30

Other 'unique' aspects of English effect accurate spelling.

English contains a number of homophones (Greek for same-sound). These are words that sound the same but with different meanings. The spelling is different for the different meanings. Students simply need to learn the correct spelling that matches the definition. The following lists some of these homophones:

| | | | | |
|---|---|---|---|---|
| ate - eight | bear - bare | be - bee | beat - beet | blew - blue |
| bread - bred | by - buy | course - coarse | dear - deer | do- due - dew |
| fair-fare | feet - feat | flee - flea | flour - flower | for - four - fore |
| grown - groan | guessed - guest | heel - heal | here - hear | heard - herd |
| hare - hair | hire - higher | horse - hoarse | I - eye | its - it's |
| know - no | load - lode | loan - lone | made - maid | mail - male |
| main - mane | mall - maul | meat - meet | new - knew | need - kneed |
| night - knight | pail - pale | pain -pane | pause - paws | peace - piece |
| peak - peek | pear -- pare | peer - pier | pen - pin | poor-pore-pour |
| pray - prey | principal - principle | rain - rein | rap - wrap | red - read |
| ring - wring | road - rode | sale-sell-cell-sail | scent - cent | see - sea |
| seen - scene | sight - site - cite | so- sew | some - sum | sore - soar |
| stare - stair | sun - son | tail -tale | there - their | tin - ten |
| to - too - two | through - threw | so - sew | stationery-stationary | steal - steel |
| waive - wave | wait - weight | way - weigh | week - weak | whole - hole |
| won - one | write - right | would - wood | your - you're | you - ewe |

The English language also has homographs (Greek for same-writing). A homograph is a word that is spelled the same as another word with a different meaning and often pronunciation. While spelling remains consonant, the only way to determine the meaning and pronunciation of the word is by context.

   bear (Grizzly bears live in Montana. He wasn't able to bear weight on his sprained ankle.)
   bow (I tied a red bow on the package. Take a bow at the end of the performance).
   close (Please close the door. He needs to sit close to the front so he can see the board.)
   dove (The white dove flew by the window. The boy dove into the water.)
   lead (My pencil lead broke. The teacher will lead the children to the bus.)
   minute (We'll leave in one minute. You need a microscope to see the minute organisms.)
   present (I got a birthday present from Dad. Please present your idea to the class.)
   read (I read the book. You need to read this book.)
   record (She broke the state record in the 3000 meter race. Can you record this song for me?)
   right (Turn right at the corner. You got the right answer.)
   sow (A mother pig is called a sow. The farmer needs to sow the seeds.)
   tear (Tear drops help clean dirt out of your eyes. Don't tear up the paper.)
   wind (The wind is blowing. Please wind up the clock.)
   wound (Cover the wound with the bandage. She wound up the clock.)

# Spelling Lesson 31

**There will be exceptions to the guidelines and expected patterns. At times spelling will be tricky and frustrating!**

Although phonetic spelling and knowledge of the guidelines are very helpful for *most* words, there will be exceptions to the guidelines and expected patterns. In other words, while these guidelines can greatly improve spelling, at times the only strategy is to simply learn the word. The solution for improved spelling is to make it easy as possible by spelling phonetically, learning expected patterns, practicing correct spelling and keeping a dictionary handy to look up words.

## Review Spelling Tips:

### ~ Spell phonetically ~
Base spelling on writing the sounds of the word instead of memorizing random letters.

### ~ Learn guidelines and expected spelling patterns ~
Learning and understanding the structure of our written language and the fundamental guidelines of 'how it works' and 'why it works' is always easier than memorizing thousands and thousands of individual words. Learning the expected spelling patterns is a valuable tool for improving spelling. A table summarizing the spelling patterns for specific sounds is located in Appendix E.

### ~ Practice Correct Spelling ~
Read and write words correctly. Avoid all incorrect representations. The more often you read and especially write words correctly the better your spelling becomes. Writing words, paying careful attention to the correct sounds as you write, is especially helpful in developing correct neural models of the word. Always practice accurate representations of our written language.

### ~ Use a Dictionary ~
The vast majority of spelling does not occur during a spelling test but rather in real life applications. If you are not sure how to spell a word, LOOK IT UP! A dictionary is a valuable tool. Looking up the word in a dictionary allows you to write the word correctly. Not only does this make your writing accurate at that point in time but it also develops and strengthens the knowledge bank of accurate representation of our written language.

### ~ Note words you misspell and practice those specific words ~
Keep a list of the words that you frequently misspell and practice those specific words. Pick a few at a time and write them in isolation.

### ~ Make short 'cheat sheet' of words you frequently find yourself looking up ~
Most individuals have a few troublesome words that they continually misspell. It seems, no matter how many times you look up and write the word you still seem to forget how to spell it correctly. If you wear out the pages of your dictionary repeatedly looking up the same words over and over, make yourself a quick reference 'cheat sheet' and tape it inside the front cover of your dictionary. (I have restaurant and museum on my list.)

### ~ Remember, spell check programs are only a tool ~
While useful, do not depend entirely on automatic spell check programs. These programs have definite limitations. They do not find all errors. In addition, the automatic features will often make inaccurate adjustments.

# APPENDIX A
# SOUND PRONUNCIATION

The following table explains correct pronunciation of the sounds and provides the key for how sounds are indicated throughout this book. This table is a reference for the parent/instructor. (Student directions are in the lessons.) ***Speech difficulties are briefly addressed following the pronunciation table. This discusses the speech developmental issues where a student has difficulty saying certain sounds.**

It is critical to teach these sounds to the student correctly from the beginning.
- Make sure you can say the isolated sound correctly before instructing the student.
- Take care to not add sounds that do not belong (for example 't' is a quick /t/ not /tuh/, r is /rr/ not /er/ or /ruh/).
- Teach the sound the letter represents in our language NOT the letter name. For most letters these are not the same thing, (the letter t is pronounced /t/ not /tee/, m is /m/ not /im/.) Students need to know the letter names for other reasons but *to read* the student must link the printed letter(s) directly to the sound the letter represents in our language.
- Some sounds must be said quickly. If these 'fast' sounds such as t, d, p, k , are not said quickly, a vowel sound is usually erroneously added (t becomes /tuh/). Always say these sounds quickly.
- Some sounds are more difficult for some students to say (such as h, r ). Other sounds are more difficult to distinguish (/t/-/d/, /b/-/p/, /k/-/g/, and /f/-/v/-the soft /th/) Pay extra attention to these sounds and be sure the student is pronouncing them correctly and distinguishing them correctly. For example, this is why in speaking some children say 'baff' for bath or 'haf' for have. They do not distinguish and say the sounds correctly. This type of error needs a little work on speech/pronunciation.

The sound pronunciation table shows:

1) The phonogram (letter or partner letters): These are listed in the same order as they are presented in the lessons.

2) The sound(s) for each phonogram: the sound is always shown between slashes /_/ (for example /m/). This pronunciation key shows how the sound will be indicated throughout the book.

3) An indicator if the sound must be said quickly: The sounds specifically listed as a 'fast' sound *must* be said quickly to prevent distortion. These 'fast' sounds such as /t/ and /d/ can NOT be said slowly. If they are said slowly, the student usually adds an additional vowel sound (/t/ becomes /tuh/). If the sound is not listed as 'fast', it can be stretched out without distorting the sound. (such as /mmmm/ or /ssssss/).

4) Notes or explanation of any pertinent information to help describe the sound. This includes descriptive notes and examples of the sound in a few words. These words can be used to check if you are saying the sound correctly and as a tool to help you determine and isolate the individual sound the letter makes.

5) An additional note of caution is included for some of the sounds that are commonly mispronounced when said in isolation. This serves as a heads up to help avoid common pronunciation errors on these sounds. Helpful tips for teaching students to pronounce the sounds correctly are included.

**\*Speech difficulties where a student has a difficulty saying certain sounds are briefly addressed following the pronunciation table (see page 265).**

# Sound Pronunciation Table

| letter or letters | sound | note if sound 'fast' | any pertinent explanation and example of the sound in words | notes of caution |
|---|---|---|---|---|
| m | /m/ | | am, mat, me | not /muh/ or /im/ |
| t | /t/ | 'fast' > | this is a quick /t/ <br> sit, at, tag | not /tuh/ |
| a | 1. /a/ <br><br> 2. /ay/ <br> -------- <br> (3)/ah/ | | 1. the /a/ sound is the 'short' vowel sound as in..... at, apple, rat <br> 2. the /ay/ sound is the 'long' vowel sound as in....... ape, late, navy <br> (3rd pronunciation /ah/ as in father about) | |
| s | 1. /s/ <br><br> 2. /z/ | | 1. sit, miss, Sam, <br> 2. /z/ is the same sound as the letter z as in.... is, as, his, use, boys | |
| d | /d/ | 'fast' > | this is a quick /d/ <br> as in..... did, dad, mad, drop | not /duh/ |
| i | 1. /i/ <br><br> 2./ie/ <br> ------- <br> 3./ee/ | | 1. the /i/ sound is the 'short' vowel sound as in....... it, pig, if, sit <br> 2. the /ie/ sound is the 'long' vowel sound as the word 'I' and as in ....... pint, time, <br> (3rd pronunciation /ee/ as in machine, trivial) | |
| f | /f/ | | if, for, flat, off | not /fuh/ |
| r | /r/ | | rat, run, rip, <br> note: this is tricky for some children to learn so they don't say /er/... have them start saying an easy word like 'rat' holding the /r/ sound saying /rrrrrraaat/. Now have them cut off before they start the /a/ sound. Practice with them until they get the hang of it. | not /er/ or /ruh/ |
| th | 1./th/ <br><br> 2./*th*/ | | 1. /th/ is the 'hard' /th/, the tickle the tongue sound as in.....this, that <br> 2. /*th*/ is the 'soft' quieter /*th*/ sound that does not vibrate the tongue as in..... bath, three, thin | not /thu/ |
| l | /l/ | | pill, tall, lid, lap | not /luh/ or /el/ |

| letter or letters | sound | note if sound 'fast' | any pertinent explanation and example of the sound in words | notes of caution |
|---|---|---|---|---|
| o | 1. /o/<br><br>2. /oa/<br><br>3. /u/ | | 1. /o/ is the 'short' vowel sound as in... **o**dd, t**o**p, l**o**ck,<br>2. /oa/ is the 'long' vowel sound as in..... **o**ld, n**o**, g**o**, m**o**st<br>3. this is the 'short' vowel u sound as in..... s**o**n, l**o**ve, fr**o**m, s**o**me | |
| n | /n/ | | **n**o, **n**ot, fi**n**, **n**est | not /in/ |
| p | /p/ | 'fast'<br>> | this is a quick /p/<br>as in....... u**p**, **p**ig, la**p**, **p**lay<br>(It is harder for some children to say /p/ fast, have them try quickly popping their lips like popping popcorn.../p//p//p/) | not /puh/ |
| e | 1. /e/<br><br>2. /ee/ | | 1. /e/ is the 'short' vowel sound as in..... g**e**t, **e**gg, s**e**t, b**e**st<br>2. /ee/ is the 'long' vowel sound<br> as in... m**e**, h**e**, sh**e** | |
| h | /h/ | 'fast'<br>> | this is a quick /h/<br>as in..... **h**at, **h**im, **h**old<br>/h/ is one of the harder sounds. It needs to be said quickly and in reading is linked directly to the following sound. If it is difficult, have the child practice feeling the short puff of air with their hand in front of their mouth as they quickly say /h/ | not /huh/ |
| v | /v/ | | **v**an, **v**ote, gi**v**e<br>Notice how the /v/ vibrates your lower lip | not /vuh/ |
| sh | /sh/ | | **sh**ip, di**sh**, **sh**ell, ma**sh**<br>you can teach proper pronunciation of this sound by using the standard 'be quiet', finger in front of your mouth /shshshshsh/ signal | not /shuh/ |
| u | 1. /u/<br><br>2. /oo/<br><br>(3. /uu/) | | 1. /u/ is the 'short' vowel sound<br>as in...**u**p, t**u**b, f**u**n, c**u**p<br>2. /oo/ is the 'long' vowel sound<br>as in..... r**u**de, t**u**be,<br>(3$^{rd}$ pronunciation /uu/ the same sound as oo in look. Found in few words...p**u**t, p**u**sh, b**u**ll,) | |
| b | /b/ | 'fast'<br>> | this is a quick /b/<br>as in.... **b**at, **b**ig, cu**b**, cra**b** | not /buh/ |

| letter or letters | sound | note if sound 'fast' | any pertinent explanation and example of the sound in words | notes of caution |
|---|---|---|---|---|
| k | /k/ | 'fast' > | this is a quick /k/ as in.... kid, seek, skate, bake | not /kuh/ |
| ck | /k/ | 'fast' > | this is a quick /k/ as in.... back, sick, duck | not /kuh/ |
| c | 1. /k/  2. /s/ | 1.'fast' > | 1. this is a quick /k/ as in.... cat, crab, cap  2. this is the /s/ sound (when the c steals the /s/ sound) it is sometimes called the 'soft c' sound as in...... city, nice, race | not/kuh/ |
| g | 1./g/  2./j/ | 1.'fast' >  2.'fast' > | 1. this is a quick /g/ as in bag, big, go, (this is sometimes called the 'hard g' sound)  2. this is a quick /j/ sound (when the g steals the /j/ sound) This is sometimes called the 'soft g' as in... page, giraffe, energy | not/guh/  not/juh/ |
| j | /j/ | 'fast' > | this is a quick /j/ as in....jam, job, jill | not /juh/ |
| w | /w/ | | win, wish, woke swish | not/wuh/ |
| ch | /ch/ | 'fast' > | the /ch/ is always said quickly chin, church, much | not/chuh/ |
| tch | /ch/ | 'fast' > | this is the alternate /ch/ spelling latch, catch, itch | not /chuh/ |
| x | /ks/ | 'fast' > | this is the quick /ks/ sound as in ax, fox, fix, tax | not /ex/ |
| z | /z/ | | zoo, zipper, amaze | |
| qu | /kw/ | | this is a tight joining of the quick /k/ with the /w/ sound to make /kw/. The 'qu' partner letters make the sound /kw/ as in.... queen, quilt, quick, equate | |
| wh | /wh/ | | the /wh/ is very similar to the /w/ except it is 'whispered'. as in... whisper, when, white, Have the child practice the quiet whispering of the /wh/ | not/whuh/ |
| a+ll | /ah/ +/l/ | | when a short a is followed by an l or ll, the a pronunciation is modified to say /ah/ as in... all, call, almost, always, walk | |

| letter or letters | sound | note if sound 'fast' | any pertinent explanation and example of the sound in words | notes of caution |
|---|---|---|---|---|
| w+a | /w/+ /ah/ | | when short a comes right after w the pronunciation is modified to say /ah/ as in…. wasp, wad, wash<br>*There are also some other words that have the /ah/ pronunciation such as in…father | |
| y | 1. /y/<br><br>2. /ee/<br><br><br>3. /ie/ | | 1. this is the beginning consonant /y/ sound as in…yes, you, yak, yet<br>2. this is the final /ee/ sound in multisyllable words (this is the most common sound for y). as in… baby, story, silly, quickly, messy<br>3. this is the final /ie/ sound when y is the only vowel ending a 1 syllable word as in.. my, by, shy, try (the /ie/ sound is also found in a few other words such as…. python, Wyoming, type) | not /yuh/ |
| ing | /eeng/ | | this /eeng/ is actually the combination of the /ee/ with the nasal /ng/ sound but it is taught as a single unit because it is so common. as in…. **sing ring string going** | |
| ink | /eenk/ | | this is actually the combination of the /ee//n//k/ sounds but is also taught as a single unit.. as in….**ink, rink sink brink** | |
| ee | /ee/ | | these partner letters have the sound /ee/ as in b**ee**, tr**ee**, m**ee**t, n**ee**d | |
| oa | /oa/ | | these partner letters have the sound /oa/ as in…. **oa**t, b**oa**t, r**oa**d, t**oa**st | |
| oe | /oa/ | | these partner letters have the sound /oa/ as in….h**oe** d**oe** f**oe** | |
| ai | /ay/ | | these partner letters have the sound /ay/ as in….r**ai**n, w**ai**t, p**ai**d | |
| ay | /ay/ | | these partner letters have the sound /ay/ as in….pl**ay**, st**ay** pr**ay** | |
| a_e | /ay/ | | in this combination, the e works with the a to make the a have the /ay/ sound as in …. **a**t**e**, t**a**p**e**, pl**a**n**e** | |

| letter or letters | sound | note if sound 'fast' | any pertinent explanation and example of the sound in words |
|---|---|---|---|
| o_e | /oa/ | | in this combination, the e works with the o to make the o have the /oa/ sound as in …. **ro**pe, **ho**me |
| i_e | /ie/ | | in this combination, the e works with the i to make the i have the /ie/ sound as in …. **ti**me, **hi**de, **i**ce |
| u_e | /oo/ | | in this combination, the e works with the u to make the u have the /oo/ sound as in …. **ru**de, **flu**te |
| e_e | /ee/ | | in this combination, the e works with the e to make the e have the /ee/ sound as in …. **e**ve, compl**e**te |
| oy | /oy/ | | these partner letters have the /oy/ sound as in…… b**oy**, t**oy**, enj**oy** |
| oi | /oy/ | | these partner letters have the /oy/ sound as in…… b**oi**l, **oi**l, c**oi**n, v**oi**ce |
| ea | 1. /ee/<br><br>2. /e/<br>-------<br>3. /ay/ | | 1. the /ee/ is the most common sound for these partner letters as in… **ea**t, t**ea**m, **ea**ch,<br>2. these partner letters sometimes have the /e/ sound as in h**ea**d, br**ea**d, r**ea**dy<br>(3. In a few words these partner letters have the /ay/ sound as in… gr**ea**t, st**ea**k) |
| ow | 1./ow/<br>2./oa/ | | 1. the /ow/ sound as in… n**ow**, br**ow**n, pl**ow**,<br>2. the /oa/ sound as in …. sn**ow**, kn**ow**, shad**ow** |
| ou | 1. /ow/<br><br>2./oo/<br>3./u/ | | 1.the /ow/ sound is the most common as in…**ou**t, l**ou**d, h**ou**se<br>2. the /oo/ sound as in ….y**ou**, s**ou**p, y**ou**th<br>3.the /u/ sound as in.. y**ou**ng, c**ou**ple, and in the -ous endings like nerv**ou**s and fam**ou**s |
| ue | /oo/ | | the long u /oo/ sound as in…. bl**ue**, cl**ue**, tr**ue** |
| ew | /oo/ | | the long u /oo/ sound as in….n**ew**, st**ew**, fl**ew** |
| ui | /oo/ | | the long u /oo/ sound as in….s**ui**t, fr**ui**t |
| oo | 1./oo/<br><br>2/uu/ | | 1. the /oo/ is the long u sound as in…… m**oo**n, c**oo**l, b**oo**t<br>2. the /uu/ sound is softer oo sound found in ….c**oo**k, b**oo**k, f**oo**t |
| ie | 1. /ie/<br>2./ee/<br>3./i/ | | 1. the /ie/ sound as in……p**ie**, d**ie**,<br>2. the /ee/ sound as in th**ie**f, bel**ie**f<br>3. the /i/ sound as in fr**ie**nd, sh**ie**ld |
| ei | 1./ee/<br>2./ay/ | | 1. the /ee/ sound as in rec**ei**ve, c**ei**ling<br>2. the /ay/ sound as in r**ei**n, n**ei**ghbor |

| letter or letters | sound | note if sound 'fast' | any pertinent explanation and example of the sound in words |
|---|---|---|---|
| ey | 1. /ee/ 2. /ay/ | | 1. these partner letters usually have the /ee/ sound as in... **key, money** 2. In a few words ey has the /ay/ sound as in... **they, obey** |
| au | /aw/ | | the /aw/ sound as in....**fault, haul, cause** |
| aw | /aw/ | | the /aw/ sound as in... **awful, law** |
| augh | /aw/ | | the /aw/ sound as in..... **caught, taught** |
| igh | /ie/ | | the /ie/ sound as in..... **high, right** |
| ar | 1. /ar/ 2. /air/ | | 1. the sound /ar/ as in......**car, star, farm** 2. the sound /air/ as in .....**carry, paradise** |
| or | 1. /or/ 2. /er/ | | 1. the usual /or/ sound as in...**corn, for, torch** 2. after w (w+or) and at the end of multisyllable words the or has the /er/ sound as in..... **work, worm, flavor, doctor** |
| or ore oar our oor | /or/ /or/ /or/ /or/ /or/ | | There are 5 combinations that have the /or/ sound **or, for, north** **more, store, chore** **board, oar, roar** **four, course, your** **door, floor** |
| er ur ir ear or | /er/ /er/ /er/ /er/ /er/ | | There are 5 combinations that have the /er/ sound **her, brother, paper, term** **hurt, churn, burp, turn** **dirt, girl, stir, birthday** **earth, search, learn** this is the w+or and or at end of multisyllable words...as in **worm, work, doctor flavor** |
| are ar air (ear) | /air/ /air/ /air/ /air/ | | There are 3 combinations that have the /air/ sound **dare, share, scare** **carry, parrot, parent** **air, hair, chair, pair** (*not common only a few words such as **bear** and **pear**) |
| ear eer ere | /eer/ /eer/ /eer/ | | There are 3 combinations that have the /eer/ sound **ear, hear, dear, near** **deer, cheer, peer** **here,** |

| letter or letters | sound | note if sound 'fast' | any pertinent explanation and example of the sound in words | |
|---|---|---|---|---|
| ear | 1./eer/ 2./er/ 3./air/ | | 1. the ear partner letters usually have the /eer/ sound as in..... **ear**, h**ear**, d**ear**, 2. sometimes the ear partner letters have the sound /er/ as in... **ear**th, s**ear**ch, l**ear**n 3. in a few words the ear partners have the /air/ sound ... b**ear**, p**ear** | |
| dge | /j/ | | these letters have the /j/ sound as in... bri**dge**, e**dge**, ba**dge** | |
| mb | /m/ | | du**mb**, cli**mb**, thu**mb** | |
| wr | /r/ | | **wr**ite, **wr**ong, **wr**ap | |
| kn | /n/ | | **kn**ow, **kn**ew, **kn**ee | |
| ph | /f/ | | **ph**rase, **ph**one, gra**ph** | |

## Additional notes on sound pronunciation:

*There is no need to teach the terminology "short", "long", "soft" or "hard" when teaching the sounds. Although it is sometimes helpful to learn these to help in describing what sound to use, it is not necessary especially with beginning reading. In fact teaching these labels can just add additional processing steps if the terminology is used as a "middle man" in learning the sounds. Students need to learn direct letter=sound relationship not letter = label to describe the sound=actual sound. Keep the sounds direct to the letter without having to first recall some label like 'short'. If the student says the wrong sound option, simply say something like "do you remember the other sound that it makes?"

*Although comprehensive, this list does not include every possible alternative pronunciation or spelling that is encountered in our language. This list includes the majority of the phonogram spellings and sounds based on frequency. For example, the printed representation of the /u/ sound is given for 'u' (run, up), for 'o' (son, from), and for 'ou' (young, couple, nervous) but not for the unusual oo spelling (flood). The infrequent 'oddball' sounds and spellings are not included. If you look you can always find exceptions, pronunciation variances and unexpected spellings.

## Variations in Pronunciation (schwa, accents, regional differences, modifying sounds)

There are variations in pronunciation that occur in speech. These therefore, are encountered when reading. In fact, dictionaries often show these variations in pronunciation.
- Some variations are due to the differences in accents (how we say the word) that vary by region or preference. For example, someone saying /dawg/ instead of /dog/).
- Many of the pronunciation differences occur with the "schwa", the unstressed short vowel sound in many multisyllable words. The schwa (shown as /ə/) is the "lazy" pronunciation of the short vowel sounds /a/ /e/ /i/ /o/ & /u/. The pronunciation varies greatly depending on the vowel, the specific word and how the individual says the word. For example, notice the sound of the schwa /ə/ in the following words: a (b**a**nana, **a**bout, miner**a**l, tradition); e (sick**e**n, pock**e**t, **e**lement); i (clar**i**ty, abil**i**ty, hurr**i**cane); o (butt**o**n, mel**o**n); and u (foc**u**s, pean**u**t) and how these words are often pronounced differently by different people. Although is important to realize that there are differences in pronunciation and accenting of the short vowel sounds, these 'schwa'

pronunciations do not have to be taught as separate sounds. You will find students unconsciously modify the pronunciation to how they say the word. If new words vocabulary words are encountered, teach the student the correct pronunciation for the specific word as 'this is how we say the word'. The schwa, lazy pronunciation does need to be specifically addressed with advanced instruction in spelling. However, for reading, it is highly effective (and far simpler) to teach straightforward short vowel sounds and then let the student adjust pronunciation appropriately as he reads specific word. In other words, don't worry about these slight differences in pronunciation. Teach the short vowel sound and you will find the student automatically and appropriately adjusts the pronunciation to how they say the word.

- Pronunciation modifications occur when we say certain sounds together (how these sounds orally blend together). These are automatically incorporated when we speak. For example, how the short /e/ sound is automatically modified to /i/ when it comes before /m/ or /n/ (hen, pen, hem). When we read we make these type pronunciation changes without even noticing (although it is helpful to point these out for accurate spelling).
- Slight variations in pronunciation of certain sounds occur in some words. If you go to split hairs, the long u sound is pronounced /oo/ in some words (rude, tune) and a slightly different /yoo/ in others (use, cute). Instead of confusing the student with several slightly different pronunciations give them one good solid pronunciation /oo/ and then you will notice that on their own the student makes those slight changes/appropriate adaptations.
- Speakers of other languages are likely to pronounce words differently than English speaking students. Accenting and proper pronunciation is more challenging for students whose primary language is not English or who are in the process of learning the language.

## Speech Difficulties

Some students have limitations in their ability to say certain sounds. These are speech development issues, not reading issues. This is where the student, for various reasons, is not saying specific sounds. Some of these children have physical limitations and others are physically capable but just have not learned to say certain sounds automatically. If a student is facing speech difficulties they need to be evaluated by a professional. Most school districts have screening processes and speech specialists who help identify and assist students with speech difficulties or recommend necessary assistance. Background information on speech development issues can be found on the internet. The National Institutes of Health NIDCD "Speech and Language Developmental Milestones" fact sheet provides general information and links to other resources. It is found at http://www.nidcd.nih.gov/health/voice/speechandlanguage.asp or you can order a hard copy of this free government publication (NIH publication No. 00-4781). Another source of information is the website www.helpforkidspeech.org established by a non-profit Scottish Rite Masonic organization under a program to help children with speech and language disorders. This parent-friendly website contains general background, informative articles and links to resources. The article *Speech Language Home Activities: Teach Specific Sounds to Your Child* and additional articles on individual sounds provide activities you can do at home to develop specific sounds.

Reading instruction does *not* replace the need for speech assistance. However, the individual attention and work on specific sounds provides an opportunity to supplement and assist students. As you work on specific sounds both in isolation and with reading words, you can sometimes help the student learn and practice correct pronunciation. Obviously this informal work on sounds is most helpful for students who do not have physical limitations and just need to learn how to make the sound. When you are working with a student with speech difficulties, the best option is to talk with the speech specialist about recommendations for helping the individual student. These specialists can usually provide specific tips. In addition, the following list shares some general information and tips that a parent or reading tutor may be able to use to help a student say specific sounds.

General Information and Tips:

- Use a small hand mirror, so the student can 'see' how they are making the sound. For example, to make the /th/ sound the student needs to 'stick out' their tongue. With the mirror, they can see the correct position.

- Face the student and make sure they are looking at you and can see your lips move as you say specific sounds. By looking carefully the student can sometimes 'see' the difference between sounds. For example, it is difficult to hear the difference between /f/ and the soft /th/. That is why many children say "It is time for a /baf/" instead of the correct /bath/. However, by looking at the lips you can 'see' the difference between the 'tongue sticking out' for soft /th/ and the teeth on the bottom lips for /f/.

- You can use the 'feel' of the sounds to help children distinguish and say specific sounds. This is helpful for distinguishing some of the sounds with vibrations (such as /v/, hard /th/, /z/) and those with 'puffs' of air (such as /h/, /p/), and the voice on-voice off differences that can be felt in the Adam's apple area between the similar 'sister sounds' (such as /t/ & /d/ or /p/&//b/ ).

- There are specific 'sister sounds' that have the same formation. The only difference is one sound is 'voice off' and the other is 'voice on'. With the closely related sounds you can feel the difference between 'voice off' and 'voice on' by touching the Adam's apple area. These closely related 'sibling' or 'sister' sounds include: /s/-/z/, /t/-/d/, /f/-/v/, /th/-/th/, /p/-/b/, /k/-/g/, /ch/-/j/

- Demonstrate to the student! Show the student how to make the sound. Let them listen, look and feel the differences between sounds. When necessary, exaggerate specific elements of position.

- There is a progression of difficulty in making specific sounds. Some sounds are more difficult to make. Talk to you speech specialist for specific details. In general the sounds /k/, /g/, /ch/, /j/, /th/ /sh/ /r/ /l/ /y/ /s/ blends and /l/ blends are more difficult.

- /s/ and /z/: "Keep the tiger in the cage". Both these sounds are made by keeping the tongue inside/behind the teeth. The /s/ and /z/ are 'sister sounds' made with the same tongue/mouth position. However the /s/ is 'voice off' and the /z/ is 'voice on'. Teach the student to make /s/, then tell them to say /z/ 'make the tiger rattle the cage'. The /z/ sound is a vibration, 'voice on' sound. The student can feel the difference in the Adam's apple and also in vibration on the tongue/teeth.

- /th/ and /th/: "Stick your tongue out!" For both the hard /th/ and the soft /th/ sound the student needs to stick their tongue out. Exaggerate sticking the tongue out to teach the sound. A mirror is particularly helpful so the student can see their tongue sticking out between the teeth. Both the /th/ and /th/ sounds are made by sticking the tongue out. The only difference is the 'voice on' 'voice off'. With the hard /th/ the student vibrates the tongue. You can feel the vibrations 'tickle the tongue'. With the soft /th/, the 'voice off' makes the quiet /th/ that does not tickle the tongue. The student can feel the difference on their tongue and also by touching their Adam's apple area.

- /t/ and /d/: The /t/ sound is made by 'tapping' the tongue on the roof of the mouth right behind the top of the teeth. Teach /t/ as a fast 'tapping' sound. Demonstrate and let the student use a mirror to see the tongue tapping. The /d/ is made the same as /t/ except for it has 'voice on'. The student can feel the difference by touching their Adam's apple area. Also remember both of these sounds are 'fast' sounds that must be said quickly. If you say slowly you distort the sound. The /d/ and /t/ are difficult for some students to orally distinguish. The phonemic awareness of the 'fast' sounds is particularly difficult when they are blended with other consonants.

- **/k/ and /g/:** These are both 'back' sounds made with the back of the tongue almost pulled back to the throat. /k/ and /g/ are also both 'fast' sounds that must be said quickly. The /k/ is made with the 'voice off' and the /g/ is made with the 'voice on. The student can feel the difference on their Adam's apple.

- **/r/:** The /r/ sound is difficult for many students. The /r/ is made by having the tongue curl up with lips apart. (If the lips are together the sound is /w/). The /r/ is a 'lift' sound where the tongue is lifted up. A mirror is helpful for teaching this sound. For speech you can exaggerate the /r/ to /er/. To say /r/ for reading have the student start to say a word such as 'run' or 'race' slowly /rrrrun/ and then have them cut off at the /rrr/. The /r/ is a tricky sound!

- **/ch/ and /j/:** The /ch/ is an 'explosive' sound. Start in the /t/ position (tongue up touching the roof of the mouth right behind the front teeth). Have the student drop their jaw as they blow out. Demonstrate and teach with an exaggerated jaw drop. Also, thanks to a little boy I worked with who loved to watch his dad chop wood, I came up with a helpful analogy. Chopping wood can effectively explain how to make this sound. An analogy between the quick force of an raised ax falling to chop the wood compares to the quick force of the tongue dropping to make the /ch/ sound /ch/ /ch/ - raise the ax (tongue) and /ch/ 'chop' (drop quickly). Also if the student has difficulty saying the /ch/ sound, start practicing with 'nch' blend words such as 'lunch', 'pinch', 'ranch' as the tongue is already raised for the /n/ sound so the /ch/ is then easier to say correctly. The /j/ is the 'voice on' sister sound for /ch/. The student can feel the /j/ in the Adam's apple area.

- **/p/ and /b/:** The /p/ is 'popping popcorn'. The /p/ is a quick sound made by 'popping' the lips together just like popcorn popping. The student can also feel the air puff at each 'pop'. Once again this is a 'fast' sound that must be said quickly. Demonstrate and use a mirror to help the student see how to make the /p/. The /b/ is the 'sister sound' made with 'voice on' that can be felt in the Adam's apple area. Both sounds are said 'quickly' with the lips and puff of air.

- **/l/:** The /l/ is a 'lift' sound that is made by lifting the tongue up behind the teeth. Exaggerate and have the student curl their tongue up, placing the tip behind the front teeth (in the /t/ position). Make sure they keep the tip of their tongue up behind/inside the teeth. Demonstrate and then have the student use a mirror to 'see' the position.

- **/f/ and /v/:** These sounds are made by the top teeth resting on the bottom lip and blowing. Exaggerate to teach how to make the sound. Demonstrate and use the mirror. The student can see the top teeth on the bottom lip. The /f/ sound is the soft sound of gently blowing. The /v/ sound is the 'voice on' sister sound. The /v/ is the 'vibration' sound (/v/=vibration). The student can feel the vibrations on the lower lip as well as feel the 'voice on' in the Adam's apple area. Also note that the phonemic awareness between /f//v/ and soft /th/ is often difficult for younger children. (Why children say 'baf' for bath, 'haf' for have and cute sayings like "My mom is a votographer') Help them develop an 'ear' for the difference by having them look at the formation differences as they hear the sounds.

- **/sh/:** This is the 'quiet' /sh/ sound. The student needs to keep their teeth together and lips rounded as they blow the air out. Demonstrate and use a mirror. The standard 'quiet' /sh/ symbol can help, except drop your finger slightly lower towards the chin so they can see the teeth together and rounded lips.

- **/h/:** The /h/ can be a tricky sound to make. Have the student feel the 'hot' puff of air on their hand. This is a 'fast' sound that must be said quickly. Also make sure they say the sound quietly as /h/ is a 'voice off' soft sound.

Remember, speech difficulties (difficulty saying a certain sound) are NOT considered reading errors.

# APPENDIX B
# EVALUATION TOOLS

## General Information on Evaluations:

An evaluation is not a 'test'. It is an informal tool to help you determine specific reading skills the student may be lacking. Evaluations help you be a more effective teacher. You need to know where specific deficiencies exist in order to help the student build and strengthen the necessary skills. This is comparable to a coach watching a player perform a task so they can determine the specific weaknesses and then coaching to strengthen those areas. Evaluation results help you effectively target instruction to develop essential reading skills. Evaluations are extremely helpful in remediation situations.

Individuals who struggle with reading vary greatly in the specific skills they are lacking. For example, one student may have poor phonemic awareness, not know the sounds and not be processing print phonetically. Instruction would need to directly establish all fundamental skills to develop the proficient phonologic pathways. Another student may be 'sounding out' words but struggling with some of the complexities because their code knowledge was incomplete. This student would need to learn the complexities and strengthen phonologic processing. Another reader may only have difficulty with multisyllable words. A different individual may decode perfectly but not pay attention to or understand what they read so would need direct work on developing comprehension strategies. The evaluation helps you identify the skills the student needs to develop and target your instruction to these necessary skills.

Before you begin evaluation, be sure to explain to the student the evaluation is not a test but rather a tool to help you target your instruction. Some students who struggle with reading, are upset with anything they view as a test. Be sure you let them know that since it is not a test there are no 'wrong answers'. Tell the student, not to worry if they 'miss' something in the evaluation. All that means is a specific skill needs to be taught to them.

**\*Important Note: The following evaluation techniques are only informal tools for indicating possible gaps in reading skills. If you have any concerns at all about the student's hearing, vision, development or other medical concern, the student must be evaluated by a doctor or other appropriate professional. These informal evaluations do not provide any medical information or official diagnostic data. If the student has difficulty hearing (for whatever reason from an ear infection to a physical disability) it significantly impacts phonemic awareness and the ability to tap into correct phonologic processors. Students with uncorrected vision impairment will have challenges seeing the print. Any and all medical concerns need to be addressed by professionals.**

## Specific Reading Skills to Evaluate:

1. Phonemic Awareness: page 269-271
2. Knowledge of the Complete Phonemic Code: page 272-274
3. Reading Performance/Accurate Decoding Skills: page 275-278
4. Spelling: page 279-281
5. Reading Comprehension: page 282

## Summarizing the Results of the Evaluation Elements (see page 283)

# 1. Evaluating Phonemic Awareness:

Assess the student's phonemic awareness by checking their ability to recognize, distinguish and manipulate sounds. If they have difficulty recognizing the sound structure of language, try and see where exactly the difficulty lies. Is it with beginning, ending or middle sounds, blended consonants, blending, segmenting or sound manipulation? Are there specific sounds that are more difficult (remember the 'fast' sounds such as /b/ /d/ /k/ /t/ /g/ /p/ ARE harder to distinguish)? Blended consonants with these 'fast' sounds are especially difficult.

Helpful tools to assess phonemic awareness include the following informal oral PA evaluation and the results of the spelling evaluation (more information under 'interpreting spelling' under the spelling portion of the evaluation). Results from these assessments can indicate what specific phonemic awareness skills you need to help the student develop.


**Interpreting Phonemic Awareness**

The results of the oral phonemic awareness evaluation and the results of the spelling evaluation are used to indicate the student's phonemic awareness.

Look at the results of the oral phonemic awareness evaluation.

- Check if the student can distinguish beginning sounds. (example starting sound for supper is /s/) If they have difficulty, where does the difficulty lie? Is it with all sounds or is it with blended consonants? (example, saying the beginning sound of 'strike' as /st/ or /str/)

- Can the student segment all sounds within a word? If they have difficulty, where is the specific difficulty? Look at the student's specific responses to determine if they have difficulty distinguishing the blended consonants (blast as /bl/ /a/ /st/) or with failing to distinguish all sounds and inappropriately lumping 'word families' ('chip' as /ch/ /ip/ and 'hug' as /h/ /ug/).

- Can the student manipulate the sound structure of words? If they run into problems, where exactly do the problems occur? Are difficulties with blended consonants, the beginning sounds, the ending sounds or the middle sounds?

In addition, look at the students spelling. Spelling often provides a useful indicator of how the student hears the sounds within a word. Look for spelling that indicates the student is missing the correct sound structure of the word. Words that are spelled phonetically incorrect with entire sounds missing often indicate poor phonemic awareness. Complete information on evaluating spelling is found in the subsequent instructions on interpreting spelling

Don't worry if the student has difficulty with phonemic awareness. Difficulty performing PA skills only indicates you likely need to help the student develop phonological skills. Direct PA instruction is effective in helping the student learn to hear, distinguish, separate and manipulate individual sounds within words. Remember phonemic awareness is essential to reading success as it permits the student to access efficient phonologic processing.

Also remember if you have any concerns with the student's ability to physically hear sounds (hearing difficulty), the student *must* be evaluated by a medical professional.

# Oral Phonemic Awareness Evaluation:

These simple oral 'sound' evaluations indicate if the student can recognize, distinguish and manipulate sounds within words. The student does *not* see the printed paper; he just listens closely and responds orally. Tell the student you are going to use some oral 'sound games' do a quick check of sound awareness. Remind him that he needs to listen carefully as you can only say the word or sounds once. Write down the student's exact response. For all activities, first demonstrate an actual example so the student understands what you are asking him to do.

### HEARING, DISTINGUISHING & SEGMENTING SOUNDS WITHIN A WORD

This activity helps see if the student can distinguish and separate individual sounds in a word. Does the student hear and recognize the phonetic structure of our language? Is he able to segment these individual sounds? How well can he distinguish and separate blended consonants?

First, I will tell you a word and then you tell me what **sound** that word started with. For example, if I say 'cat' you would tell me the sound /k/ that starts the word cat. If the student tells you letter names, say something like 'yes that is the letter but I need the sound.

| | | | |
|---|---|---|---|
| supper _____ (/s/) | | speaking _____ (/s/) |
| mistake _____ (/m/) | | dribble _____ (/d/) |
| porch _____ (/p/) | | strike _____ (/s/) |
| fantastic _____ (/f/) | | flashing _____ (/f/) |
| capable _____ (/k/) | | stench _____ (/s/) |
| healthy _____ (/h/) | | group _____ (/g/) |
| shiver _____ (/sh/) | | plaster _____ (/p/) |
| tracking _____ (/t/) | | |

In this next sound activity, I will tell you a word once and then you tell me all the sounds that you hear in that word. Make sure you give me the sounds separately (slight pause between sounds). Give an example so the student understands what you want him to do..I say "cat" you tell me /c/ /a/ /t/. (if he gives letter names, ask for the sounds) Write down exactly how the student says/segments the sounds.

| | | | |
|---|---|---|---|
| chip ___ ___ ___ ( /ch/ /i/ /p/ ) | | drop ___ ___ ___ ___ ( /d/ /r/ /o/ /p/ ) |
| vat ___ ___ ___ (/v/ /a/ /t/ ) | | crash ___ ___ ___ ___ ( /c/ /r/ /a/ /sh/ ) |
| shun ___ ___ ___ ( /sh/ /u/ /n/ ) | | munch ___ ___ ___ ___ ( /m/ /u/ /n/ /ch/) |
| hug ___ ___ ___ ( /h/ /u/ /g/ ) | | strap ___ ___ ___ ___ ___ ( /s/ /t/ /r/ /a/ /p/) |
| slap ___ ___ ___ (/s/ /l/ /a/ /p/ ) | | clown ___ ___ ___ ___ ( /k/ /l/ /ow/ /n/ ) |
| trip ___ ___ ___ ___ ( /t/ /r/ /i/ /p/ ) | | bleach ___ ___ ___ ___ (/b/ /l/ /ee/ /ch/) |
| blast ___ ___ ___ ___ ___ ( /b/ /l/ /a/ /s/ /t/ ) | | |

**SOUND PROCESSING/SOUND MANIPULATION:** This evaluates how well the student can distinguish and manipulate individual sounds within a word. Tell the student in this activity he will make changes to the word that you ask him to. (Give an example "say cat without the /k/" "you would say "at".)

(These manipulate beginning sounds)

say **rest** without the /r/ _____ (est)    say **sick** without the /s/ _____ (ick)

say **matter** without the /m/ _____(atter)    say **chip** without the /ch/ _____ (ip)

say **popsicle** without the /p/ _____(opsicle)    say **rate** without the /r/ _____ (ate)

(These beginning sounds with blended consonants are more difficult to separate and distinguish)

say **drive** without the /d/ _____(rive)    say **clay** without the /c/ _____(lay)

say **grab** without the /g/ _____(rab)    say **bring** without the /b/ _____(ring)

say **flipper** without the /f/ _____(lipper)    say **train** without the /t/ _____(rain)

say **step** without the /s/ _____(tep)    say **shrimp** without the /sh/ _____(rimp)

(These manipulate the ending sound)

say **splat** without the /t/ _____(spla)    say **cheese** without the /z/ _____(chee)

say **smack** without the /k/ _____(sma)    say **groom** without the /m/ _____(groo)

say **group** without the /p/ _____(grou)    say **strip** without the /p/ _____ (stri)

(These manipulate the ending sound with blended consonants)

say **lost** without the /t/ _____(los)    say **lunch** without the /ch/ _____(lun)

say **grand** without the /d/ _____(gran)    say **cramp** without the /p/ _____(cram)

say **hold** without the /d/ _____ (hol)    say **wilt** without the /t/ _____(wil)

(These manipulate sounds within a word and are more difficult…younger children may have a hard time with these even when they have good phonemic awareness)

say **flip** without the /l/ _____(fip)    say **transit** without the /r/ _____(tansit)

say **vest** without the /s/ _____(vet)    say **strain** without the /t/ _____(srain)

say **class** without the /l/ _____(cass)    say **count** without the /n/ _____(cout)

## 2. Checking Knowledge of the Printed Phonemic Code

Evaluate the student's knowledge of the complete phonemic code. This simply checks to see if the student knows the complete necessary print=sound code of our written language. The reading skill objective/knowledge base that you are evaluating includes:

- Does the student know the direct print to sound relationship?
- Is this knowledge complete? (This includes all the alternate sounds, vowel combinations, r-controlled combinations, and other complexities)
- Is sound pronunciation correct?
- Is print to sound knowledge automatic?(If the student takes awhile to give you the sound and does not know it 'instantly' the code knowledge is not automatic)

The tools for checking the code knowledge include checking knowledge of sounds in isolation on a list and evaluating the results of the student's spelling and reading.

The first evaluation tool is simply a list of all sounds in isolation. The list is used to check the student's direct print = sound knowledge of all basic sounds, alternate vowel sounds, vowel combinations, r-controlled vowel combinations and other complexities. Determine if they have specific gaps in their code knowledge. Also check that the code knowledge is direct and automatic. It is not a coincidence that most struggling readers have major gaps in their code knowledge especially of the vowel combinations and other complexities.

## Interpreting Knowledge of the Code

Checking the knowledge of the complete phonemic code is fairly straightforward. Give the student the list and simply ask them what sound the letter(s) would make if it was within a word. The student should be able to quickly provide the sounds. On your copy note down exactly what the student tells you. If the student responds correctly after a long pause, ask the student how they figured it out. Often the student will tell you "I thought of the word _____" This is important to note as it indicates inefficient, indirect processing.

For students who are having difficulties reading, this check is often enlightening. Frequently, you will find out the student simply does not know their sounds. Deficiencies are commonly associated with incorrect pronunciation and lacking knowledge of the vowel combinations, r-controlled vowel combinations, or alternate sounds.

The knowledge of the complete phonemic code is also reflected in the spelling and reading performance evaluations. Frequent errors with specific sounds in both spelling and reading can indicate gaps in the student's knowledge base of certain sounds.

# Check of Phonemic Code:

In this assessment, there are 2 copies of the sounds; one for the student to look at and one for you to make notes on. Point at the letters/phonograms on the student's copy one at a time and ask the student "if you saw this in a word, what sound would it make?" The student looks at the various letters or other phonograms and tells you the sound that they make. Write down exactly what the student tells you. If he gives you letter names, say "yes, that is the letter name but I need to know what sound it makes" If they say the letter name again just write that down and go on to the next letter on the list. For the letters/phonograms that have more than one sound simply ask the student, "Do you know another sound this letter/ letters make?" The student should know these sounds quickly/automatically. If they can answer only after a long pause, *ask* the student how they figured it out (Their answer of how they determined the sound often reveals indirect processing such as "I thought of the word ___" ) If they do not know the sound, tell them they can tell you "I don't know".

<u>Parent or Evaluator's copy</u> (for you to record the student's responses on)

| | | | |
|---|---|---|---|
| m ___ | b ___ | oe ___ | igh ___ |
| t ___ | k ___ | ai ___ | ar ___ |
| a ___ ___ ___ | ck ___ | ay ___ | or ___ |
| s ___ ___ | c ___ ___ | oy ___ | ore ___ |
| d ___ | g ___ ___ | oi ___ | oar ___ |
| i ___ ___ | j ___ | ea ___ ___ ___ | our ___ |
| f ___ | w ___ | ow ___ ___ | oor ___ |
| r ___ | ch ___ | ou ___ ___ ___ | er ___ |
| th ___ ___ | tch ___ | ue ___ | ur ___ |
| l ___ | x ___ | ew ___ | ir ___ |
| o ___ ___ ___ | z ___ | ui ___ | ear ___ |
| n ___ | qu ___ | oo ___ ___ | are ___ |
| p ___ | wh ___ | ie ___ ___ | eer ___ |
| e ___ ___ | y ___ ___ ___ | ei ___ | ere ___ |
| h ___ | ing ___ | ey ___ | dge ___ |
| v ___ | ink ___ | au ___ | wr ___ |
| sh ___ | ee ___ | aw ___ | kn ___ |
| u ___ ___ | oa ___ | augh ___ | ph ___ |

Student's Copy

| | | | |
|---|---|---|---|
| m | b | oe | igh |
| t | k | ai | ar |
| a | ck | ay | or |
| s | c | oy | ore |
| d | g | oi | oar |
| i | j | ea | our |
| f | w | ow | oor |
| r | ch | ou | er |
| th | tch | ue | ur |
| l | x | ew | ir |
| o | z | ui | ear |
| n | qu | oo | are |
| p | wh | ie | eer |
| e | y | ei | ere |
| h | ing | ey | dge |
| v | ink | au | wr |
| sh | ee | aw | kn |
| u | oa | augh | ph |

# 3. Evaluate the Student's Reading Performance (decoding skills)

In this evaluation technique, you give the student an oral reading evaluation. You listen to the student read and record their exact performance. Although there are many established reading test, this informal evaluation of exact decoding accuracy, speed and ability is very helpful. It is enlightening to carefully look at and evaluate errors that struggling readers make and think about why the student made those errors. Frequent, persistent, repeated patterns of errors are very helpful in both indicating deficiencies in specific reading skills and importantly in identifying the skills that you need to help the student develop. This reading performance evaluation of accurate decoding skills is particularly helpful in establishing an effective remediation plan to build proficient reader skills in struggling readers.

Select 4 or 5 pages of grade level material the student has NOT previously read. Avoid material where text can be guessed from the pictures or a book with repetitive or predictable text the student can guess or memorize. It is very helpful to make a copy of the pages the student will be reading so you can write your notes directly on your copy of the text as the student reads.

The student simply reads this material out loud to you. Make sure you are looking at the material he is reading so you can see exactly what he is reading. At this time, do not stop or correct the student. Simply listen to the student read and record the student's exact reading performance. It is important to record every error, no mater how small. Be sure and record the exact error the student makes (not just that he missed the word but precisely what he said when he missed the word). Indicate all skipped words (even the little words 'a' 'an' and 'the'), incorrectly read words (write down precisely what the student says), replacing one word for another , missing part of the word, or difficulty with multisyllable words. While you do not correct the student at this time, note any self correction the student does on his own. In summary, you record the student's exact reading performance. Also make notes on any of your observations or overall impressions concerning reading skills such as 'reading was slow and laborious', 'reading was fast', 'seemed to be rushing and missing words', 'student corrected self when made an error', 'frequently student did not notice errors', 'student's reading was choppy and slow', or 'difficulty appears to be with multisyllable words'.

## Interpreting Reading - Accurate Decoding Skills

Close scrutiny of the student's exact mistakes when reading is enlightening. Careful evaluation often reveals patterns of errors. Patterns with particular types of reading errors can indicate deficiencies in specific skills such as tracking, blending, attention to detail, and absence of phonologic processing.

Although it is not precise science, you can generally evaluate the specific errors the student makes when he reads and interpret some of the common mistakes. Look for common patterns that may indicate specific deficiencies. What types of words did the student miss? Is he skipping words when he reads? Is he simply not tracking? Does he only struggle with vowel combinations or just with multisyllable words? Carefully scrutinize exactly what the student says when he misreads a word. The exact error helps point to what he is doing wrong. When there is a pattern of errors, think about why he made the error.

The following examples show common errors that students make and the types of problems these errors may indicate. Once again, it is not a single error but the patterns of repeated mistakes that are informative. Although these examples came from experiences with actual students, each individual is different and these examples may not apply to your student. These examples illustrate how you can gain valuable information from a student's errors. Remember, these are not clear-cut categories and overlap is common. (For examples 'whole word' readers often are not tracking and often do not know their sounds).

**"Whole Word" Errors:** These types of errors occur when the student is attempting to 'see' or 'visually recognize' entire words as a unit instead of processing the print by sound. The student tries to recognize the overall visual appearance of the word. Often the words 'look similar' to words the student has already learned as 'sight' words. Words usually contain some visually similar letters or structure. Frequent 'whole word' type errors indicate the student is not processing print phonetically. Examples of 'whole word' type errors include:

| | | | | | |
|---|---|---|---|---|---|
| exit → next | every → very | simple → smile | sprout → poured | van → have | roam → more |
| dim → made | years → yours | value → volume | afraid → after | include → locating | agree → argue |
| lord → rod | speed → sleep | cork → clock | text → next | vane → have | being → belong |
| navy → very | clang → change | adult → about | spread → prize | will → while | shift → finish |
| since → nice | scrape → escape | when → then | district → distance | swallowed → shallow | |

**"Word Guessing" Errors**: Frequent 'word guessing' errors are somewhat similar to 'whole word' errors because the student is not processing print phonetically. In 'word guessing' the student often only looks at the first letter and then guesses a word. Frequently, errors are completely 'off'. Sometimes a recently used word will be used or a word will be guessed from an illustration. Sometimes the student will look at you (instead of the print) and in quick succession chant several options. Word substitutions are considered 'word guessing' errors as the student is not reading the print but instead guessing their own word from context. Occasionally these are the 'I have absolutely no idea where that come from' type errors. These types of word guessing errors are closely associated with students who do not process print phonetically and instead are relying on 'whole word' visual recognition techniques. There is usually overlap between 'whole word' errors and 'word guessing' errors. Examples of 'word guessing' errors include:

pencil → pear     spoil → special    hound → hundred     gentle → great..giant..     graft → giraffe
hound → hundred    true → tunnel    plenty → prehistoric    command → computer     detest → dentist
chart → chimp (read a book with the word 'chimp' so now says 'chimp' for any word starting with 'ch')
value → Valentine (because it is February and student was recently exposed to 'Valentine')
shell → shark (because there was an illustration of a shark on the page)
never → nurse (because there was an illustration of a nurse on the previous page)
stir → shirt..sister..sitter (student looking at me while guessing various words)
angry → mad or class → school (word substitutions guessed on context instead of reading print)

**Tracking Errors:** These errors can sometimes appear similar to 'whole word' errors. The distinction is that the student appears to be attempting to sound out words. However, they are not properly tracking left to right. The words they say often contain the same sounds but are out of order. These tracking errors are closely related to 'whole word' processing. If the student looks at the word as a 'whole' instead of processing correctly in an orderly left to right manner they frequently 'mix up' the sounds within the word. Students can also make tracking errors if they are 'hopping' around looking for familiar bits and pieces that they 'recognize'. These types of errors indicate the student need to develop proper left to right directional tracking. Examples of tracking errors include:

| | | | | |
|---|---|---|---|---|
| was → saw | no → on | slip → spill | left → felt | step → pest | lots → lost |
| slot → lots | form → from | miles → smiles | balk → black | last → salt | tired → tried |

**Lack of Code Knowledge/Difficulty with Complexities**: When the student makes frequent errors or has difficulty with words that contain vowel combination and r-controlled vowel combinations it often indicates they lack knowledge of the complete phonemic code. If the student did not know the complexities in isolation and has difficulty reading words that contain these sounds, often the student needs is some direct instruction and practice in these sounds. These students sometimes read correctly and accurately with the basic sounds and are attempting to sound out words but lack the complete code knowledge therefore struggle with the complexities. Examples of difficulty with code knowledge include:
--mispronunciations where the sounds of vowel combinations are sounded out separately such as
        sound → /s/ /o/ /u/ /n/ /d/     tease as /t/ /ee/ /a/ /z/    'compete' as /k/ /o/ /m/ /p/ /e/ /t/ /ee/

--difficulty with words that contain complexities when simple code is read accurately and easily
--lack of knowledge of the alternate sounds, for example every time the student comes across 'ow' they use the /ow/ sound and do not know and apply the /oa/ sound
--student will start sounding out the word and then 'word guess' because they don't have knowledge to sound out correctly

**Consonant Cluster Errors**: These errors occur primarily with common 'blended clusters' such as s-st, st-str, d-dr, c-cl, c-cr, t-tr, g-gr, f-fr and ending clusters p-mp, and d-nd. In these types of errors the student will insert the 'blended cluster' sounds into words even when it is NOT present. These type of errors occur frequently in students who were taught consonant clusters as a unit (student learned the consonant cluster as a unit such as st, str, tr, mp, gr, fr, dr...) The student consequently 'sees' and processes the blended sounds even when they are actually not present in a word. Often the student will look at the word several times repeating the same error. Examples of 'consonant cluster' errors include:

| | | | | | |
|---|---|---|---|---|---|
| flip → flimp | clip → climp | cap → camp | stiff → striff | gab → grab | tying → trying |
| dip → drip | cop → crop | speak → spreak | sand → stand | tide → tride | fog → frog |
| chat → chant | tease → trease | stout → strout | steak → streak | tendency → trendency | |

**Attention to Detail Errors:** These types of errors are when the student does not pay close attention detail, carefully processing all the letters in order. Attention to detail is closely associated with proper tracking and correct phonologic processing. The 'attention to detail' errors are when the student misses bits and parts of the word. Consonant cluster errors are a type of attention to detail error. Sometimes the student will be sounding out the words correctly but misses parts. The 'fast and sloppy' readers often make frequent errors with the details. Examples of attention to detail errors include:

| | | | | |
|---|---|---|---|---|
| inspect → insect | father → farther | must → most | son → soon | explain → exclaim |
| explore → explode | invent → invert | powder → power | retorted → reported | adapt → adopt |

+ missing details with plural words (inaccurately leaving off or adding /s/ /es/)
+ changing or missing other endings (such as ing, ed)

**Word Family Errors**: These errors occur when the student inappropriately 'pulls' common word families out of words when they are reading. Hopping around looking for 'word families' that they recognize also confuses proper tracking. Often in these errors you can recognize the inappropriate use of 'word family'. Examples include:

| | | | |
|---|---|---|---|
| train → into | page → /p/ /ag/ /ee/ | training → /tr/ /in/ /ing/ | manager → /man//ag//er/ |
| stream → /str//ee//am/ | indicate → /in//dic//at//ee/ | | |

**Difficulty with Multisyllable Words:** These type of errors occur when the student appears to sound out and accurately read the shorter words without problem and yet struggles with multisyllable words. If fundamental reading skills are established (processed phonologically, knows sounds, tracks correctly) then often the student simply needs instruction in handling these more complex multisyllable words. Errors with multisyllable words tend to include missing or changing parts of the word, dropping or adding sounds inappropriately, difficulty putting the words together and general trouble handling the longer words. Examples of multisyllable errors include:

| | | |
|---|---|---|
| inconsistent → inconstant | opportunity → oppority | eliminate → elimate |
| committed → commititated | determine → deterimmine | objective → objectactive |
| representative → repsetive | fundamental → funmental | encountering → encouting |

**Slow Processing:** If the student is 'sounding out' words but the phonetic decoding is slow and difficult, it may be that the reader is relying on indirect processing to phonologically process the print. For efficient reading the student needs to automatically convert print to the correct sound. If the student must first recall another word that contains the sound, extract the correct sound and then apply it to the new word, it involves slow indirect 'long way' processing pathways. While the student is able to extract the necessary sound knowledge it takes lots of effort. In this case the student needs to practice the direct print=sound relationship so the print can be processed rapidly and efficiently. In addition, once correct phonologic processing is established it still takes repeated practice of each word to develop fluency. Remember fluency is build word by word and requires repeated phonologic processing. Practice is necessary to build this 'fast' fluent reading.

**Blending Difficulty**: Difficulty blending is evident by the 'choppy' or 'segmented' sounding out. The sounds are said broken apart instead of being blended smoothly together. The 'choppy' sounding out is usually very noticeable. Sometimes the student says all individual sounds correctly but because they are segmented/separated they are not able to combine them back together. The student needs to learn to smoothly blend sounds. Have them take a deep breath before starting and if necessary sing the word. Directly teach smooth blending.

**'Fast and Sloppy'**: This is where students appear to be rushing through the reading, moving so fast and careless they miss entire words and sections. When they slow down their accuracy and reading improves dramatically. They appear to have necessary skills but are in too much of a hurry to apply them. These types of 'going too fast' errors often correspond with the personality of certain students. They are simply in too much of a hurry to be careful. These types of students simply need training in careful reading! These students have the necessary skills, they simply have to slow down and apply their skills. Guided reading, where you stop the student at every error is the best way to help these students develop careful reading skills. They usually do not like to stop so forcing them to stop and go back usually motivates them to improve their accuracy!

**Letter Confusion:** Letter confusion is most commonly encountered with the visually similar letters b - d - and p. For example:

    big→dig    drag→brag    brown→drown

Letter confusion with other letters can also be created by certain writing styles. For example loopy cursive crossover print can create confusion with additional letters. The loopy cursive writing can create confusion between i-j-l. When curves and loops are added, *i-j-l*, these letters which are distinct under normal block print also become visually similar. Loopy writing of k & h as *k-h* can create confusion not just between k-h but also with ch-ck. As a result, some students who learn these loopy cursive crossover styles will make errors such as:

    ask → ash    much → muck    mash → mask    racket → rachet    basket → bashet
    hill → kill    joint → loint

Remediation for these letter confusion errors is to have the student repeatedly print the letters with proper formation in normal block style print. While print or font style is usually irrelevant for skilled readers it can create additional difficulty in students who are learning the printed language.

These are just a few of the many types of errors that struggling readers make. For evaluation purposes, note and carefully evaluate the exact errors the student makes. Identify common patterns in the errors and ask yourself, "why did the student make that error?" Once again the precise errors and patterns of errors are enlightening in helping determine what skills the individual student lacks and also which specific skills you need to teach the student to help them achieve proficient reading.

# 4. Evaluate the Student's Spelling:

Spelling indicates how the student is converting sound to print. This is not a spelling test but rather a tool to see how the student understands our written language. Remember spelling (writing down words of our language) is the converse process of reading (translating print back to language). Often a close look at how the student approaches spelling/writing language is very helpful in seeing how the student understands and processes our phonemic language.

Evaluate spelling by having the student spell a list of words they have NOT studied. A suggested list is provided. An alternative to a spelling list is to evaluate samples of the student's uncorrected writing from notes, a journal entry or other written assignment. Do not use a corrected proofed report or a spelling test they have studied for. Rather use a representative sample of how they spell when they are writing so you can see how the student perceives written language. Patterns in spelling often indicate how the student is processing print. Spelling errors can also reveal phonemic weakness.

Another important tool for evaluating the students spelling is to ask the student how they write words when they spell. If the student attempts to write words by the sounds, (even if not perfect spelling) indicates they are processing print phonetically. If they are writing words by trying to remember what the word looks like or by memorizing letter names it may indicate they are not processing print phonetically. Watch the student as they spell. If they are 'saying the sounds' as they write, it is a good indicator they are trying to process print phonetically.

## Interpreting Spelling

Once again, this informal evaluation requires interpretation. Look for patterns in their spelling errors to determine which skills need to be strengthened. One spelling error does not mean the student has a specific difficulty. However, patterns of similar errors may indicate deficiencies. Look closely at how the student spelled the word and think about why they spelled the word the way they did. The following general interpretations arranged into groups provide examples of areas to consider. While an individual's exact spelling errors may not fit neatly into one of these general descriptive categories they provide an idea of how to interpret spelling. Remember you are looking for indicators of necessary reading skills in phonemic awareness, knowledge of the complete accurate phonemic code and correct phonologic processing of print.

**Phonologic Processing Errors**: If the student is not processing print phonetically, they tend to make frequent spelling errors reflective of their failure to recognize the phonetic structure of print. These are the spelling errors that are 'way off' phonetically. They are similar to the 'whole word' reading errors. Sometimes the student has some of the correct letters but they are 'out of order'. At other times will write correct portions of another word (not the one being spelled). Another indicator of absence of phonologic processing is when a student can memorize a list of words for a spelling test, make a 100% on the test and then the following week can not spell any of the words. This indicates 'memorizing' letters not phonologic processing. Examples of phonologic processing errors include:
- replace as 'rlpece'
- stability as 'satbile'
- plastic as 'paltsic'
- furnish as 'finish' (another similar appearing word the student has memorized)
- marks as 'makes'
- persistent as 'president'

**Phonemic Weakness Errors**: Frequently missing sounds within words may indicate poor phonemic awareness. Although the student is trying to write by sound he misses sounds. Frequently these type of

'phonemic awareness' errors involve the blended consonants that are harder to hear. The student does not distinguish all the sounds. Generally these patterns of spelling errors indicate the student if processing most of the word phonetically but misses some of the sounds. Generally these types of errors indicate a need to develop phonemic awareness. If difficulties are with 'fast' blended consonants, this indicates those are the skills that specifically need to be developed.
- brown as 'bown' (missing the /r/ sound)
- drastic as 'dastic' (missing the /r/ sound)
- predict as 'predit' (missing the fast 'c' when it is next to the /t/)

**Letter Name Errors**: Some errors indicate the student is spelling words by letter name instead of the correct sound the letter represents. Depending on the type of error, these sometimes indicate the student is attempting to process print phonetically but lacks the correct sound pronunciation knowledge for the sounds. They use letter name instead of correct sound such as 'x' /ex/ not correct /ks/, 't' /tee/ not correct /t/, 'm' /im/ not correct /m/, 'd' /dee/ not correct /d/. A few examples of errors that indicate 'letter name' processing include spellings such as:
- empty as 'mt'
- determine and 'dtrmn'
- expel as 'xpl'

**Difficulty with Vowel Combinations**: If the student has good phonemic awareness, appears to be processing print phonetically but has persistent difficulty with the vowel combinations it may be that the student lacks direct knowledge of these complexities. Systematic direct instruction of the complete code usually improves these types of errors. You can often identify the sounds the student needs to learn through the patterns of errors. Examples of vowel combination errors include:
- growth as 'groth'
- proof as 'pruf'
- appear as 'apper'
- include as 'includ'
- nominate as 'nominat'

**"Spelling" Errors**: Making 'spelling' errors is completely different from difficulty or misunderstanding of the structure of our written language. Words that are spelled phonetically correct but 'misspelled' are what I consider 'spelling mistakes'. In these types of errors the student hears and processes the sounds correctly, they simply use the incorrect spelling. Learning some of the general spelling guidelines helps many of these types of spelling errors. This includes errors such as spelling:
- picnic as 'picnick' (used 'ck' spelling for /k/ instead of 'c')
- speaking as 'speeking' (using incorrect vowel combination spelling for the /ee/ sound)
- common as 'commun' (spelling how it sounds instead of 'shwaw' lazy vowel o= /u/)

Spelling List for Evaluation:

Have the student spell the following list of words. Do not give the words to the student to study. Simply see how he writes the words as he hears you say the words. Be sure to say the word clearly and repeat the word at least once. Feel free to shorten or change the following spelling list. Tell the student it is not a spelling test. It is simply for you to help see how they are writing the words.

## Basic Sounds + alternate vowel:

| | | | | | | |
|---|---|---|---|---|---|---|
| smack | brunch | sprint | blank | swamp | camping | within |
| inject | vanish | complex | inspect | problem | expand | plastic |
| stranded | closet | predict | extend | program | consist | migrant |
| basic | stable | install | washing | tundra | simply | identify |
| yelping | trinket | | | | | |

## vowel combinations & r-controlled vowel combinations:

| | | | | | | |
|---|---|---|---|---|---|---|
| speechless | indeed | unload | reclaim | payment | donate | landscape |
| provide | preclude | balance | postage | hoisted | destroy | release |
| healthy | growling | renounce | withdrew | continue | smoothly | defraud |
| discover | ordinary | terminate | furnish | harvest | forceful | hanger |
| research | compare | | | | | |

## Multisyllable (3+ syllable words) & Advanced:

| | | | | | | |
|---|---|---|---|---|---|---|
| invasion | application | artificial | adventure | invitation | knowledge | cumulative |
| adaptation | appropriate | percentage | terminated | announcement | | |

# 5. Evaluate the Student's Reading Comprehension:

To evaluate comprehension, you check how well the student understands the material they are reading. Assess if the student is able to answer questions about what he read, remember what he read, pull out pertinent information, summarize the main points, and for higher level comprehension infer and predict. If the student is having difficulty with comprehension you also need to determine if their poor comprehension is based on decoding difficulty, lack of comprehension skills or both.

To evaluate comprehension, have the student read several pages to a chapter of appropriate level material to you. Do not correct decoding errors at this point. Just listen to the student read. Stop the student at ends of paragraphs or other appropriate locations and ask *specific* content based questions to determine if the student can:
- Remember what they just read (basic comprehension)
- Pull out important points
- Summarize the content
- Infer and predict (higher level skills)

Also notice:
- Does the student independently go back and re-read to answer questions?
- If the student misreads a word, is he able to catch himself?
- How accurate is the reading (accurate few errors or struggling with lots decoding errors)
- How much 'effort' (quick/effortless or slow/laborious)

If the reading itself is difficult for the student (lots of effort) or if the reading/decoding contains frequent errors, comprehension is usually blocked. If the student is struggling with both the decoding and comprehension, STOP his reading. Instead you read the material to him and ask him questions based on your oral presentation. This checks comprehension separately from reading/decoding skills. If the student who had poor comprehension when he was struggling in reading the material to you, turns around and can fully understand and answer detailed questions when the material is read to him, it indicates the student's primary problem with comprehension is an inability to proficiently decode the print. Many bright students who struggle with decoding actually have the advanced comprehension skills. Their apparent struggles with 'reading comprehension' are in fact struggles with decoding. Their inability to easily and accurately decode print limits their comprehension when they read. These students need to develop proficient reader pathways so they can easily and accurately decode the print.

In contrast, if the student is reading quickly and accurately and still can not understand what they are reading they are lacking comprehension skills. The student needs to learn how to pay attention to what they are reading, think about and understand the text. They likely need direct instruction in comprehension strategies to develop comprehension skills.

Some students struggle with both the decoding and the comprehension skills. These students are the ones that had difficulty understanding both when they read to you and also when you read the material to them. These students would likely need skill development first in proficient decoding and then also in comprehension skills.

In evaluating specific comprehension skills, note exactly the types of comprehension skills the student both completes easily and which areas he needs work in. For example, the student may be able to tell you exactly what he read yet not be able to pull out the overall important points. This is where the student can relate bit by bit trivial detail but misses the main point. This student needs instruction in how to pull out important information. Another student may be able to pull out some important points but not yet be able to infer or predict. Refer to *Section 9: Developing Reading Comprehension Skills* for detailed information on how to help students develop comprehension skills.

# Summarizing the Results of the Evaluation Elements

After you have completed the individual evaluation elements, you need to combine and interpret the overall results. The combined results of phonemic awareness, knowledge of the complete phonemic code and performance in reading and spelling provide a useful 'picture' of the exact skills you need to help your student develop. Students who struggle with reading do so because they are lacking specific skills. Look at all the evaluation elements together. The combined results usually indicate specific weakness in certain fundamental skills. You then can target instruction to build these necessary skills.

Remember the focus is on establishing necessary skills for proficient reading. To read proficiently the student must first process print phonetically. This requires the integration of essential subskills in phonemic awareness, blending, tracking, attention to detail and knowledge of the complete phonemic code. After the student develops the fundamental skills they need to work on advanced skills in handling multisyllable words, fluency, vocabulary and comprehension.

If the student is weak in **any** of the fundamental skills including phonemic awareness, blending, directional tracking, direct knowledge of the complete phonemic code **or if you have any indications the student is not processing print phonologically** the student needs to first establish these essential skills. Start at the beginning of the program to ensure the student masters the essential skills in phonemic awareness, tracking, blending, direct knowledge of the basic code and phonologic processing skills.

If the student has strong fundamental skills (strong PA, proper directional tracking, smooth blending, automatic knowledge of basic code, and well established phonologic processing) and is only lacking knowledge of the complete code, you can sometimes start at section #2 (lesson 10). However, be sure they have learned the multiple sounds for the vowels and letters like s, and have mastered the basic tracking and blending skills before advancing to all the vowel combination and r-controlled vowel combinations. If you are in doubt, it is best to start at the beginning to ensure the student establishes a strong foundation. If you repeat a skill the student already knows, they simply gain a little extra practice. (Remember, even the professional elite players practice fundamental drills). Problems arise when the student fails to acquire a necessary foundational skill. Older students, especially those with some of the skills in place, advance very rapidly. Don't cut out lessons just to save time. An extra day or two is cheap insurance for making sure fundamental skills are established and practiced.

If the student has strong foundational skills but processing is slow because they are processing the phonemic code indirectly (for example having to think of another word, extract the sound and then apply to the new word), you need to back up and directly teach the print=sound code. The student needs to directly practice the print=sound relationship until it is automatic. Since the fundamental skills are in place these students usually rapidly progress. Practice writing the sounds is the quickest way to establish this direct print=sound knowledge.

If the student has strong foundational skills and is only having difficulty with some of the complexities, then you can systematically teach the specific advanced code knowledge the student is missing.

If the student has strong foundational skills and is only struggling with multisyllable words, then you can start with Section 6 on handling multisyllable words.

If the students decoding skills are strong (fast and accurate decoding with no indications of deficiencies in foundational skills) but they are struggling with comprehension you can begin with guided reading and specific actions to develop comprehension skills.

# APPENDIX C
# LESSON PROGRESS CHART

| | | |
|---|---|---|
| 1 | 27 | 53 |
| 2 | 28 | 54 |
| 3 | 29 | 55 |
| 4 | 30 | 56 |
| 5 | 31 | 57 |
| 6 | 32 | 58 |
| 7 | 33 | 59 |
| 8 | 34 | 60 |
| 9 | 35 | 61 |
| 10 | 36 | 62 |
| 11 | 37 | 63 |
| 12 | 38 | 64 |
| 13 | 39 | 65 |
| 14 | 40 | 66 |
| 15 | 41 | 67 |
| 16 | 42 | 68 |
| 17 | 43 | 69 |
| 18 | 44 | 70 |
| 19 | 45 | 71 |
| 20 | 46 | 72 |
| 21 | 47 | 73 |
| 22 | 48 | 74 |
| 23 | 49 | 75 |
| 24 | 50 | 76 |
| 25 | 51 | |
| 26 | 52 | |

# APPENDIX D ~ LETTER FORMATION INSTRUCTIONS

The following notes and tips on letter formation are for the parent to review before teaching the student.

Use normal block print or manuscript style and take the time to teach correct formation from the beginning. Attention to correct formation helps prevent common problems and makes letter writing and reading easier for the student.

- Letters sit on the line or "stand on the ground". A few letters have parts that go below ground (g, j, p, q, y)
- For most letters, you write the entire letter without picking up the pencil. You do need to pick up your pencil for the letters with crosses (f, t, q) and dots (i, j) and for k x and y.
- Usually you write letters from the top to the bottom.
- It is important to begin writing the letters that start with curves/circles (a, c, d, f, g, o, q, s) from the correct position. These letters begin at the 2 o'clock position. Tell younger students to picture a little smiley face and to start the letter where the right ear would be and go up and around counterclockwise. Demonstrate where to start and which direction to move.

*For a, c, d, f, g, o, q and s... start at the ear and go up and around!

The following table shows how to form each of the letters. The dot • indicates where to start the letter and the directional arrow → shows which way to write. On the letters that require picking up the pencil a number 1 is given to show which part you write first. Other letters are made without lifting the pencil.

Correct letter formation is especially important for the visually similar letters b, d and p. These letters, (b, d, and p) are different orientations of the same shape. Therefore, they are visually similar. Proper formation helps student learn to differentiate these letters. A highly effective technique for both preventing and overcoming letter confusion is to focus on correct formation.

- d - Write the letter with the 'round part' first. Start at the 2 o'clock position and go around and then up. A fun way for young children to learn this is 'donut for dad' /d/ make the 'donut' or round part first
- b - Start at the top and make the full down stroke first, then go up and around. A fun way to help young children learn the correct 'b' formation is 'big board for the big building'; make the big tall board first
- p - Start at the top and go down below the line and then up and around. A fun way for young children to remember this is 'pony tails hang down' so go down first.

Notice the distinct formation of the properly printed letters d, b, and p. The kinetic motion of correct formation engrains the proper shape and gives the student a way to differentiate these visually similar letters.

If a student has difficulty with writing (penmanship), I recommend the *Zaner-Bloser* manuscript handwriting program. This effective handwriting program teaches the specific steps involved in correct penmanship from how to hold the pencil, to correct position, formation and spacing. I would like to thank, Mr. Clint Hackney for introducing and sharing this very effective writing program with me. The step-by-step instructions illustrating details such as how to correctly hold the pencil and proper paper position are fantastic. Many students have difficulty writing because they never learned 'how' to write. It sounds surprising but many students who struggle with writing do not even hold the pencil correctly. Direct instruction in the exact skills of skilled writing is highly beneficial and effective in helping students improve penmanship skills. The student workbooks cost approximately $12 and are suitable and effective for individual tutoring situations. Classroom programs which include the teacher materials are also available. More information on the *Zaner-Bloser* program can be found at their website http://www.zaner-bloser.com/html/hwgen.html.

# APPENDIX E ~ Summary of Spelling Patterns for Specific Sounds

The following table provides the different phonograms or spelling patterns for each sound. The spelling patterns for each sound are listed in general order of frequency of occurrence with the more common ways of writing a sound listed before the less frequent spelling patterns. The 'unexpected' spellings are indicated with an asterisk (*). The list is organized with the consonant sounds listed first, followed by vowel, vowel-combinations and then r-controlled vowel sounds. A few special endings are listed at the end. Although this list covers the most common spellings it does not include all the possible spellings for every sound. Also pronunciation can vary for some of the sounds.

| Sound | Spelling Pattern (Examples) |
|---|---|
| | The spellings alternatives for each sound are listed in order of frequency with * = unexpected pattern |
| /b/ | b (bass, bring, grab) |
| /d/ | d (did, drop, sad, wild) |
| /f/ | f (fun, draft, flip, gift) <br> ff (off, stiff, staff) used to end single-syllable short-vowel words <br> *ph ( phrase, graph, photograph, phone, orphan) |
| /g/ | g (gum, grip, bag, tangle) |
| /h/ | h (hum, hold, help, hide) |
| /j/ | j (jump, jug, job, enjoy) <br> g+e (age, angel, strange, lunge) <br> dge (ledge, badge, fudge, bridge) used to end single-short-vowel words <br> g+i (giraffe, giant) <br> g+y (gym, bicycle) |
| /k/ | c (cold, came, scare, act, class) <br> k (kid, soak, keep, kite, rake) <br> ck (back, sick, luck, sock, racket) used at end of syllables w/ single short vowel <br> *ch (school, Christmas, ache, scheme) |
| /l/ | l (learn, love, cold, slap, clam) <br> ll (all, call, roll) used to end single-vowel, single-syllable words |
| /m/ | m (map, mark, mom, storm, smear) <br> *mb (dumb, climb, comb, lamb) |
| /n/ | n (not, ran, nothing, never, land, went, snap) <br> *kn (know, knew, knee, knife) |
| /p/ | p (puppy, plug, gulp, spell, space) |
| /kw/ | qu (quick, quilt, quiet, equal) |
| /r/ | r (run, ride, rest, brick, string) <br> *wr (write, wrong, wrote, wrap) |
| /s/ | s (sun, see, swing, mist) <br> c+e (cent, race, cell, nice, space, price, trace) <br> c+i (city, cinnamon, Pacific, Cindy) <br> c+y (bicycle, cylinder, cyst, lacy) <br> ss (pass, toss, miss, mess, boss) used to end single-syllable short-vowel words |
| /t/ | t (told, tip, tall, stop, test, last, kitten) |
| /v/ | v (vest, vent, have, love) |
| /w/ | w (west, wild, winter, swell, swat) |
| /y/ | y (yes, you, yellow, beyond) when 'y' is a consonant beginning syllables |
| /ks/ | x (fix, box, exit, expand) |

| | | |
|---|---|---|
| /z/ | s | (is, was, has, rose, use, risen, raisin and numerous plural words) |
| | z | (zoo, zipper, zebra) |
| | zz | (buzz, fizz, jazz) used at end of single-syllable short-vowel words |
| | *x | (only in a few Greek origin words starting with x, xylophone, xeric, xylem) |
| /ch/ | ch | (child, chop, choke, munch, reach) |
| | *tch | (watch, latch, itch, match) used ending single syllable single-vowel words |
| /sh/ | sh | (shut, ship, wish, mash) |
| | *ch | (only in a few French origin words machine, chivalry, chalet, Cheyenne) |
| /th/ | th | (this, that, those, mother) |
| /th/ (soft) | th | (math, bath, thin) |
| wh | wh | (whisper, when, whip) |
| /a/ | a | (had, at, am, as, mad, apple) |
| /ay/ | a_e | (ate, made, rate, space, grace, page, game, bake) |
| | ai | (rain, pain, wait, aid, aim, waist, train) |
| | a | (rang, bang, bank, navy, thank, gravy) |
| | ay | (play, stay, may, pay) |
| | *ei | (vein, rein, veil) |
| | *eigh | (eight, sleigh, weigh) |
| | *ea | (great, steak) |
| | *ey | (they, obey) |
| /e/ | e | (egg, set, check, elk, felt, west, mess, wet) |
| | ea | (bread, head, ready, instead, health, tread, steady, heaven) |
| /ee/ | ee | (bee, see, green, need, deep, street, meet, sheep) |
| | ea | (eat, team, seat, leap, peach, reach, heat, seal) |
| | y | (baby, silly, candy, picky, quickly) Used for /ee/ end of multisyllable words |
| | e | (he, she, be, me, and in the prefix pre- , re- and de-) |
| | *e_e | (eve, Pete, precede, concrete) |
| | *ie | (grief, brief, brownie, collie) |
| | *ey | (key, money, monkey, honey, turkey) |
| | *i | (machine, brilliant, material, radiate) |
| /i/ | i | (hid, it, is, if, grip, instead, hit, sit) |
| | *y | (gym, typical, system, syllable, mystery, symbol) |
| | *ie | (friend, shield, yield) |
| | *ai | (again, captain, mountain, certain) |
| /ie/ | i_e | (pine, fine, time, nice, ride, hide, ice) |
| | i | (wild, child) |
| | y | (shy, cry, by, fly, my, try) |
| | igh | (high, tight, right, sight, night, fright, might, sigh) |
| | *ie | (pie, die, lie) |
| /o/ | o | (not, mop, hop, sob, sock, hog) |
| /oa/ | o_e | (vote, home, hope, tote, shone, globe, rode, choke, hose) |
| | o | (no, go, so, old, told, most) |
| | ow | (snow, glow, own, show, blow, owner) |
| | oa | (boat, oat, goat, roam, shoal, coal, loan, soap) |
| | *oe | (toe, foe, doe, hoe) |
| | *ough | (dough, though) |
| /u/ | u | (up, us, cup, fun, must, hung, until, under) |
| | o | (son, from, love, some, contain, money, month, front, of ) |
| | *ou | (couple, cousin, famous, nervous) often found in 'ous' ending multisyllable words |

| | | |
|---|---|---|
| /oo/ or /yoo/ (long-u is pronounced as /yoo/ in some words such as cute) | oo<br>u_e<br>ew<br>*ue<br>*ou<br>*ui<br>*u<br>*ough | (moon, soon, cool, hoop, boot,<br>(use, rule, tune, flute, cube, mule, bugle)<br>(stew, drew, chew, threw, few)<br>(blue, blue, true)<br>(you, group, youth)<br>(fruit, suit, bruise, cruise)<br>(music, tuba, pupil)<br>(through) |
| /uu/ | oo<br>*u | (cook, book, took, foot, )<br>(put, push ) |
| /ow/ | ou<br>ow<br>*ough | (out, pound, ground, stout, )<br>(now, how, owl )<br>(plough) |
| /oy/ | oi<br>oy | (choice, coin, oil, boil, moist )<br>(boy, toy, employ, |
| /aw/ | aw<br>au<br>a+l & a+ll<br>*augh<br>*ough | (law, paw, lawn, crawl)<br>(haul, cause, fault)<br>(almost, all, call, also, talk) pronunciation of a+l<br>(taught, caught)<br>(bought, thought) |
| /ar/ | ar | (arm, car, star, artist, market) |
| /er/ | er<br>ur<br>ir<br>or<br>*ear<br>*ar | (her, term, sister, over, hunter)<br>(nurse, turn, lurch, curve)<br>(stir, bird, thirst, shirt, girl)<br>(w+or as in work, word & ending some multisyllable words visitor, doctor)<br>(early, learn, earth, heard)<br>(dollar, collar, solar, lunar, orchard) |
| /or/ | or<br>ore<br>oar<br>*our<br>*oor | (or, for, torn, north)<br>(more, tore, snore, score)<br>(oar, roar, board)<br>(four, pour, tour, your)<br>(door, poor, floor) |
| /air/ | are<br>ar<br>air<br>*ear | (mare, dare, share)<br>(carry, parent, barren)<br>(air, hair, stair, chair)<br>(bear, pear, wear) |
| /eer/ | ear<br>eer<br>*ere | (ear, dear, near, clear)<br>(deer, cheer, peer)<br>(here, mere) |
| | **Special endings for multisyllable words** | |
| /shun/ | tion<br>sion<br>*cian<br>*cion | (nation, station, motion, correction)<br>(vision, confession, mission)<br>(electrician, magician, technician) used for an occupation<br>(suspicion, coercion ) rarely used |
| /shul/ | cial<br>*tial | (special, artificial, financial)<br>(partial, potential) |
| /shus/ | tious<br>cious | (cautious, infectious, nutritious)<br>(precious, spacious, ferocious) |
| /chur/ | ture | (fracture, picture, nature, future, mixture) |
| /zhur/ | sure | (measure, pleasure, treasure, closure) |

~ Free Reading Information ~
~ Comments & Questions ~
~ Ordering Information ~

# www.righttrackreaading.com

**Free Information on Teaching Children to Read:**

    Informative articles
    Useful resources
    Links to other resources and research

**Questions & Comments:**

    The author welcomes any questions or comments on *Back on the Right Track Reading Lessons*. Feedback on the program is appreciated as this information helps the author fine tune and improve the program.

    Please send any questions or comments to mail@righttrackreading.com or to Right Track Reading, PO Box 1952, Livingston MT 59047.

**Ordering:**

    To order additional copies of *Back on the Right Track Reading Lessons* please go to the website. Several options for ordering copies of the program are available.
1. The book can be directly ordered and purchased from www.righttrackreading.com using the Paypal ordering and payment system.
2. Print off a hard copy of the order form and include a check or money order for full amount payable to Right Track Reading LLC. Mail the order form with payment to: Right Track Reading LLC, PO Box 1952, Livingston MT 59047
3. The book is available in some bookstores. See the website for a list of bookstores where you may directly purchase the book.

    Shipping details and additional contact information are located on the website.

## Empowering parents and teachers.
## Improving reading proficiency, one student at a time!